SPIRIT
HACKING

SHAMANIC KEYS TO RECLAIM YOUR
PERSONAL POWER, TRANSFORM YOURSELF,
AND LIGHT UP THE WORLD

SHAMAN DUREK

First published in Great Britain in 2019 by Yellow Kite
An imprint of Hodder & Stoughton
An Hachette UK company

First published in the United States in 2019 by St Martin's Press

1

A CIP catalogue record for this title is
available from the British Library

Trade Paperback ISBN 978 1 529 37668 5
eBook ISBN 978 1 529 38088 0

Printed and bound in Great Britain by Clays Ltd, Elcograf S.p.A.

Hodder & Stoughton policy is to use papers that are natural, renewable
and recyclable products and made from wood grown in sustainable
forests. The logging and manufacturing processes are expected to conform to
the environmental regulations of the country of origin.

Hodder & Stoughton Ltd
Carmelite House
50 Victoria Embankment
London EC4Y 0DZ

www.yellowkitebooks.co.uk

I dedicate this book to my father.

CONTENTS

FOREWORD

Have you ever seen one of those movies like *The Matrix* or *Mission Impossible*, where one character has an incredible knack for doing something like hacking a computer, something that seems superhuman? It's a reflection of the world we live in, where some people are amazing artists, some people can sing songs like no others, and others can design the Internet or rockets to go to the moon. Some people can dunk or run faster than any other.

Perhaps you believe, as is enshrined in the Declaration of Independence, that "all men are created equal"? Or more accurately, "all people are created equal" when you take into account the 51 percent of humans who are women.

It's not true. We have equal rights, yet some people are wired to be exceptional in a special way. For two decades, I have studied these people on my path to become a higher performing, better human being via any means possible. At first, that meant doing the things that are supposed to work. Working out all the time. Diets that didn't work. Working harder so I could have the things that make you happy. Studying. Pushing. Staying up late. Getting an Ivy League MBA. Making $6 million before I turned twenty-seven. Unfortunately, I was exhausted and miserable, because I thought my brain was in charge of my happiness, and I didn't know there are emotional and spiritual components to tapping into whatever special-ness we carry inside ourselves.

Eventually, I spent more than $1 million to improve my biology at every level, from subcellular all the way to the highest spiritual levels I could find. Along the way, I created the modern field of biohacking, which was added to the *Merriam-Webster* dictionary as a new word in our language. It is the art and science of changing the environment inside and outside our bodies so that we have full control of our own biology. It even led me to create Bul-letproof, my company dedicated to helping people tap into the unlimited power of being human (and butter in coffee), that has raised $68 million in venture funding and served about 200 million cups of brain-enhancing cof-fee. I've written *New York Times* bestsellers about the brain and willpower, interviewed hundreds of researchers on consciousness and brains and biology on my Webby Award–winning podcast, and started a neuroscience facility for upgrading the human brain.

When I ran out of things that were supposed to work for a computer hacker like me, I decided to try the things that aren't supposed to work. I've traveled to Tibet to learn meditation from the masters. I used ayahuasca with a plant shaman in Peru twenty years ago, before it was trendy or even easy to find. I learned Chinese energy medicine techniques. I studied shamanism, although I am not a shaman. This is not to say I didn't study mitochondria or hormones or antiaging; the truth is that these things coex-ist with whatever spiritual energies exist, and you can learn to see both.

I also learned that there is a small number of people out there who see things that others don't, or sense things that are hard to see, but they can do it reliably, *and they see the same things as others like them*. In fact, every society has been studying, honing, and pursuing knowledge of these things since the dawn of history. By many different names, shamans have traveled the spirit world, healing sick people, finding lost souls, interpreting dreams, and just knowing things without a scientific explanation. Real scientists are drawn to things without explanations because that's where learning happens.

In fact, the local First Nations Cowichan tribe, which is located near where I live on Vancouver Island, has an oral history going back more than ten thousand years, recalling how their medicine man had a dream of a great tidal wave. He told his villagers to get in their canoes and paddle out into the ocean. They rode over the top of the giant wave before it crested, while the wave decimated most other tribes on the island as it reshaped the landscape into what we know today. How did he know? Is it possible some of us can do that?

It is not only possible but there are now studies showing that humans are capable of more than we think. I am blessed to know a good number of special humans, some of whom call themselves shamans, some of whom just know they can do or see things that most people don't. I have also come to know a larger number of people who desperately want to be one of these special humans, hang up shingles calling themselves shamans, and even acquire some of the skills of full-blown shamans.

There are a lot of people who can dunk. There are a lot fewer Michael Jordans.

Shaman Durek is unusual in that he comes from a mix of shamanic lineages and has a powerful ability to tap into things I don't know how to explain. I've seen his eyes roll up in his head as he starts speaking languages he does not know. Not gibberish, but fluent languages, switching rapidly between them as he swaps out healing techniques.

He's simply very plugged in to a world that is around us but mostly invisible, and he's been that way since he was born. That's why he's uniquely equipped to offer a vision of the world that can powerfully benefit you, one where your spirit is real and matters as much as your brain or your body.

You could even call him a spirit hacker. I do.

—Dave Asprey
founder of Bulletproof
New York Times bestselling author of
Head Strong and *The Bulletproof Diet*

SPIRIT HACKING

INTRODUCTION

E ven though the medicine woman told me I was going to die two days
before it happened, it still shocked the hell out of me when I actually
did. I mean, it was hard enough for a robust twenty-seven-year-old
man to wrap his mind around his mortality while training with shamanic
elders in the jungles of Belize, but when the seizures kicked in, and my organs started shutting down, and my dead grandmother appeared in the
hospital room, and told me to relax into the pain, and to let death take me—
well, that's the kind of experience that really knocks you on your ass, know
what I mean?

Dying was one of my rites of passage as a shaman—another brutal initiation that wrecked my body, and annihilated my ego, and flooded my

consciousness with sacred teachings, and lessons, and insights, and illuminations that completely shifted my understanding of reality. The experience left me very raw, and very humble. It strengthened my powers and fortified my devotion to Spirit, thereby allowing me to be of greater service to humanity, and of greater service to the planet—but only after I came out of the coma, and healed the brain damage, and taught myself to walk again.

It's not like I hadn't already been studying shamanism and practicing shamanism since the ancestors first started coming to me when I was a kid. Still, when I died, everything shifted. When I died, the mark of the shaman was indelibly etched inside my body, mind, and spirit; because, despite all New Age fads to the contrary, you don't become a shaman because you went to Peru, bought a poncho, sang some sacred plant songs, and learned how to mix a booming batch of ayahuasca. You become a shaman because the spirits choose you to be a shaman.

SHAMANISM 101

Shamans have been an integral part of every tribe and every culture since the first humans walked the Earth. The word "shaman" means "one who knows." Shamans gather their knowledge by traveling between dimensional planes, acting as ambassadors between the physical world and the spirit world. Shamans utilize a vast array of spiritual tools and techniques to communicate with spirits, and ancestors, and elements, and all sorts of unseen energies, entities, and intelligences in service to the health and well-being of everyone in the tribe.

Shamans perceive reality through an expanded perspective that acknowledges the life force, the sacredness, and the divinity in all earthly lifeforms, including those in the animal kingdom and in the plant kingdom. Shamans are bound by neither third-dimensional constraints nor the five senses. No one is, really. But most humans are programmed to reject their extrasensory capabilities, and to reject the existence of nonmaterial reality, and to reject the spiritual realms altogether. But mostly, humans are programmed to reject their own power, which has a lot of people stubbornly beholden to a very narrow, very limited material experience of reality as perceived through the standard-issue five senses.

Because shamans perceive reality beyond this third-dimensional construct, shamans understand that everything is animate, and that everything has intelligence. That's not to say that everything has the capacity for complex cognitive exchange. Let's not be ridiculous. I'm not going to have an in-depth conversation about Shakespeare or quantum mechanics with a sycamore tree. But trees stand tall, and trees have deep roots and a lot of wisdom to share in their own way. Shamans utilize spiritual tools to access certain doorways of perception that allow us to communicate and share relationships with these other intelligences that share the planet with us.

THIS IS NOT AN AYAHUASCA THING

These days, people confuse shamans with people who name themselves after their spirit animal, and wear beads, and burn palo santo, and give people plant medicine. I can't tell you how often it happens that people hear I'm a shaman and just automatically assume I get people high, meaning that I work with psychedelic plant medicine, which I do not.

In fact, there are many different types of shamans. There are root shamans, who work specifically with root medicines, and root spirits. There are water shamans, like in Indonesia, who work only with the water element, and the water spirits. There are shamans who work with animals, and who administer the toxins that they extract from them. And yes, there are shamans who work with entheogenic plants—meaning, plants that open up certain doorways of perception that allow people to commune with Spirit— plants like peyote, and iboga, and San Pedro, and ayahuasca.

Now that plant medicine is trending, and ayahuasca is the new black, you have all these people spending their weekends wearing white, and drinking psychedelics, and puking into Tupperware bowls, and having their minds blown. They come out of a ceremony, all wide-eyed and radiant, with these beatific smiles, and this incredible love for humanity and for the planet, and this profound understanding of the interconnectedness of all beings. Then, they tell their friends about this amazing mystical experience, and they get all this spiritual street cred, and all this social cachet; and then two weeks later, someone cuts them off in traffic, and all their holiness goes right out the window as they flip the person the finger, topped off with a hearty "fuck off!"

People are not using plant medicine in the right way. Traditionally, shamans give people plant medicine to activate certain doorways, and certain awarenesses, and certain perceptions, not to give people something to check off their bucket lists, or to brag about at dinner parties, or even just to take them on a wild-ass ride. Plant medicine exists to show us what is possible when we engage beyond the false limitations that we have allowed to shape our reality. But plant medicine is only an entryway; it is not a place to hang out.

A lot of people confuse plant medicines with the states of consciousness they induce, and then they develop dependencies upon these medicines, as though they are the only way to access these states, and as though these states do not already exist inside them and cannot be accessed at any time. This is very limiting for those who then become reliant upon these plant medicines and these shamans, whom they place on pedestals, and worship like golden calves.

BE YOUR OWN DAMN GURU

Shamans are not gurus, and shamans sure as hell aren't perfect. So many spiritual teachers make it seem like they have it all figured out, like they're these higher luminaries of perfected human embodiment who never trip, never fart, and never get down on themselves. It's bullshit. If you're in a biological spacesuit—which is what I call the body—then your shit's getting fucked up on some level. I mean, we're living in duality, peeps! That means that we are dealing with real darkness, and with real challenges—all of us. Sure, I might be more adept at dealing with the darkness, and with life's challenges, because I have all these shamanic tools to support me—not to mention the spirits and the ancestors—but that doesn't mean I don't get affected by the same challenges that afflict the rest of humanity. It doesn't mean I don't get angry, or that I don't ever act out of character, or that I don't engage in patterns that run counter to my best interests. I'm just as human as everyone else.

But people love to worship their golden calves, and so they are quick to place shamans on pedestals. It's really annoying. If you're going to put me on a pedestal, then you'd better climb onto your own version so that we can see eye to eye, because I'm not going to strain my neck to talk down to you. Either show up as my equal, or don't show up at all. I'm not here to be your guru. Be your own damn guru.

SPIRIT SHAMANISM

I am what is known as a spirit shaman. Spirit shamanism is one of the oldest shamanic traditions on the planet, which is why our rites of passage are generally so intense (aka: I literally died, remember?). Spirit shamans don't rely on medicine, or plants, or on any earthly tools to do our healing. We go directly to the source. We go to the spirits themselves.

Every life-form on the planet has a spirit. Spirit shamans cultivate relationships with these spirits to facilitate clear communication in times of breakdown or imbalance, so they can determine what adjustments need to be made in order to restore harmony to the being, or the situation.

When the ancestors came to visit me when I was a kid, and started to train me in the ways of shamanism, they mostly took me to different realms so they could introduce me to the spirits, so that I could start to cultivate my own relationships with them. So much of my shamanic training involved networking with the spirits—just getting to know them, and learning their energy, and offering my support to them in their realms, just as I would learn to call upon their support to help the people in this dimension.

Instead of relying on a plant, or a drum, or a breathing exercise to tap into the spirit realm, spirit shamans pretty much live there 24-7. When I'm working with people, and I open myself up as a vessel to the spirit realm, all kinds of different beings and energies come through me. So, in any one given session, I might sing, I might dance, I might speak in tongues, I might make shapes or mudras with my hands. I might pray in a language I've never studied. I might channel an African elder, or an Asian monk, or an Aboriginal tribesman, or a Tibetan rinpoche. Shamans are equal opportunity spirit vessels. We don't discriminate against other cultures, or religions, or traditions, or dimensional entities. We're very evolved.

JUST BECAUSE YOU'RE NOT HIP TO IT, DOESN'T MEAN THE SPIRIT WORLD ISN'T A THING

A lot of people have a hard time wrapping their minds around what I do and how I engage reality. They don't have a context for spirits, or for unseen energies, and they don't have a framework for other-dimensional realms of perception and existence. You can't really blame them. It's not like they teach us this stuff in school. Children are only taught about material reality as it is perceived through a very limited, third-dimensional lens that accesses only a tiny portion of the whole picture. But just because we have not been taught about the spirit world, and just because we don't yet know how to perceive the spirit world, or how to navigate the spirit world, doesn't mean the spirit world isn't a thing. It's just means we haven't educated ourselves yet.

MY LINEAGE IS MYSTICAL AF

My great-grandmother Mamal started visiting me in my dreams when I was five. But my mom says it was clear by the time I was three that I wasn't like the other kids, because I used to go up to strangers in the grocery store and give them hugs while breaking down all their issues, and telling them that I loved them. Even though my traditional shamanic powers come from my father's side of the family, my mother comes from a long line of Norwegian oracles, as well as Native American medicine men/women. She is no stranger to the spirit realm, and she said that my spiritual powers started to make themselves known early on.

Mamal was a powerful medicine woman from Ghana, where she worked with spirits, and herbs, and music, in service to her tribe—a mix of Mende, Yoruba, and Bantu traditions. When the slave traders infiltrated the African tribes, Mamal fled to Haiti where she studied hoodoo and became a spiritualist before ending up in New Orleans. Mamal's shamanic powers are legendary in my family, and I've heard countless stories of her miraculous healings. My father told me that when he was a kid in New Orleans, people used to line up around the block to see her. Mamal would lay them down on a wooden table that stood in the center of her healing room. She would rub oil and various herbs into her hands, while praying and singing. Then, she would spit into her hands, and rub them together, while waving them over the person's body and chanting to the spirits. Mamal would sing and dance, all while rubbing her hands, and rubbing her hands, and rubbing her hands. Then she would smack the person, and she would keep smacking them; and with every smack, the person would shake, and the person would cough, and sometimes, the person would throw up into a metal bucket that Mamal kept under the table, and then they would be healed. It didn't matter what the sickness was, this was Mamal's technique, and—apparently—it worked wonders to heal any imbalance that presented itself. Granted, it was a different time. You can't just go smacking people healed these days. That kind of thing doesn't fly anymore.

My mother is a powerful seer and a fountain of wisdom. Ancient Viking spirituality runs deep in her roots. Rejected by her stepfamily early on because they were black, and she was white, my mother spent the bulk of her childhood apprenticing to a woman she referred to as her spiritual mother—a Romanian gypsy who started training my mother in the ways of seeing, and knowing, and working with energy from the time she was eight. My mother says she knew that I was going to be a powerful shaman while I was still in her womb, because my ancestors came to her while she was pregnant and taught her all these chants and spirituals that she'd never heard before but that she sang to me constantly, between prayers. She says my ancestors also guided her to place certain power objects in my nursery—drums to teach me the musical ways of the Mende tribe; feathers to teach me to fly, so that I could always lift myself above the mundane world; and a special blanket that was woven in Africa, that she says I used to kneel on to pray and to meditate when I was just a toddler.

THE CALL

Given how deep and how diverse these spiritual powers run in my bloodline, I didn't think it was weird that dead relatives and strange spirits were showing up in my room at night, and speaking to me, because I thought everyone was having that type of experience. That is, until I was ostracized as a freak by kids who were not, in fact, having those experiences and who excluded me, and bullied me accordingly.

A lot of times, when I mention spirits, people think of ghosts, or ghouls, or see-through entities levitating above the ground. But that's not how spirits show up. Spirits look exactly like regular people, except sometimes their clothes and accessories give them away. That's why it was so disconcerting as a kid, because I'd wake up to see an African man wearing a crown of stones, and a red velvet cape, just sitting in my chair, staring at me. Or I'd walk into my room to discover a Viking draped in animal pelts throwing bones on my floor, while a Native woman stood behind him, pointing to the formations they were making on the carpet, trying to teach me the ways of divination. I'd figured out that other people couldn't see the spirits, except for a handful of folks in my family who followed the old ways, but I didn't myself know how to deal with them.

At a certain point, my powers were getting stronger and stronger, and I knew I needed to start training to be able to navigate these realms, and deal with these experiences that I was having more and more of. I was seeing colors around people's bodies. I was starting to feel other people's emotions and hear other people's spirit guides, which was getting noisy, and distracting, and overwhelming. Not to mention I started seeing these swirling balls of light that would disappear into the walls in different parts of my house. They were spirit portals, but I didn't know that then. I was in elementary school. I didn't know what a spirit portal even was, let alone how to make sure it was properly sealed.

I told my dad that my powers were getting more intense, and that it was time for me to start my training. He asked if I was hearing the ancestors' voices, and if they had started asking me to do things for them. When I told him that yes, the ancestors were asking me to do a lot of things, my father told me that he used to hear the ancestors' voices, too. That's when the beatings started, and that's when my grandpa Leon started calling me the devil's child.

That Time on the Playground . . .

When I was very young—around seven or eight years old—I was playing with some kids at recess, and all of a sudden, I saw this one girl throwing up blood while all her hair fell out. It scared me so much, I started screaming, and screaming, and screaming. It became this ordeal, and the girl and I were taken to the principal's office, where we had to wait for our parents to come get us. When our parents arrived, the principal kept pressing me to explain why I was screaming so much, and I finally fessed up, and told them what I saw, at which point both the mother and the little girl started to cry.

"My baby has leukemia!" the woman sobbed.

My father leaped to his feet, grabbed my arm, and said, "We have to go now," and rushed us out the door, practically dragging me across the parking lot to his truck.

"You are drawing attention to yourself," he growled once we got inside the cab. "People will find out about your powers. You cannot use them. Those powers are bad. You must shut them down."

Because we come from a long line of shamans, both my grandfather and my father knew the kinds of hardships the shamanic path entails. My dad used to apprentice for his grandmother (Mamal) and for his aunt—both of whom practiced shamanism in New Orleans. So he had witnessed firsthand the trials and tribulations I would have to endure if I was to choose to step into my power. He knew that I would be shamed and ostracized for being different. And, though he would never admit it, he was terrified of the powers that he himself had suppressed his whole life. It didn't help that, according to my father's religion, I was evil, which was why he tried as hard as he could to beat my powers out of me. I spent the bulk of my childhood bloodied and bruised, and told—repeatedly—that I was evil, and that I was a curse from the devil.

But the ancestors kept insisting that I needed to start my training, and I was literally being inundated by spirits day and night. So my mother (who had divorced my father and moved to New York when I was three) stepped in on my behalf, and demanded that my father allow me to start training in shamanism, and in the ways of Spirit.

SHAMAN TRAINING: THE EARLY YEARS

That's when the ancestors started sending teachers and mentors and healers and elders my way; and that's when I started to learn how to navigate the realms of Spirit; and that's when I learned that those spinning vortexes in my house were spirit portals, and figured out how to seal them shut. Some of my teachers were incarnate, and some of my teachers were spirits. This is part of what makes shamanism so unique—our training and practice take place in the realms of the physical as well as in the realms of Spirit. So shamans learn from physical teachers, and shamans also learn from spirits, who come at nighttime, in many forms. The spirits might come as a Native American chief, or as an Egyptian temple guard, or as a woman with the body of a snake who shakes you out of your sleep to bring you a message, or to teach you a prayer, or because it's time for you to learn to summon the wind, or to make an offering to a tree seven blocks away, even though it's two o'clock in the morning and it's pouring rain outside.

The spirits would often work in tandem with physical teachers. I remember one time, a girl I went to school with invited me over to her house after school. Her mother, Diana, was a witch, and she said that my ancestors had visited her and asked her to train me in the dark arts—not because they wanted me to practice them, but so that I would know how to protect myself when I came across them. Diana gave me books to study, which I hid under my mattress, lest my father and stepmother beat me for having them.

My aunt Hazel, who practiced the old ways from Haiti, would teach me on the sly, because she knew how much my father feared the family powers.

"Don't tell your father," she would remind me at the end of our visits.

Aunt Hazel taught me how to ride my breath into the spirit world, where I would connect with the ancestors and the spirits who are still teaching me new things to this day. I remember the first time I rode my breath into that realm. I met a spirit who instructed me to wake up at 4:00 A.M. and go to a place where there was mud, and water, and birds. I set the alarm and snuck out of the house, and when I got to the park with the mud, and all the rest of it, the spirit was waiting for me next to about a half dozen dead birds on the shore of the pond. The spirit told me to bury the birds, and to trace circles around them with a stick, and to sit there and meditate on bird energy. As I did, the birds flew up out of the earth from where I buried them, and went right into my body, infusing me with their energy. That experience taught me how to navigate the spirit realm through flight, while changing the way I perceived things in this realm by expanding my vision considerably.

Unfortunately, my father was waiting up for me by the time I got home with mud-caked shoes, and dirt under my fingernails; I endured yet another beating for sneaking out, and practicing the powers he kept telling me to shut down.

SHAMAN TRAINING IS SUPER DIVERSE, AND EXTRA INCLUSIVE

Because spirit shamans work with spirits from every culture and every tradition, all over the world, and across all timelines, spirit shamans must study other peoples' cultures, religions, and philosophies, in addition to their own tribal lineages. I continue traveling the world, studying other cultures, and other religions, and other shamanic traditions. I am always learning, and I am always training, and I am always stretching myself.

My family comes from the West African tribal traditions, as well as the Toscuran and the Scandinavian. So, of course, my ancestors have trained me extensively in those practices and beliefs. I have also trained in Native American shamanism with the Lakota and the Cherokee tribes. I've trained in Haitian shamanism, and Nigerian shamanism, and Hawaiian shamanism, as well as in the Cuban babalawo, and the African Kuba mystical traditions. I studied Judaism and Kabbalah with rabbis in Israel, Sufism in Turkey, and Christianity, Catholicism, and Christian mysticism through-out Europe. Plus, I have spirits from all kinds of cultures and traditions and religions and mystery schools who train me, and who advise me, and who work through me—spirits from the Maori tribe, elders from Valhalla, and spirits from Angola, and Thailand, and Vietnam.

My shamanic studies haven't necessarily been linear or logical. For example, it wasn't until I went to Israel to study Jewish mysticism that I really understood the symbolism in those books about black magic that Diana had given me as a child. It was through my studies of Hebrew and the Torah that I understood the codes that were hidden in language, and the power of those codes to create, and to destroy, and to transform.

While I was in Israel, I almost got run over by the number 4 bus. As the bus careened toward me, a Hassidic man pulled me out of the way and threw me against the window of a travel agency. As I collected myself, and shook off the scare, I saw a poster in the window that said VISIT TURKEY, and I knew that Spirit wanted me to go there. In Turkey, I met a Nigerian shaman who took me into the forest to participate in a powerful ceremony, during which I met a Kuba spirit who taught me many things, and who still advises me in my healing sessions, and in the dreamtime.

So, a lot of my shamanic training and immersion comes from following signs and availing myself to the wily ways of Spirit, which aren't as cut-and-dried as, say, your average university curriculum.

THAT TIME I DIED FOR FOUR MINUTES

Two days after I left the jungle and was told I was going to die, I woke up in the middle of the night to find a spirit sitting on top of me, reaching into my body. The next thing I knew, I was strapped to a gurney in an ambulance with my friend Marcus sitting next to me, looking all kinds of freaked out.

"What's going on?" I wheezed.

According to the paramedic, I'd had five seizures in a row, which was strange, given that I wasn't epileptic and that I'd never had even one seizure before in my life. I had two more seizures before we got to the hospital. I realized that it was really happening, and that I was dying. I was terrified.

A luminous woman walked into my hospital room just as everything started to glow and turn into liquid.

You're going to feel a lot of pain, she said. *Don't fight it. Just let go.*

She disappeared just as the pain kicked in, and what felt like a thousand flaming knives started stabbing every square inch of my body. Apparently this is what happens when your potassium levels skyrocket to 10 mEq/L and all your organs shut down, and you're a sixth-generation shaman. One by one, my organs went off-line while I just kept right on convulsing. When my lungs gave out, I started hitting my throat with my fist as I struggled for air. The doctors rushed to give me a tracheotomy, but I still couldn't manage to get any oxygen, because my lungs were no longer operational.

Beloved child, I heard the woman's voice say, *let go.*

Marcus told me later that, while I was being drawn toward this soothing voice and this luminous light, and this peaceful energy, the doctors and the nurses were struggling to hold down my herky-jerky body, and to push my eyeballs back into their sockets.

Let go, child . . .

That time it was my grandmother's voice. That's when I stopped fighting, and I let go, and I died.

Everything became very clear, and very expansive. I went from seeing just the ceiling above my head, to seeing the entire hospital room, and then the entire hospital, and the parking lot outside, and then the whole block, and then the whole city. Then my grandmother was with me, telling me to relax into the pain, and telling me it was all okay. Then I was floating in a black ocean, infused with love and energy. I realized that I was in my mother's womb, and I watched her give birth to me, which was bizarre, because I wasn't used to perceiving from both the inside and the outside at the same time.

I then simultaneously watched and experienced my entire life. I was with every person I'd ever known. I saw everything I'd ever seen. I relived every fight I'd ever gotten into. Not only did I live through my whole life, but I also saw how my every action impacted all the people around me. The images and the memories kept flooding my mind until I reached the point where I could accept it all, and let it go with love. That's when I was released from this plane altogether.

I melted into an incredible bright light that was pure love, and I knew I was home. I found myself on a beach without a body. The luminous woman reappeared and gave me back my hands, but without the bones, and asked me if I had any questions.

"Lots," I said, and then proceeded to grill her about the situation here on planet Earth. I asked why people hurt each other, and why people suffer, and why we have borders, and why we have disease, and why we have war.

For every question I asked, the answer was always the same: *malfunction in thinking.*

I was officially dead for four minutes and twenty-five seconds, but the time I spent on the other side felt like at least a couple dozen eternities. After a while, and many conversations with many different spirits, another being came to me and told me that I didn't have to stay, and that I could go back to my Earth life if I wanted to. As much as I wanted to stay on that love beach, with my bone-free hands, and the sky that made happy sounds whenever I looked at it, I knew that I had to go back to Earth, to teach the people what I'd learned.

I walked into the water and was swallowed up by deep space, which I was now shooting through at warp speed. I stopped just above Earth and hovered for a while before I dropped down through the atmosphere, and through the ceiling of my hospital room, where I saw myself lying beneath a sheet, with a giant hypodermic needle poking out of my chest, and defibrillator paddles shocking the shit out of me. As I came back into my body, I felt a rush of pain, and I gasped loudly, just like people do in the movies when they're brought back to life. I reached to pull the tube out of my mouth but realized I couldn't move my hands, or my arms—not because my bones were still missing, but because I was paralyzed.

I spent the next two months in a coma. When I regained consciousness, I couldn't speak, and I couldn't move. I was told that I had brain damage, and that I would never walk again. My kidneys were in such bad shape that I spent the next eight years of my life on dialysis—an experience that forced me to walk through the fires of human suffering, and human hopelessness so as to allow me to understand others' pain in profound ways that I wouldn't have otherwise been able to tap into if I hadn't gone through it myself.

The road to recovery was long and painful. The spirits came to me in the hospital. They explained that the brain is a conductor, and that mine was transmitting faulty messages. They explained that if I wanted to recover, and if I wanted to heal, I needed to start thinking with my expansive soul and not with my limiting brain. I took their words to heart and worked diligently, every day, to heal my body with my thoughts, and with my words. I beat every odd, and I proved every doctor wrong, and I experienced a full and complete recovery, all because I trained myself to think properly.

THE PROPHECY

While I was dead, and while I was hanging out with the spirits on the beach, they showed me this extraordinary moment in human history— this planetary initiation that we, as a global citizenry, are navigating right now.

Many shamanic, tribal, and indigenous traditions have prophesied about this epic transitional time for our species. They call it the Great Upheaval—the dark point before dawn—that threshold moment where humanity is forced to wake up from their slumber, and their separation, and their destructive ways, and to choose to consciously evolve the species and the planet, or to perish.

I call it the Blackout. Blackouts are pivotal moments that demand quantum leaps in evolution to ensure the species' survival. They are sink-or-swim junctures that present themselves when planetary conditions reach extreme levels of imbalance, and when large swaths of the population have become stuck and stagnant in their ability to recognize the tools and the knowledge they already have inside them, and to make dramatic and necessary shifts in service to the survival and the adaptation of their species.

THE BLACKOUT

The Blackout is here to shine a light on everything that is broken, imbalanced, and out of alignment—not only within ourselves, as individuals, but also within the world at large. We are currently navigating a period of great disconnect that has us bearing witness to disruptive weather patterns, large-scale natural disasters, and tremendous amounts of social, political, cultural, and technological upheaval.

The Blackout is a crossroads. It is a time for human beings to look at the mess we've made of our planet, and our systems, and our society, and to make the shifts we need to make if we are to survive, and to level-up. We are teetering upon the edge of a remarkable shift that is poised to alter humanity's trajectory, and humanity's MO, in some pretty giant ways. The Blackout is inviting human beings to decide whether we are going to continue to think against ourselves and continue to steer the planet into darkness; or if we are going to wrangle our thoughts for the supportive, and take responsibility for ourselves, and for our situation here on planet Earth, and embrace the light. This decision is both personal and collective, because the only way we can change the world is to change ourselves.

SHAMANISM TO THE RESCUE

It is the shaman's task to venture into the dark places most people avoid. And it is the shaman's task to embrace that darkness as a means of investigating the human condition, and a means of understanding the nature of the things that humans grapple with. The shaman's connection to Spirit is what allows us to brave the darkness again, and again, and again, because it is that connection which allows us to know we are always, always safe. This is the function of the shamanic initiation. To obliterate the shaman again, and again, and again, so that the shaman learns—not by indoctrination, but by experience—that he cannot be obliterated. But most humans do not endure these rites of passage, which means that most humans do not have this connection to Spirit, and so most humans do not experience the feelings of enduring safety that come along with it, even those who claim to be religious or spiritual.

I have compiled the spirit hacks in this book to help you develop this kind of connection with Spirit, and to help you to cultivate this same sense of safety that I have cultivated through my experience with the spirit world. By regularly applying these tools in our individual lives, every one of us will be able to navigate the world with confidence, and with love, while inspiring and educating others to do the same. Then, before you know it, we've generated this giant self-correcting spiral that's lifting and shifting the world, one lit leader at a time. So many people are so busy, and frantic, and stressed out, racing to figure out intricate, complex solutions to all the planet's ills, that we've lost sight of the real solution: for the world to get better, the people living in the world must feel better. This means feeling more safe, more whole, more fulfilled, more nurtured, more connected, more empowered, and more authentic. This is what these spirit hacks are for.

Because shamanism is inclusive, and expansive, and relational, and quantum, it is uniquely positioned to offer humanity a pretty massive array of poprocks integrative tools found both in nature, as well as in our own human operating systems. My vision is for humanity to utilize these tools as a means of adapting, and evolving, and thriving throughout the Blackout. These tools have been handpicked and carefully curated to support you in becoming a greater and more powerful version of yourself, while living and thriving in harmony with all life and getting lit AF.

SHAMANISM IS NOT RELIGION; IT'S A LIFESTYLE

While the spirits have chosen me to be a shaman, and while I have endured the rites of passage, and have undergone the training that being a shaman entails, shamanism is a lifestyle choice that is available to everyone.

Shamanism is not a religion. It's not about rules, or sin, or hierarchy, or punishment; and it's not about rewards, or righteousness, or austerity, or a heavenly afterlife. Shamanism is not about placing figureheads between you and God, as though you need anyone else to connect you to your own divinity. As a shaman, I am not here to stand between you and Spirit, and I am not here to tell you how to live your life, or how to be a spiritual person. I am here to empower you to cultivate your own relationship with Spirit, and I am here to help you empower yourself by teaching you spirit hacks that will support you in lifting and shifting, and living giant.

Shamanism is a way of perceiving life in a more expansive, engaged, loving, inclusive, impartial way. What you hold in your hands is not a religious text or rule book. This is an invitation to take a sacred journey into the depths of your spirit, and to go on discovery, and to step into the unknown, where you will connect with that infinitely loving, limitless power that resides inside each and every one of us, and you will learn to cultivate that power, and you will learn to harness that power, in service to the evolution of this planet, and this species, and yourself.

GLOSSARY OF TERMS

While I will explain and contextualize all the terms listed below as we move forward, I've compiled them into their very own section for easy reference, because I want you to focus on empowering yourself, and getting lit, instead of straining your brain trying to remember how I defined *sensorium* on page whatever. A lot of these definitions are tailored to my own personal lexicon and won't necessarily match up with the dictionary definitions. Welcome to my world, love.

BIOLOGICAL SPACESUIT: the human body

BLACKOUT: a period/magnetic energy frequency that sheds light on humanity's density, so that we can see it, and take responsibility for it, and transmute it, such that we can realize the highest potential of love consciousness on planet Earth

BOBBLEHEAD: a person who mindlessly follows the herd and does what they are told without thinking

DARKNESS: an energetic void that houses everything that is not held in the field of love

DEVOTION: the observance of energy, and the focus of attention guided by love

DUALITY: the perceived separation of light and darkness as they reflect off one another in this dimensional realm

EGO: the great paperweight; the part of human consciousness that creates and sustains the realities we choose

ENERGETIC SIGNATURE: your unique baseline vibrational frequency

GIANT: epic, living large, playing full out, embodying your highest truth for yourself; also, a quantum leap in evolution

GIANT AGE: the forthcoming golden era that follows the Blackout; a period of global peace, prosperity, joy, health, and harmony for every being on Earth

GLAMOUR: a class of energies geared to distract you away from yourself by hijacking your attention with sparkle, and glitter, and glitz

GOD: a sustainable energy source of pure, unconditional love that constantly creates itself within itself (see also: *Spirit* and *Source*)

JUNKERY: discordant energy frequencies the shadow holds on to for us until we are ready to take responsibility for them

KEEPING IT ON BLAZE: being so empowered in who you are that nothing can get in your way

THE LIGHT: the emanation from God, which is pure, unconditional love and supports growth and expansion (see also: *light intelligence*)

LIT: high energy driven by passion and purpose

LIT TRAIN: a divine energetic source that fuels your joy, your fun, your energy, and your expansion

MANTRA: words or phrases uttered in rhythmic repetition to entrain the mind with specific frequencies

THE MATRIX: a system put into place by the darkness that generates rules and regulations people must follow to support the system

MAYA: Hindu concept of earthly illusion

MEDICINE: the element that creates movement in what has been stagnant

POPROCKS: explosive, amazing, energy driven, exciting, new, fun

QUANTUM: operating on multiple dimensions simultaneously

RESPONSIBILITY: the ability to show up with love

SELF: the divinity inside you; the purest, most authentic aspect of your being

SENSORIUM: the body's sensory apparatus, or faculties considered as a whole

SHADOW: the part of your being that is the light, and that holds all the things you haven't taken responsibility for, with unconditional love and acceptance

SKETCHER: the voice of an underworld spirit resonating in your head

SPIRIT: a conscious energy source; also—in some instances—God

SYNTHESIS: the means through which our sensory mechanisms communicate with one another

THE SYSTEM: the authority structures that enforce the limitations of the matrix and that tether you to survival consciousness

THE WILL: the action of energy brought forth by thought and feeling

PART I

FROM DARKNESS TO LIT

1

THE BLACKOUT

B lackouts aren't anything new. They happen when a portion of the species goes off the rails and veers so far out of alignment that they need to experience a quantum leap in awakening to restore harmony to themselves, and to the planet. Basically, they need a big ol' shake-up to wake up. Human beings have incurred plenty of Blackouts throughout the ages. What makes this particular one unique is its scale. This Blackout is happening on a global level, rather than on a single continent, or in one particular state or region. This Blackout is the all-inclusive, superdeluxe variety, because this Blackout is affecting every single being on the planet.

We are already witnessing massive disruptions in the natural world as Earth attempts to restore balance to itself by way of accelerated climate change and increasingly violent weather patterns. Our societal constructs are teetering on the edge of similarly massive and tumultuous shifts. We are living in unsustainable structures that are hogging far too many resources and taking a major toll on the ecosystem. We eat processed food infused with deadly chemicals that wreak all kinds of havoc on our bodies, to say nothing of what they are doing to Earth itself. We spend weekends polluting our systems with disruptive media and poisonous intoxicants to get a temporary break from the stress and monotony of survival. We think and speak to ourselves and others in demeaning and self-defamatory ways that have far-reaching negative effects on our physical, emotional, and psychological well-being. We divide. We gossip. We consume. We slaughter entire groups of people who believe differently than we do. We condemn criminals to death, instead of seeking to rehabilitate them. We kill animals for food, clothes, science, and sport, because we don't value them as sentient beings carrying the life code inside them, because we don't value the life code, period. It's crazy the extent to which humans will try to convince themselves that they have the right to destroy life for profit.

Then there's the infighting and the intolerance, which have a lot of people hung up on things like racism, and sexism, and discrimination, without realizing that these issues are merely symptoms of a much larger malfunction. So now we have people fighting the symptoms of social inequality with the same shortsighted tactics we see the Western medical model using to fight disease, completely oblivious to the fact that the more we try to fight these symptoms, the sicker our society gets, because the root of the issues remains unexamined. Therefore, the sickness continues to manifest more and more symptoms, while the source of the problem just grows bigger and bigger, and stronger and stronger.

AS WITHOUT, SO WITHIN

We have to understand that everything we are experiencing in our here-and-now reality is a manifestation of the energies we are holding on to inside ourselves, and that anything we are uncomfortable or displeased with in the world is a reflection of something we are uncomfortable or displeased with in ourselves. The Blackout is asking us to take a long, hard look at ourselves, and to acknowledge all the stuff we have been denying, and avoiding, and stuffing under the rug, and pretending isn't broken, or distorted, or happening on any level whatsoever. The Blackout is demanding that we—as individuals, as well as a collective—face the things that we've been running from.

This is why we are experiencing so much discord on the planet. The Blackout is creating a magnetic energy stream that is pulling everything we've been shoving under our rugs to the surface for us to examine, so we can put it back into balance. This is why we are witnessing so many polarizing leaders stepping into high-profile sociopolitical positions, and getting people so riled up. Shamans call these figures the *great agitators*. The great agitators serve a very valuable function in reflecting back to us the things inside ourselves that we don't want to look at, and all the shit we need to deal with to get back into alignment. People get confused and project their anger and their issues onto the great agitators themselves, when in reality it's just their hurt that they haven't worked through yet.

The great agitators are a gift from Spirit, sent to assist us in our evolution. On some level, we all know that something's got to give. The consciousness of this knowledge is the Blackout. It is the understanding that we must shift the old to bring our world back into alignment, so that new forms and new structures can emerge. This means that everything that has not been created or transformed through the lens of love, and the lens of harmony, and the lens of balance for all humanity, as well as for every other plant and animal species on the planet, is surfacing so that we can get a clear look at the choices that have led us to this collective experience, so that we can restructure our world from a place of love.

Human progress has been pushed forward at a breakneck pace in a drive for power, domination, and achievement that has served the interests of individual nations and corporations far more than it has served the species as a whole. Until now, technological advancement has been driven by consciousness of competition—by the desire to innovate first, best, biggest, and fastest.

This strategy has divided people across artificial boundaries while creating technologies that destroy life. It's like, the Manhattan Project got America props for creating the first nuclear bomb. Great. That's quite an achievement in terms of innovation and engineering. But maybe we should have engaged a little discernment, and asked ourselves if this was the kind of technology we actually wanted on our planet in the first place, and checked in to make sure it was going to serve the good of mankind before going about mass-producing atomic bombs for profit.

If we want the species to endure, we cannot continue to let our egos drive progress. Evolution is not a power play; it is a collaborative endeavor meant to serve the betterment of life. We can no longer innovate for the sheer sake of innovating. We must employ discernment, and we must make sure that our every action honors the life code and improves the quality of life for all people and all beings, as well as for the planet itself.

The Blackout marks a choice point for humanity—a crossroads where human beings get to choose if we want to continue to thrive on planet Earth, or if we decide to let it all fall apart. It can still go either way. If we continue to shove our heads in the sand, and pretend like nothing's wrong, and that it's all working out fine because we have eleven thousand Instagram followers, and our manicure is on fleek, then it's gonna be painful, and we might very well blow it. But if we choose to get real, and take a long, hard look at the core issues humanity is facing, and take responsibility for the imbalances we have created, then we can ring in a Giant Age here on Earth.

You see, that's part of the prophecy as well. Sure, the shamans, and the indigenous people, and even Nostradamus himself foresaw the cataclysmic events that were to threaten humanity during this time. But they also spoke of a golden age—an era marked by incredible peace, joy, harmony, and prosperity that follows the Blackout. It's not a done deal; but if we set the house on fire, thereby burning down all the old programs that are stealing our light; and if we choose to evolve out of love instead of fear, utilizing higher intelligence to create new structures that support the well-being of *all* beings—not just the ones who were born on the coast, and went to prep school, and got rich, or famous, or both—then we can level up this world, and create what I call the Giant Age. But the only way we're going to experience heaven on Earth is if we transmute the darkness that's blinding us to the light that is our birthright.

THE DARKNESS

A lot of New Age love-and-light types like to pretend that there's no such thing as darkness. Well, I'm here to tell you that there *is*. It doesn't matter how holy you claim to be, or how powerful you think you are, or how many times you chant Ganesha's name while fingering your mala beads and staring at your third eye, if you've incarnated on planet Earth, you're dealing with darkness on some level or another.

One of the most mind-blowing things the spirits showed me when I died was the incredible array of multidimensional realities comprising the Earth plane. And when I say incredible array of multidimensional realities, I'm not talking, like, a hundred, or a thousand. I'm talking about millions, and billions, and zillions of different earthly realities that all exist simultaneously, now. People have a hard time wrapping their heads around that one, which I get if you haven't flatlined and had the spirits spell it out for you while your spirit left your body and soared throughout the cosmos for what felt like an eternity. Still, that's what it means to live in a quantum reality, wherein every possibility you can imagine—and about a million, billion more that you can't (or rather, *haven't yet*)—all exist on their own dimensional plane.

Darkness is one of these possibilities that exists. The darkness is a very real dimensional realm that thrives on fear, lack, and separation. Darkness is prevalent in this particular region of the cosmos because this part of the galaxy happens to contain dark matter. Just like Arizona has cacti, and Switzerland has mountains, and Antarctica has glaciers, the Milky Way has dark matter—lots of it.

Dark matter is an extremely dense energy frequency held within an extremely dense form. Human beings experience the darkness it generates like a void, or a black hole. When a being's consciousness gets sucked into that black hole, it synchronizes with the frequencies of the darkness. These frequencies affect our entire reality through our thoughts, words, and actions, which are manipulated by the darkness to generate more darkness.

THE MATRIX

The darkness operates through the matrix—an intricate system steeped in rules, and patterns, and programs that exist to keep us enslaved. Once we're caught in the grips of the system, the darkness hacks into our unconscious minds so as to dominate and restrict our behavior, while generating the frequencies of fear, doubt, lack, and conflict in order to feed its own realm. The matrix programs us to believe we are free, while generating a distortion frequency within our energy patterns that actually blocks us from taking conscious action to exert our free will. It does this by planting a belief into our collective psyche that we must follow the rules of the matrix if we are to survive.

The matrix is all about boxes. It exists to keep us living in boxes, and thinking in boxes, and doing the same things everyone else is doing, all day, every day, for the rest of our lives, because boxes, and patterns, and the status quo make humans easy to control. Think about it. We've all been indoctrinated with the standard-issue life dream formula the system tells us we're supposed to be living. It goes like this: go to school, get brainwashed, go to college, get more brainwashed, drink beer, get a degree, get a job, get married, have kids, get promoted, get a mortgage, take a yearly vacation, buy stuff on the holidays, retire, take up golf, be a grandparent, get cancer and die. The matrix exists to make sure you follow this formula, so that you can do your part to support the very system that's enslaving you. Except you think you're free because you went to Maui for a week last June. That's not freedom, my love. That's a bone.

The matrix gets you to follow these rules by programming your consciousness to believe that if you don't, then something bad is going to happen. Sometimes the bad thing is a concrete vision—like, that you're going to lose all your savings, and be destitute, and have to survive on whatever change you can collect while panhandling on the side of the freeway off-ramp. But at other times you don't even know what that bad thing is. It's just this vague, nebulous feeling of doom and gloom, and you know that if you don't follow the rules, and do what you're supposed to do, something terrible is definitely going to happen.

Except it isn't. That's just the darkness fucking with you. And that's why I wrote this book—to give you all the tools you need to take your power back from the matrix, and not go falling for darkness's shenanigans.

THE MAYA

Remember, the matrix was built by the darkness to maintain control over humanity by locking us inside a bubble we cannot see, and programming us to think we're free, so we will continue to blindly do its bidding. The system depends on human beings remaining stuck in the Hindu concept of *maya,* which means "illusion." When we're stuck in the maya, we're caught in survival mode, suffocating and in perpetual overwhelm, while juggling have-tos, jumping through hoops, and trying *not* to drown in an endless sea of red tape, media input, and OS updates. Survival consciousness is what generates the fear and separation frequencies that keep the darkness alive, while blinding us to the fact that there's more to life than third-dimensional slavery and the rules, structure, and shackles the matrix places upon us.

The thing is, we did not incarnate on this planet just to survive. We came here to create joy, and love, and magic. Every human being is created out of the great light fold of the continuum, which is what we call *God*—that omnipresent, omnipotent, all-encompassing orgasmic energy field—and is here to be a creator. Because that's what God is—a pure, unconditionally loving, infinite, everywhere-at-once, all-knowing, all-loving, all-powerful, creative energy source.

A lot of people get all tripped up about what God really is because religion—which is absolutely, positively a tool of the matrix—has given God a bad rap. Religion has painted God as this twisted pervert, perched high up on a throne in the sky, where he gets off on punishing folks because they didn't say enough Hail Marys, or bow to Mecca the right way. As though God is petty and has self-esteem issues. *Please.* God doesn't punish, and God doesn't judge. All God does is love, and create, and love, and create, and love, and create, and create, and create.

As children of God, that's exactly what we're meant to do, too. Human beings are creation. Creation is our very essence. Our entire purpose here on planet Earth is to create. It is to lift and to shift, and to thrive, while living the lives of our dreams, and creating a better world for our brothers and sisters, and all beings.

The matrix exists to make you forget that you are a quantum creator by keeping you operating in survival mode, and making you a slave to the system, which sustains itself by stifling your life force, and dumbing you down by: pumping you up with sugar, jacking you up on caffeine, dulling you down with fluoride, poisoning your body with pills, programming your consciousness with fear and lies and celebrity gossip, and whacking you so far out that you don't even notice when things are imbalanced and out of alignment—kind of like our planet right now. I call it being a bobblehead, which means acting like a sheep. Because once your brain has been hijacked by the darkness, you become more concerned with following the herd, and being like everyone else, than with thinking for yourself, let alone with living a lit life as a quantum creator.

DARKNESS JUST *IS*

As whacked as it all sounds, the darkness isn't actually bad. It's not jacking human beings up on judgment and scarcity while manipulating us to be brain-dead minions because it hates us. Darkness is just doing what it needs to do to survive, which means generating enough discord and enough conflict to maintain its realm.

One of the darkness's primary survival strategies is to convince human beings that we are separate through the pretense of lines and divisions, such as class, color, gender, ethnicity, religion, politics, and sexual orientation—all relatively meaningless constructs that, at this point in human evolution, are only holding us back. The illusion of separation serves the darkness by generating isolation and conflict, which generate the frequencies of fear and discord, which empower its dimension. The matrix goes to great lengths to keep us disconnected from ourselves and from others, as well as from nature. The state of the world today is a confronting reflection of how destructive the *us*-versus-*them* mentality that darkness generates actually is.

DUALITY

The concepts of *us* versus *them, black* versus *white,* and even *dark* versus *light* come from our fundamental misunderstanding of duality. Let's break it down, shall we?

The darkness's realm emits a reflective energy that is illuminated by the light of all that is. The perceived separation of light and darkness as they reflect off one another in this universe is what we call *duality*. The way we experience it on this planet, duality is a construct comprised of two polar opposites interacting with each other in an allegedly separate experience but that is, in fact, a perpetual quantum entanglement. This plays itself out here on Earth through the idea of *right* versus *wrong, men* versus *women, Left* versus *Right,* etc. The act of framing these alleged "sides" in opposition to one another tethers them together in an ongoing exchange of tension and friction in a continuous fight for autonomy that is impossible to resolve in light of the opposition they are identified with and defined by.

Culture programs us to judge these polarity constructs as *good* or *bad*. The thing is, *good* and *bad* are subjective opinions that don't actually exist of their own accord. *Good* and *bad* are arbitrary judgments defined by our social structure. For instance, whereas we in the States judge the idea of serving dog for dinner as wrong and bad, in Cambodia, the idea of dressing your Chihuahua in a sweater and letting it sleep in your bed and lick you on the mouth is just as appalling.

Duality is a culturally indoctrinated lens of perception. We don't have this in shamanism. Shamans don't classify things as good or evil. We understand that the beings and the circumstances that are creating pain and resistance in our lives are gifts from Spirit that are supporting our growth. We don't label them as *good* or *bad,* or *right* or *wrong.* We have darkness, and we have light. Darkness isn't bad. Darkness is just an energy frequency that needs love to return it to the light.

Think of darkness like a drop of ink that's been added to a glass of water, which is the light. The presence of the ink doesn't invalidate the water's existence. The water just needs to be purified to return to its original state. But the ink isn't bad, and the water isn't better, because duality doesn't work like that. Duality is an evolutionary construct that allows us to understand what *is* and what *isn't*. The purpose of duality isn't about choosing sides; it's about transcending the illusion of sides altogether, and learning to embrace the whole.

The Blackout is asking us to evolve beyond duality, which means our task is not to blame the darkness, or to shame the darkness, or to fight the darkness. Our task is to embrace the darkness, and all the lessons it is illuminating, while taking responsibility for the world we have cocreated, stepping into our rightful place as quantum creators, and lifting and shifting ourselves, and the planet.

EMBRACE THE DARKNESS

Darkness is light distorted through consciousness. Distorted, fragmented, and seemingly separate though it is, darkness is still light. Our purpose here on Earth is to bring these fragmented aspects of duality—*our* fragmented aspects of duality—back into wholeness. We are here to bring the darkness home. When we incarnate, we agree to allow darkness into our beings so that we can understand it, and learn from it. This relationship allows us to cultivate the ability to meet the darkness with love, which is what—ultimately—allows the darkness to be redeemed and to return home to the light.

Remember, shamanism is relational, and shamanism is inclusive. We don't cut things out, or write them off with judgment and intolerance. We engage every aspect of life from a place of openness and humility, so that we can learn and grow.

Our species has been stuck on the wheel of suffering for quite some time, stubbornly believing that the only way we can evolve is through pain, or tragedy, or destruction, or calamity, or heartbreak; and that only after enduring whatever terrible things we endure, will we then be ready to change our behavior, make smarter choices, connect to our spirituality, and transform. The problem with this approach is that fear and suffering do not make for very efficient adaptation tools. They're infused with darkness, they're not in alignment with divine will, and—quite frankly—they don't make the evolutionary process all that inviting.

The matrix has been driving the pain and suffering narrative for quite some time, programming people with this ridiculous notion of a spiteful God who punishes the bad and rewards the good, and gets his panties in a bunch if you don't prostrate yourself before his imaginary God feet while chanting in some dead language with your eyes crossed, or whatever other nonsense the gatekeepers try to shove down our throats to keep us in line. Religion is a tool the matrix uses to make us fear God, and to follow more rules, and to keep us from knowing our true divinity, and from knowing ourselves as quantum creators in an unconditionally loving universe. Because, if the truth got out, then we wouldn't be putting money in the collection plate, or signing on to some stifling hierarchical system that has us believing we need a priest or a rabbi to talk to Spirit for us. I talk to spirits all day, every day, and believe me—you don't.

Our choice to evolve through pain, and suffering, and discomfort is exactly that—a choice. The Blackout is playing out on parallel energy fields being informed by the frequencies of duality that human beings have created on Earth. The Blackout is demanding that we evolve, but we get to choose how we want to go about it. We can do it the old way, and evolve through fear, pain, and suffering, or we can make the choice to evolve through love, for love's sake.

EVOLUTION, LOVE STYLE

When we evolve through love, we make a deliberate choice to take responsibility for our experience here on Earth. Responsibility means *the ability to show up with love*. Taking responsibility means we respond to all things with love, no matter what those things may be, without exception. When we respond with love, the universe creates an energetic opening that allows evolution to expand through us. By choosing to evolve through love, we are able to observe imbalance objectively, without leaping to shame, or blame, or deny, or separate; instead, by perceiving reality through the lens of unconditional love and acceptance, we can thereby easily discern what needs to shift to be put back in order.

The Blackout is a call for humanity to evolve through love. It is an opportunity for us to level-up our every global structure through higher intelligence, and to create life-affirming frameworks that support all beings in thriving and living lit, poprocks lives. The Giant Age can only be created by human beings living and loving in alignment, unified by a shared vision of a balanced, sustainable system that supports everyone in being fulfilled on all levels of their being. The key is to empower ourselves—to take our energy and our attention away from the matrix, and to refocus it on the Giant Age we are choosing to create.

2

THE FEMININE FACTOR

As the Blackout unfolds, we find ourselves navigating more and more chaos in our relationships, as well as within the collective social construct. People are creating conflict, manifesting drama, breaking down, breaking up, and freaking out. This turmoil is a reflection of humans' lack of emotional intelligence.

Our emotional intelligence deficiency is a direct result of the devaluing of the feminine, in all her many expressions, which means that to raise our emotional intelligence—as individuals, as well as a collective—we must understand how masculine and feminine energetics function in this reality.

EQUAL + OPPOSITE

Everything in our world is composed of energetic polarities. The interplay between equal and opposite energetic forces is what holds this reality construct together. Masculine and feminine are equal and opposite energetic forces that must be properly balanced if we are to live in harmony here on planet Earth. Our world is out of balance because, for quite some time, we have been overemphasizing the masculine while disregarding the importance of the feminine. This is why humanity's emotional intelligence levels are so stunted—because we haven't valued the feminine to the same extent as we have the masculine.

The Blackout is presenting us with an amazing opportunity to evolve into a new awareness of higher intelligence. To do this, we must restore balance and alignment to Earth, which means we must lift the feminine. Of course, this means empowering women to step into their greatness, and to be giant, and to lead the planet back into alignment. At the same time, we must also elevate feminine qualities in all people, regardless of biological (or even psychological) gender, while incorporating feminine energies into our society and our world. This can only happen when we acknowledge that men and women are different, and that masculine and feminine energies consist of very different qualities, and that both are valuable and necessary for the survival of the species.

MASCULINE + FEMININE ENERGETICS 101

The feminine is, by nature, intuitive and emotional. The feminine is about feeling, and flowing, and merging, and connecting, and relating. Masculine energy, on the other hand, is about structure, and placement, and task. It's about patterns, and regimen, and routine. Masculine is about doing, and fixing, and achieving, and accomplishing stuff.

The feminine—which is, by nature, unstructured—is meant to be harmonized by the directed orientation of the masculine. Notice I said *harmonized by,* not dominated by. The masculine has long dominated the feminine by incorrectly equating emotion with weakness, and intuition with nonsense. In devaluing these qualities, both men and women have suffered, as has society, and Earth itself.

When the masculine and the feminine are in sync, they complement each other in a beautiful symbiosis. But when the ordered, problem-solving nature of the masculine is not balanced by the expanded, emotional perspective of the feminine, both become distorted.

While women tend to embody mostly feminine energy, and men tend to embody more masculine energy, we all carry masculine and feminine energetics inside us. Therefore, when I say *masculine* and *feminine,* I am referencing not just men and women, but I am also speaking to the natural polarity distinctions that determine how we perceive and engage reality.

When men and women are relating to one another from masculine and feminine energies that are balanced, they bring out each other's strengths, and amplify them. The same goes for the world. When we, as a collective, bring the masculine and the feminine energetics informing our politics, and our culture, and our education, and our environment, and our economics, and our everything into balance, that's when we will find ourselves thriving on a poprocks planet in a Giant Age for all.

LOGIC VERSUS INTUITION

Logic and intuition are fundamental masculine/feminine polarities. Logic is an intellectual reasoning construct that relies on facts, figures, data points, and deductive reasoning to establish whether or not something is true. Intuition is a means of perceiving reality through a far more subtle and intricate internal cognition process. Fundamentally, intuition is the synthesis of emotions and empathic energies, combined with the machinations of the central nervous system, the sympathetic nervous system, and the parasympathetic nervous system. These perceptual instruments collaborate to create a comprehensive sensory apparatus that allows us to perceive which energy frequencies are in alignment with our being, and with our environment, and which ones are not. Basically, our intuition is our internal *yes,* and our internal *no.*

Spirit Hack: Calibrating Your INS

To fully integrate these ideas, we cannot just process them with the cognitive mind. The mental body is amazing and all, but to get any kind of integrated understanding of anything, we must have our own personal experience of it. Shamanism is all about experience. It's not about believing someone else's words, or signing on to someone else's so-called authority. Shamanism is about empowering ourselves by way of our own embodied experience. That's what the spirit hacks are for.

This is a spirit hack to calibrate your internal navigation system (INS). Ancient shamans—who happened to be women—utilized this technique as a way to figure out where their itinerant tribes should settle, as it allowed them to decipher if there was water nearby, and if there was game nearby, as well as which plants were safe to ingest, and which ones were poisonous. Calibrating your INS is a way of connecting to your own personal compass, so that you can know when something is aligned for you, and when something is not.

- Ground into your body with a few deep breaths. Place your awareness on your internal state by observing the rise and fall of your belly with each inhale and exhale.

- Say, out loud: "Body, show me *yes,* so that I can feel it."

- Scan your body for sensations.

Notice what you feel, and where you feel it. It might be tingles in your solar plexus. It might be throbbing behind your eye. It might be a rush of energy in your chest. It might be a twitch in your elbow. It might be a scratchiness in your throat. It could be any sensation, anywhere in your body. When you identify a feeling and a location, you want to speak those details out loud (I'll explain why in Part II, when we delve deeper into the spirit hacks).

- Say, out loud: "I feel _____ in my _____."

- Then, say, out loud: "Body, show me *no*, so that I can feel it."

- Scan your body for sensations.

- Say, out loud: "I feel _____ in my _____."

You can use this spirit hack anytime you want to get clarity on a question or a situation. Like, if you want to go to the beach but you're supposed to work, you can ask yourself: "Is it in my highest and best interests to go to the beach today?" Or, if you're not sure the person you've been messaging with on that dating app is really worth the energy, you can ask yourself, "Is there any authentic alignment or connection worth exploring with this person?" And then listen for your body's unique *yes* or *no*, and make an informed decision from there.

Now, in case it's not already completely obvious, intuitive knowingness is not any less relevant than knowledge we deduce by logic. But because this culture has sought to demonize the feminine, and invalidate the feminine, intuitive knowingness is often derided and cast aside as nonsense, while logic has been elevated as the be-all and end-all of cognitive processes, much to the detriment of the species. You see, intuition is an extremely valuable asset when it comes to survival and adaptation, because it is the faculty that allows us to sense danger and imbalance before they actually manifest. The choice to elevate logic over intuition has had a profoundly negative impact on humans' ability to clue into and correct the imbalances threatening our planet. It has also seriously hindered our ability and our willingness to develop our sensory faculties, as well as our emotional intelligence.

When "Logical" People Act Illogically

Shamanism is all about the feminine. It's about feeling, and sensing, and trusting subtle inner cues. I deal with mysterious unseen energetic forces all day, every day; and I also deal with a bunch of so-called logical people trying to discount my practices, my healings, my experience, and my shamanic lineage as so much imaginary woo-woo, framed through their ignorant, distorted, masculine lens of perception. Can you imagine the nerve of these people, invalidating the entire spirit realm as bullshit just because they haven't seen it, and they haven't explored it, and they haven't studied it, and they don't understand it? I mean, the arrogance of human unconsciousness is just ridiculous.

For the record, logic is an assessment strategy that entails going on discovery, and doing one's due diligence to either affirm or deny the veracity of the structure in question. A truly logical person has an idea about something, and then goes on the discovery process to gather data and proof to validate their idea as true or false. An illogical person spouts their opinion with no actual knowledge to back it up, while claiming the stuff coming out of their mouth is "logical," because they're parroting their indoctrination. It's absurd.

If we are going to make it through the Blackout, people really need to start questioning their thoughts, and their beliefs, and start figuring out the truth for themselves. I mean, if people are going to claim to be logical, then they need to get freakin' logical.

THE FEMININE UNIFIES; THE MASCULINE DIVIDES

The masculine is naturally oriented toward itself, and therefore, it priori-tizes what it wants, and what it needs, and what's going to serve it over the well-being of the whole, and the parts making up that whole. Now, let's be clear. I'm not saying that men are divisive, or incapable of caring about the collective. I'm talking about how the masculine polarity is naturally oriented, and how it inherently expresses without its feminine counterpart balancing it out.

Fighting, warring, winning, dominating—these are all masculine con-cepts. The masculine sees the world through an *us* versus *them/me* versus *you* lens, framing others as adversaries to be triumphed over, rather than as allies to collaborate with. This orientation is informed by thousands and thousands of years of biological imprinting and survival programming from way back when we were tribal nomads living in very, very different conditions than we are today. These leanings and perspectives weren't an issue when the feminine was equally empowered and respected, and when women were honored for their intuition, their sensitivity, and their emo-tional intelligence, because men and women were balancing one another out, and the planet was aligned and thriving.

Our modern world paints a very, very different picture, wherein we are disconnected from the feminine, while the masculine runs the show. This imbalance has us operating from an *every man for himself* kind of mentality, instead of attuning to the bigger picture of community and what serves the good of all. Having overemphasized the masculine to such an extreme, we identify as separate individuals competing against one another for limited resources, rather than as a unified species devoted to everyone's well-being on a planet of abundance. When we entertain thoughts that tell us there isn't enough for everyone, we are under the influence of the darkness, and thereby stuck in the maya, and operating in survival mode, where thriving is impossible, and the lit train makes no stops.

THE MASCULINE HOARDS; THE FEMININE GIVES

Lack consciousness wants us to believe that there is never enough, and that we have to fight over a limited amount of finite resources if we are to survive. The collective willingness to buy into the idea of scarcity, hook, line, and sinker is a direct result of our disconnection from the feminine nature of the planet itself.

The feminine gives. That's what it does. Look at all that women give— to their children, to their partners, to their families, to their friends. Women will empty their well of every last drop, giving water to everyone in the village, and in their lives, so that everyone's thirst can be quenched. It's why I call women *the divine givers*.

Guess what else gives? Nature. The Earth is a feminine planet, animated by a distinctly feminine spirit, named Gaia. Gaia's function is to provide—to constantly provide—because that providing is what generates harmony and balance on planet Earth. The sun gives. The moon gives. The trees give. The oceans give. Nature is always, always giving. If any part of nature was to suddenly get greedy and start hoarding its gifts, and withholding its offerings, every living species would die.

Humans limit, and hoard, and give their power away to lack consciousness because they are perceiving reality through the distorted masculine lens of *you versus me*. They don't understand that the entire *you-versus-me* perspective is completely absurd. *You versus me* makes no logical sense, because it implies that it has to be one or the other. Like there's not enough room or oxygen for both of us to exist. Earth doesn't work like that. This isn't an either/or planet. It's a *yes, and* planet. It's not like because the sun shines, the moon's got to take a hike, or that for glaciers to exist, volcanoes have to be eradicated. Yes the sun shines, and yes the moon shifts the tides, and yes the volcanoes rumble, and yes all of nature does all its unique nature things without any lame separation hang-ups, because nature knows how to coexist. Humans are also part of nature, which means that if we're gonna make it through the Blackout, we have to learn how to coexist as well. That means we have to embrace the feminine.

SEPARATION IS A SLIPPERY-ASS SLOPE

Whereas the masculine is primarily self-serving and therefore prone to employing division and competition to get what it wants, the feminine operates from an integrated perspective, seeking to harmonize, connect, and serve. The feminine utilizes emotion and intuition to attune to the well-being of the larger construct, as well as the parts it contains.

When we overemphasize the masculine, as human beings have done for centuries, we shut down our emotional and intuitive faculties, as well as our connection to/compassion for the whole. Thus disconnected from our planet, ourselves, and one another, we misperceive the world through the lens of separation. This allows us to rationalize the use of violence and aggression to achieve power and control, instead of promoting nurturing, heart-centered action in service to the greatest good of all. Today we are bearing witness to what happens when the balance swings too far in one direction for too long. We are witnessing a world starving for the feminine.

The imbalance between the masculine and the feminine has not only created the conditions for a hostile global environment, and for the Blackout itself, but it has also created cracks in our collective energy field—cracks through which we have allowed the darkness to seep in.

ENTER THE DARKNESS . . .

The darkness goes to great lengths to disempower the feminine, because women are wired for peace and inclusivity—neither of which feeds the dark realm. The matrix has to keep women down, because the conflict and the divisiveness the overbearing masculine continues to create are keeping the underworld alive and kicking.

In ancient times, when humans were aligned with nature and with spirit, there was harmony between men and women. Back then, each person played their role in service to the well-being of the whole in a beautiful, coherent symbiosis. Then the darkness up and shoved its nose in humanity's business and infected men and women with a distortion frequency that has allowed the darkness to maintain a considerable amount of control over humanity.

The matrix knows it needs the feminine off-line to survive, which is why it infiltrates the minds of men and manipulates them into believing that feminine energy is weak. As we have bought into the programming that devalues and disconnects us from feminine energetics, we have also underestimated the power of women and disrespected the deep wisdom they hold. The darkness knows that if women were in power, and if emotion and intuition were valued and respected in our society, then we—as a harmonized collective—would sense the distortions and the imbalances in the system, tear the whole thing down, and redo it in a loving, sustainable way. But that doesn't really serve the darkness's agenda all that well, now does it?

THE LIFE CODE

You see, the darkness is smart. It knows that women carry the life code, and that women are wired to honor and protect life. The ancient Egyptians knew this as well, which is why the ankh is featured so prominently in their mythology. The symbol, which looks a lot like the whole vagina/ birth canal situation, represents eternal life, because women are life givers. Women are the ones who continue to bring life to this planet, generation after generation after generation. Women's wombs are imprinted with the life code inside them, meaning that the walls of a woman's uterus are literally encoded with geometric symbols (the ankh included), which act as portals and sensory mechanisms that attune women to the balance and well-being of life on the planet.

Men don't have the life code inside them. They are not concerned with the inner workings that allow an organism to sustain life and consciousness. Men are attuned to structure and function. This is why when a little boy encounters a butterfly for the first time, he wants to know how it works, and what it's made of, and whether or not it bleeds; and he will go about trying to figure these things out by tearing off its wings and poking it with a stick. The feminine, on the other hand, is operating through a multitude of sensory apparatuses that allow females to intuitively understand that the butterfly contains the life code. So instead of hurting it, or mutilating it, or trying to figure out what its guts look like, the little girl will simply cradle the butterfly in her hands while marveling at its beauty, and its intricacies, intuitively sensing the creature's delicate nature, its gentleness, and its majesty.

The life code is what allows females to sense quantumly. As we've already established, quantum means *operating on multiple dimensions simultaneously*. The feminine is quantum. Women's sensory apparatus is quantum. And sure, we all have masculine and feminine energies inside us, but given that women carry the life code, women are sensing on a whole different level—make that level*s*.

THE MASCULINE IS LINEAR; THE FEMININE IS QUANTUM

Think of the masculine as a line, and the feminine as a circle. As a line, the masculine moves on a straightforward linear trajectory, which—when it comes to getting shit done—is amazing. Following the circular feminine is more like riding the loop on a roller coaster. One moment, you're heading toward the sky; and the next one, you're upside down; and then suddenly, you're speeding down a steep drop into a giant pool of water. It's a totally different experience.

Whereas women's quantum, intuitive nature allows them to feel how a system functions internally, men are more drawn to the external structure that contains those functions. Women's connection to the internal allows them to also understand why the external structure is misaligned but from a more expanded, informed perspective.

When we are assessing a situation through the lens of the linear masculine, we are sensing through a very narrow lens of perception that seeks to understand, and to problem solve, and to get what it wants and what it needs. When we are sensing through the quantum feminine, we are attuning to a multitude of factors—internal, external, visible, and invisible—while devoting ourselves to finding coherent balance among all constituent parts and players for the greater good of the whole. It's a completely different frame of reference.

The matrix doesn't want us sensing internal and external imbalances, and it certainly doesn't want us sensing quantumly. When it comes right down to it, the matrix doesn't want us sensing anything at all, ever, period, because were humans to be able to feel and perceive how imbalanced our world has become, we would take action to change it immediately.

SENSORIUM

One of the biggest reasons why humans are so deficient in emotional intelligence is because humans can't feel their feelings. It's very challenging to master our emotional state when we can't actually sense our emotions in the first place. We've lost touch with our feelings because we've lost touch with our sensorium.

Sensorium is the body's sensory apparatus. It allows us to not only feel our own feelings and energies, but also to feel other beings' feelings and energies. When I say *beings,* I don't just mean people. I mean trees, plants, insects, and animals, as well.

Shamans know what we know, and shamans can do what we do, because shamans' sensorium is on point AF. Let me tell you, it is a very, very different experience of reality when we can actually feel the world we are living in—when we can feel the discord, and we can feel the love, and we can feel the anguish, and we can feel the joy, and we can feel the all of it. Most people are operating with a completely shut-down sensorium and have no idea what they feel, let alone what the trees, or the birds, or the parks, or the people around them are feeling. It's sad, because most people have no idea how much they are missing out on.

It's why I don't drink alcohol, and I don't do drugs, and I don't smoke pot, and I don't sip champagne at weddings, or bar mitzvahs, or on international flights. I don't dibble-dabble—ever—because I'm a shaman, and even just the occasional dibble-dabble would quell my sensorium, and interfere with my ability to communicate with the spirits who come through me. Shamans maintain very clean, very pure vessels so that we can commune with the spirit realm. Especially spirit shamans, who aren't using plant or animal medicines to move between worlds. I don't intoxicate myself because my work as a shaman is dependent upon my having a strong sensorium. My sensorium is what allows me to be in a dynamic, engaged, communicative relationship with my surroundings at all times, which is crucial to being a shaman, because I never know when a spirit or an ancestor is going to come through, or give me instructions, or guidance, or a teaching, or a task to carry out.

The matrix doesn't want you to have a strong sensorium. The matrix wants you to be a bobblehead. It wants you numb, and dumb, and disconnected, and checked out, so that you don't notice that you're a slave to a system that's feeding off the misery that you can't even feel is there. The matrix cuts us off from our sensorium by polluting our consciousnesses with a constant stream of disruptive, fear-based media input transmitted by way of news, advertisements, pop music, scary movies, and blinking neon signs perpetually screaming *BANG! BANG!! BLOOD! GUTS! TERROR! FEAR! HORROR! DESTRUCTION! AWFULNESS!!!!!!!* in our faces, all the time.

This onslaught of what I call *aggravated stimulation* disconnects people from their sensorium by flooding their systems with information that is wholly unnecessary for them to adapt and to thrive. The only thing aggravated stimulation serves is the darkness. Aggravated stimulation overwhelms us and creates disturbance frequencies in the body, mind, and spirit that further separate us from our intuitive capabilities and make it that much harder for people to feel the imbalances that are threatening the well-being of this planet at this time.

THE EMOTIONAL INTELLIGENCE THING

A quantum leap in emotional intelligence is absolutely, 100 percent necessary if humanity is to make it through the Blackout. There is no way around it. Emotional intelligence is key.

Because the feminine has been so degraded on this planet, humans have not been taught to engage their emotions in a healthy, useful manner. To society's great detriment, the system has elevated the masculine propensity for reasoning over the feminine penchant for feeling. This imbalance has humans misidentifying emotions as some kind of shortcoming, thereby disregarding them, and barreling over them, while totally disrespecting the emotions' sacred function to help us grow. This is actually what those New Age, goddessy types are referring to when they speak about the "return of the divine feminine." They are talking about the healing of humanity's emotional body. They are talking about this pivotal moment in human history when our species chooses to consciously evolve, and to realign this planet by raising our emotional intelligence.

EMOTIONS GET A BAD RAP

Humans have a lot of fear and judgment around their emotions, as though certain emotions are bad or wrong, and that if we feel those emotions, we are terrible people. The truth is: emotions are never wrong, and emotions are never bad. Emotions are energetic tools that allow us to feel what it is we are experiencing. They are markers from the universe saying *You are here, now.* Feeling our feelings is what allows us to connect to truth. How we choose to act upon those feelings is another matter entirely. That's where emotional intelligence comes in. But judging our feelings for simply existing is straight-up absurd.

The problem is the mind, which is the masculine. The mind hijacks the emotions and tells the emotions that they are wrong, and tries to bully the emotions into pretending they are entirely different emotions altogether— emotions that are nicer, and more appropriate, and more socially acceptable. The kicker is that the mind's attempts to control the emotions distract us from feeling the things we really are feeling, which only furthers the disconnect. When the mind tries to dominate and suppress the emotions, we experience conflict and imbalance in our beings. Kind of like what we're seeing externally, on the planet itself. *As above, so below. As without, so within.*

This imbalance has led to a collective emotional intelligence deficiency, which manifests as repression and mismanagement of our emotions, as well as an overreliance on logic and reasoning as dominant life-navigation and reality-creation strategies.

EMOTIONAL MISMANAGEMENT

Because human beings have not been taught how to effectively manage, or relate to their emotions, they are easily overwhelmed by them. Emotional overwhelm manifests as emotional reactivity, which is a major, *major* issue on this planet.

Here's how it works: we receive some upsetting news that triggers an emotional response in the body. The instant that data registers marks a choice point. In that moment, we can choose how we want to interpret those emotions, and how we want to express those emotions, and whether or not we want to take the opportunity to learn from those emotions. Those of us riding the lit train will absolutely milk those emotions for all the lessons they have to teach us, because we're all about lifting and shifting, and we know that our emotions are here to help us evolve. But most people don't take advantage of that opportunity, or that choice point. Most people don't even know that such an opportunity exists, and that choosing different emotional responses is an option they can exercise in any moment. Humans don't know these things, because they don't teach us this stuff in school. Instead they teach us algebra, and how to regurgitate useless facts for even more useless grades, because schools are institutions of the matrix.

When we react, and we allow our emotions to overtake us, we generate an output expression that matches the exact same frequency band as the input stimulus that upset us to begin with. It's really quite ridiculous, because all it does is perpetuate the emotions that are causing our suffering in the first place, while spreading discordant vibrations into the world, bumming other people out, and shaping our realities in kind.

You see, emotions color our reality. When we are in love, we experience the world as loving. We are vibrating at the frequency of love, and so we see love everywhere, because reality is being filtered through that lens, and that resonance. Just like if we're sad, the world breaks our heart over, and over, and over again. But emotions don't affect just our perception of reality; they also determine how reality manifests by sending out electromagnetic frequencies that attract people and events that vibrate in kind. Like, when we are feeling frustrated and impatient, the universe sends us red lights, and detours, and interruptions, and complications, because the emotional frequencies of impatience and frustration are attracting matching experiences. This is why it's so important for people to stop giving their power away to fleeting emotions they don't want to be feeling in the first place, because those vibrational frequencies are organizing our reality.

DOORWAYS TO POSSIBILITY

When we allow our emotions to overwhelm us, and we react, and we spew them back out onto others, and into the world, without having filtered them through the lens of consciousness, we limit ourselves from accessing the full spectrum of possibilities that are available to us as quantum creators. The whole reason we incarnate on this planet, in this dimensional construct, is so that we can walk through as many doorways and have as many different experiences as possible. So why do humans choose to impose so many unnecessary limitations upon themselves by narrowing their emotional output expression options through unconscious reaction patterns? It makes no sense. I mean, that's what getting lit and living giant, poprocks lives is all about—expanding possibilities, not limiting them.

Shamans know that we are not our emotions. We don't identify with them, and we don't confuse them with the personalized construct of Self, which is why we don't feel the need to defend our feelings. When shamans get triggered, it's not about fighting, or lashing out, or shutting down, or freaking out. It's about bringing consciousness to the feeling, and then managing it accordingly: *I am having an emotion. An emotion is moving through me, and is animating my spirit. How interesting. Let me feel it, because I know it is fleeting, and that another emotion will soon be visiting my vessel.*

In shamanism, we don't relinquish our freedom to our emotions. We don't give our power away to our feelings. Shamans train to raise our emotional intelligence so that we can consciously choose the emotional frequencies we want to generate, instead of defaulting to the frequency of the emotional stimulus, which only enslaves us to that input. We do this by utilizing shamanic principles of awareness and emotional perception that allow us to consciously generate our own authentic emotional responses, instead of having something from the outside world generate them for us. We do this by spirit hacking.

When we use shamanic principles to raise our emotional intelligence, we cultivate the ability to perceive our emotions with clarity and consciousness. This allows us to pause before we react, and to decide for ourselves if the emotional frequency that's been triggered is one we want to generate more of, or if the emotional frequency that's been triggered is one we want to let go. The act of bringing consciousness to our emotions in real time, as they are stimulated, and then deliberately choosing how we respond gives us the ability to perceive reality in many different ways. Emotional intelligence allows us to expand our perception and to access different pathways of thought, as well as action, by generating a new emotional response to something that would have overtaken us in the past, and then seeing which doorway that new emotional frequency opens, and where it's going to lead us.

YOU ARE RESPONSIBLE FOR YOUR EMOTIONS

Emotional intelligence means taking responsibility for our own emotional state. So often people blame others for their internal experience in saying: *You made me feel like this,* or *He made me feel like that,* as though anyone has the power to make us feel anything, ever. It's ridiculous. Feelings are internally generated energies. We are responsible for our own emotions.

I'm a no-bullshit kind of shaman, and I don't beat around the bush, which means that sometimes my clients get upset at me for calling them out on things that they don't want to look at. I once had a client say to me during our session: "Shaman Durek, you make me feel like shit."

Now, if I were a narcissist or an underworld spirit, I probably would have been flattered by the idea that I was so powerful as to have control over someone else's emotions. But the fact is that I am a love being, and a shaman, which means I wasn't, and that I know better.

"I'm just being me, and showing up as I am," I explained to my client. "Out of the hundreds of thousands of different frequencies of emotional experiences that you could possibly pull from the universal field of consciousness, and generate for yourself, you are choosing the *feel like shit* frequency. That's on you, my love. But I am honored to be able to show up as a powerful reflection for you to be able to see what is already transpiring inside you."

My client really didn't like hearing that. Very few people want to hear that they are responsible for their experience of reality, and that if they want their reality to shift, then they must shift themselves. My client wanted me to sign on to her story, which painted her as a victim to my imaginary emotional control—not because me signing on to the story would make her feel any less shitty, but because me signing on to the story would allow her to be right.

HUMANS LOVE TO BE RIGHT

Pride has human beings thinking that they need to be right in order to feel safe. We lean on pride to keep us from feeling vulnerable, which is unfortunate, because being right is so dark ages.

Religious indoctrination has crippled humans with an almost debilitating fear of not being good enough, having programmed humans to think they need to embody some kind of idealized perfection to earn God's love. As though God hoards love, and withholds love, and only doles out little bits of love sparingly to supermodels, overachievers, and Olympic gold medalists. It's so ridiculous. This fear has made humans stubborn and arrogant when it comes to their ability—make that *inability*—to take responsibility for their issues, and their shortcomings, and for any form of discord in their lives. It's a really misguided orientation, because Earth is a planet of refinement, but not perfection. There is no such thing as perfection, people! We are here on this planet to learn and to grow, and we do that by making mistakes, and by learning from them.

Humans have to evolve beyond the idea that having faults, and having weaknesses, and making mistakes necessarily make us wrong or bad. And humans also have to learn how to receive feedback about our issues with humility, and to learn how to put that feedback to good use. I count on my friends and family to call me on my shit, and to keep me humble. My assistant calls me out for being high maintenance. He's right. I am very high maintenance. And even though it can be uncomfortable to hear that about myself when I'm caught up in the moment, and acting entitled and difficult, I appreciate that he cares enough to reflect back to me how I'm behaving, and how it's not serving anyone, including myself. How else am I going to see what I need to see about myself, so that I can lift and shift, and expand my superhuman capacities? I mean, if I were playing the pain game, and defaulting to some *evolve through pain* nonsense, then sure, I could manifest some sort of terrible crisis to see what I need to see about myself. But I'm riding the lit train, which means that I choose to evolve through love. I choose to evolve through joy, and through consciousness, and through my relationships, while strengthening my connection to my tribe. Calling each other out on our bullshit is a generous and loving act, because when we do, we are choosing to step toward the other in reflecting back to them what their evolution is asking them to see about themselves so that they can grow.

THE FEMININE FACTOR

The Blackout is here, now, because the imbalance between the masculine and the feminine has reached a crescendo. The imbalance of emphasis we have placed on the masculine has infected all our foundational societal structures, which are steeped in rules, regulations, hierarchy, red tape, power plays, and authority issues. We see this narrow, logical, structural toxicity infusing our schools, our government, and our social services, just as we see it in justice, law enforcement, and religion, where—as it is currently functioning—it only serves to make us feel *more* separate from source than we would without all these churches and temples and mosques alleging to tell us how we're supposed to worship Spirit, and live our lives.

The Blackout is an opportunity for us to tear down our already crumbling societal constructs, and to reenvision them through the lens of the feminine. We are being called to employ what I call the *feminine factor* to level-up our actions, our structures, our environment, our perspectives, and our relationships, so that they function harmoniously, in service to the well-being of all.

To do this, we must first foster the feminine in ourselves. We do this by balancing the masculine and the feminine in our own beings. We do this by raising our emotional intelligence, and empowering ourselves as quantum creators in a loving universe of infinite abundance.

PART II

SHAKE UP TO WAKE UP

3

GET REALER

et's be very clear: the matrix has its shit together. Like, *really* together. The matrix knows what it wants. It wants fear, and lack, and discord, and conflict, and separation. And it has created an efficient system of control to generate and extract these energies from the human beings it enslaves. We need only look at the rapid acceleration of the Blackout to indicate how much momentum the matrix has backing its agenda, which is to continue to provoke more and more discord among humans to feed the darkness. If we are going to rebalance this planet and manifest a Giant Age here on Earth, then we have to get real, and we have to get aligned, and we have to get aware, and we have to get empowered. And the only way we're going to do any of these things, is to level-up our wills.

WEAK WILLS MAKE FOR BOBBLEHEADS AND BLACKOUTS

The people who have bought into the matrix (aka: the majority of human beings on the planet) are weak-willed. They are driven by a strong need for external approval, and a strong need for external acknowledgment, and a strong need to achieve to convince themselves that they deserve the external approval, and the external acknowledgment they are striving for. Still, their wills remain weak.

When our will is weak, our actions are governed by the need to fit in, and the need for other people's approval, instead of by what is authentically aligned with our spirit. Most people don't even know what it means to be authentically aligned with their spirit, let alone how to embody it, or how to act from it. They are too distracted by the matrix, and by the various carrots of status, success, and happiness the system dangles in front of them—the ones the bobbleheads hustle to achieve to feel worthy of the love and acceptance that are everyone's birthright.

ALIGNMENT

Every human being on the planet has a unique energetic signature that connects them to specific energies and frequencies that are meant to support them on their path. Our signatures determine things like whether we are aligned to live in the city, or in nature; or if we do best working in solitude outside, or in an office with other people; or if we are inspired by creative pursuits over academic ones. If someone is meant to work with their hands, in nature, but instead they are hustling on Wall Street, they are going to suffer, because they are making choices that are not aligned with their signature.

When we are aligned with our signatures, we connect with people, and opportunities, and experiences that are harmonic and supportive. But when we make choices that are shaped by other people's ideas, opinions, or belief systems—as the vast majority of humans are currently doing—we betray our energetic signatures and craft lives for ourselves that are not aligned with who we authentically are, or what we really believe. The sad truth is that very few humans are living in alignment with their signatures.

WHAT ARE YOU DREAMING?

To have a strong will means to be committed to our truth, our authenticity, and ourselves with unwavering conviction. It means that we are in charge of our own ship, and that our actions are aligned with our desires. When our will is on point, we know who we are, we know what we want, we know where we are going, and we know what we need. Leveling up our will is the first step in getting lit, and living life as a quantum creator, wherein we not only get to dream giant but also to manifest those giant dreams quickly and easily.

As it is now, what with the Blackout and all, people are not dreaming their own dreams, let alone manifesting them. People are playing out the singular dream the system is programming them to follow. Sure, there are different flavors and expressions that give the construct the appearance of freedom—like, you can get rich being a lawyer, or a doctor, or a rapper, or a real estate developer—but they're just different means of getting rich, which is considered the crowning achievement in this culture, second only to getting rich *and famous*.

Billionaires Aren't Enlightened

I do shamanic work with a bunch of millionaires, and billionaires. You'd be surprised to know how many of them are miserable. These people have spent their entire lives out of alignment with their energetic signatures, and with their soul's true purpose, accumulating all the things the system told them would make them happy, and whole, and successful, and worthy, and lovable. They now have everything they've ever dreamed of, and all this external validation, and they're still empty. It's very confusing for these people, because they can fly anywhere in the world, and they can do anything they want to do, whenever they want to do it, which means they can't blame their misery on money problems the way everyone else does. Their despair comes from knowing that they let the system take from them the thing that mattered most—themselves.

The dream we are indoctrinated with isn't just about money or fame. It's about the spouse, the house, the family, the success, the car, the watch, the wardrobe, and whatever other external things the system tells us we need to accumulate to be somebody, and to matter. It's all bullshit. You don't have to achieve anything to matter. You matter because you are. Your presence, and your purpose, and your breath are sacred. You don't need to chant mantras, or wash lepers' feet, or marry a surgeon, or win a Nobel Prize or a Grammy to be sacred, and to be worthy, and to matter. God's will is for you to be happy, to be free, to be easy, to have love, to have joy, to have prosperity, to have good health, to have everything you could possibly want. And there is nothing you have to do or achieve to earn the right to have these experiences.

But the matrix doesn't want you to know this, because if we knew ourselves as whole, and as worthy of unconditional love, and acceptance, and ease, and joy, and health, and prosperity, and fulfillment exactly as we are right now, then we wouldn't yearn for all the things the system needs us to yearn for to keep it running.

THE DESIRE CYCLE

The dream the system indoctrinates in us is a lie. It doesn't deliver. It never delivers, and it never will. That would defeat the purpose of the matrix, which is to keep those it enslaves in a constant state of yearning, so that they will keep doing the darkness's bidding, so that they will continue to drive the system forward by way of unsustainable consumption, and all the discord the desire cycle creates.

Yearning is an energetic frequency the matrix generates to keep human beings in a constant state of craving. That craving drives humans to chase and to consume, which generates more craving, and more chasing, and more consuming, because chasing programmed desires doesn't satisfy programmed desires. It only creates more desires while helping the system to create more and more things for us to desire, to keep humans forever chasing the next best thing . . . and the next . . . and the next . . . and the next. . . .

That's why the big tech companies keep changing their ports and their accessories, and "upgrading" their phones, and computers, and operating systems. It's why car companies roll out new models every year, and why fashion houses drop new collections every season. It's because these corporations—which are tools of the matrix—know that human beings will always want bigger, and better, and shinier, and happier, and more, and more, and more, and more to try to fill that empty vacuous space inside them that has been deliberately put there by the matrix.

LACK

The system enslaves us through our desires by manipulating the mind to believe that something is missing. It does this through media and advertising that are constantly, constantly telling us we are not enough. This false notion of lack activates the yearning frequency in the emotional body, where it churns out negative energies like envy, hierarchy, and separation, as well as a bunch of distorted thoughts and beliefs that try to convince us that the grass is always greener on someone else's social media account, and that our value is based on the price of our handbag, or the make of our car, or the cup size of the woman on our arm. This endless desire influences the worst of human behavior, which throws dignity and integrity to the wind to get what it (thinks it) wants. The thing is: desire is a sham. The matrix uses desire to lure us into chasing external things that promise to quell the yearning it is manipulating, which is impossible. The dissonance the setup generates in human beings is what drives the system, because the more lack we see in ourselves, the more desire we generate, and the more external things we chase and consume in our efforts to quell the incessant longing the darkness has programmed in us.

The way it works is that the matrix flashes this shiny, sparkly thing in our face and puts on this whole song-and-dance routine to convince us that if we buy this widget, and if we follow this path, and if we look like this, and if we talk like this, and if we act like this, and if we do what they tell us to do, we're going to get the shiny, sparkly thing that we've been yearning for. Not only will we get the shiny, sparkly thing that we've been yearning for, but that shiny, sparkly thing will also give us all the happiness, success, fulfill-ment, and freedom we could possibly desire.

People with weak wills (aka bobbleheads) are susceptible to this trap because their discernment mechanism is off-line, which means they do whatever the matrix tells them to do, without ever stopping to ask them-selves if they actually want to be doing the thing the matrix is telling them to do, or what it actually is they really do want to be doing. So they just keep doing what everyone else is doing.

THE GRAND GLAMOUR

In shamanism, we call those shiny, sparkly things the system waves in front of our faces the *grand glamour*. It doesn't matter what form the thing actu-ally takes—whether it's a material object, or an experience, or a personal-ity, or a movement, or a lifestyle—the grand glamour is an enticing illusion that would-be manipulators use to distract people from what is actually important, and valuable, and authentic, and aligned. The system generates a steady stream of glamour by way of media, sports, fashion, technology, and advertising that exists to make us feel poor, ugly, and less than, while distracting us from our own authentic purpose and desires, as well as what's really happening on the planet.

Entertainment is the matrix's number one method of hypnotizing humanity, which is why actors make so much money. Playing make-believe might not seem like that important of a job in the grand scheme of how society functions, but when it comes to distracting the populace such that they will be so enchanted with the glamour that they continue to feed the matrix, entertainers turn out to be among the most important players in the system.

The grand glamour exists to mesmerize people with all the sparkle, and all the glitz, and all the hype so they won't notice how discordant the world actually is, and how out of alignment with themselves they really are. When we are under the spell of the glamour, our attention and our devotion are consumed by the theatrics of the matrix—by the pageantry, and the decadence, or by the absurdity and the outrage; and we become so consumed with the masquerade being played out, that we don't perceive all the fucked-up shit that's happening right underneath our noses.

The advertising industry uses the grand glamour to get us to buy stuff. You open a magazine, and what do you see? You see a glossy picture of a Greek god of a man wearing a Gucci suit, holding a half-naked supermodel on his lap, who's staring at him with bedroom eyes, and red lips, looking like she's four seconds away from unzipping his pants and mounting him. The image manipulates the consciousness of the person reading the magazine to envy, and to yearn, and to think: *Wow. If I just had that suit, I'd get to fuck a model, and everyone would envy me. Hell, that suit would probably even get me a raise, and a Benz. Sold!*

The same goes for women. They starve themselves to fit into sexy clothes, and they go into debt to buy the expensive Louboutin heels with the red bottoms, so that when they walk around town, everyone knows that their shoes are on trend, and that they're someone special. The problem is that when we are driven by the idea of being admired by everyone, we become a slave to those everyones. We become people's bitch. Which means that what all those red-bottomed shoes are really saying is: *I need you to approve of me so I can feel good about myself.* That's all status symbols ever really say: *I will do whatever the herd tells me to do so that I can fit in, because I don't actually know who I am.*

Rolex Schmolex

A friend of mine once offered me a Rolex and was really thrown when I told him I didn't want it. I don't wear a watch, and I'm not into status, so why would I want a Rolex? Why do people even care about Rolex anyway? It's not like Rolex is curing cancer, or creating positive change in the world. The only point of having a Rolex is to tell other people: *I'm rollin', man. I'm rollin'.* But that message, and those status symbols, just create more divisiveness, and more separation. I don't want to trigger other people's jealousy, or other people's envy, or other people's lack consciousness. I mean, it would be one thing if I were into watches, or I was into the history of Rolex, or I genuinely loved how wearing a Rolex made me feel. But most people are not buying Rolex watches because they're really into the mechanics that make Rolex a luxury item. Most people are buying Rolex watches so they can let everyone know that they are successful, and important, and worthy of your admiration, because they spent $8,000 on a watch. Whatever. I'd rather wear a really cool crystal that has natural wisdom and intelligence, and looks just as fierce.

The desire cycle is a trap, because yearning for fulfillment outside of ourselves only generates more desire. The desire for anything outside of ourselves is a distortion, which means those desire frequencies can't ever be satisfied, thereby making the desire cycle a continuous, self-sustaining loop. Sure, the dopamine rush of instant gratification is there in the beginning, but it dissipates just as quickly, landing us back in lack, and back in yearning, which starts the desire cycle all over again. The thing is, it doesn't matter how many things we acquire, or accumulate, or achieve, the yearning doesn't go away; the yearning won't ever go away. And the real kicker is that our efforts to satisfy the yearning by accumulating things outside of ourselves only puts us into energetic bondage with all those things through what we call quantum entanglement.

QUANTUM ENTANGLEMENT

Quantum entanglement binds us to energies in such a way that they influence our internal state of homeostasis—physically, psychologically, emotionally, and energetically. In the case of the desire cycle, the accumulation of so many external things that aren't truly aligned with our internal signatures tethers us to discordant energies that don't actually support our well-being. This creates a lot of disruption in people who've gone the distance to acquire the various things the matrix has enticed them to acquire, given that these things haven't brought the love and the happiness they promised, and are now only complicating their lives.

DEVOTION

In case it isn't totally obvious by now, the matrix isn't fucking around. It's got its system dialed. It's actually quite brilliant, from a design standpoint, because the way it's set up, all the people who the matrix is working against are the ones who are driving it forward. It's very efficient this way. Still, the system isn't foolproof. The darkness, and the yearning, and all the rest of it, can really only manipulate us when our will is weak. This is why it is so important that we level-up our wills, so that our devotion to love, and to

Spirit, and to truth, and to authenticity is so lit, and so poprocks, and so giant, that we can't be distracted by the matrix's tricks, traps, or theatrics.

Devotion is the energy that focuses our will, which—as I've already said, and am going to keep on saying, because it really is that important—is absolutely, unequivocally crucial for us to strengthen if we are to free ourselves from the grip of the matrix, and the darkness it serves. The will is the mechanism in the human vessel that allows us to take deliberate action. The will is what generates our devotion into third-dimensional form, and what manifests our devotion into third-dimensional form. When we are devoted to uplifting ourselves and the planet, and those energies are fortified by a strong will, then we are empowered to make positive change in the world, undeterred by the matrix's attempts to distract us.

When I talk about being strong in our will, I am talking about having the ability to consciously direct our attention toward anything we choose, and to hold it there with unwavering devotion, which is what fuels us to take positive, deliberate action. It is only when our devotion is aligned with light intelligence, as well as with our authentic path, and with our authentic purpose, and with our authentic joy, and with our authentic inspiration, that we can actually shift our planet back into balance.

It all begs the question: What are you devoted to? Are you devoted to checking your *Likes*? Are you devoted to talking shit about celebrities, or Republicans, or your friends? Are you devoted to partying, and zoning out in front of video games, or porn? Or are you devoted to lifting and shifting, and to raising your emotional intelligence, and to radiating positivity, and joy, and inspiration, while riding the lit train with your tribe, and raising the vibrations here on planet Earth for the greatest good of all?

THE FIRE ELEMENT

The fire element has been used as a tool for reflection by tribal cultures for centuries. In African shamanism, fire is known as "the perceiver"—the one who can see in all directions, and who sharpens our psychic abilities. Shamans call upon the fire element to understand how the mind is operating in conjunction with the will. Ancient tribespeople would peer into a fire while holding their energy on a specific intention, or a specific experience, or a specific outcome, because the fire energy ignites the spark of life in whatever we concentrate our devotion upon. It's called *fire scrying*.

Spirit Hack: Fire Scrying

Fire scrying allows us to strengthen the will by learning to direct our energy in one place, and to sustain it for an extended length of time. The longer we can hold our gaze upon something, and focus our devotion upon it, the more we absorb the energy of that thing, which allows us to align ourselves and our vibrational frequencies with our devotion. What we are training ourselves to do is to ground into that which we *choose* to ground into. We are training ourselves to take authority over our lives, and to choose where, when, and how we direct, commit, and devote our energy.

It's best to practice this spirit hack in seclusion, free from distractions, preferably, in a dark room, with your phone off, while wearing loose clothing. The intention is to liberate yourself from anything that could take your attention away from you, be it an incoming text, a wandering pet, or a swath of stiff, tight fabric digging into your thighs.

For this spirit hack you will need five candles.

- Sit cross-legged in a circle comprised of four lit candles, each representing the four directions.

- Light the remaining candle, and place it on the floor in front of you.

- Set a timer for five minutes.

- Stare at the candle while summoning a thought, or an energy, in your mind.

The thought can be anything you want to strengthen, or call in: love, money, your dream job, a chocolate chip cookie—whatever you want.

- Hold that thought/energy in your mind while gazing at the flame without diverting your eyes, or allowing any other thoughts to distract you.

The thought is your devotion. Your gaze is your commitment. Commit your devotion to that flame while focusing on nothing else for as long as you can.

- When the timer rings, snuff out the four candles surrounding you.

CLOSING THE PRACTICE

- Set the timer for five more minutes.
- Say: "I increase the fire inside of my being to allow me to see in all directions."
- Breathe consciously and deliberately, then repeat: "I increase the fire inside of my being to allow me to see in all directions."
- Keep breathing, and keep saying this aloud, until the timer goes off.

It is important to finish all fire scrying sessions with this short closing practice, because a will that is fortified with the sight of the four directions is one strong-ass will.

I encourage my students to practice fire scrying every day, *at least* once a day, and to challenge themselves to hold their gaze on the candle flame for longer and longer stretches of time as they progress. I recommend adding five minutes to your practice each week until you can hold your attention on the flame for an hour at a time.

Strengthening our will is crucial because it is only when our devotion to love is really strong—like, giant strong—that we can't be swayed, and we can't be distracted. Weak wills make us easy to control. The lack consciousness they generate makes us vulnerable to the programming of the matrix, and keeps us from questioning the indoctrination being foisted upon us. We don't think to pause and ask ourselves if what's being dangled in front of us is aligned with love, or with our own authentic truth, because without a strong will, we don't know what our authentic truth even is. If we knew ourselves, and valued ourselves, we wouldn't give our belief and our allegiance over so easily—especially to all the nonsense the mainstream media machine tries to shove down our throats. When our will is strong, we can't be controlled, and we can't be indoctrinated, because we know who we are, and that knowingness protects us from the darkness.

KNOW THYSELF WHOLE

When the will is weak, the desire to fit in and be a part of the in crowd overrides our devotion to alignment. This is why the darkness doesn't want us to know ourselves as whole, doesn't want us to attune to our authentic desires, and doesn't want us connected to each other, or to the planet, or to ourselves—because the entire matrix construct is dependent upon our belief in separation, and conditional love, and our inherent brokenness to function, and maintain the status quo.

The system has a vested interest in our insecurity and our crappy self-esteem, which is why it programs human beings to think they are fundamentally defective, and that safety can be found only in the cozy confines of the herd, which we are supposed to blindly follow without ever questioning its direction, its motives, or its sanity. This setup has humans afraid to be themselves, when that is exactly what we must do. The quickest, most effective way for us to take our power back from the matrix is to ground into our authentic selves—to know and embody ourselves so well, and be so lit, that there are no cracks in our consciousness for the darkness to seep in through. The way we take our power back from the matrix is to root so deeply into the truth of our wholeness, and our connectedness, and our unconditionally loving natures, that we become impervious to all the ways the system tries to steal our sovereignty, and our life force.

KNOW THYSELF UNIQUE, AND COMPLEX, AND NUANCED

Because people are not grounded in their wills, they do not have a clear, rooted sense of Self. People know themselves only through what they consume, and who they follow, and how many *Likes* their latest selfie got. So instead of cultivating an authentic, harmonious relationship with themselves, and learning about themselves, and using spirit hacks and shamanic principles to transform themselves, they just grab onto some prefab, off-the-rack identity—like, the type of thing you get at Target that was mass-produced at a factory in Cambodia, and that's hanging next to dozens and dozens just like it. It makes no sense. Wouldn't you rather wear a one-of-a-kind, couture masterpiece that you craft yourself, stitch by stitch, given that it is *your* life, and all? Most people don't do that. Most people don't take the time, or the care, or the effort to cultivate an authentic sense of Self. Instead they just slip on the Target version and pretend it fits, and then confuse their distorted, humdrum, store-bought identity as being *me*.

Black Wasn't Always Beautiful to Me

I used to hate being black. At first I hated it because when my mother divorced my father and moved across the country when I was three, I thought she left because she wasn't black, and I was. Plus, my stepmother told me that was the case between beatings.

Then I hated being black because of all the programming around it. I grew up in a wealthy white neighborhood, so the only thing I knew about being black in America was what I saw on television, where all the black people were poor, dumb thugs who lived in ghettos, drank 40s, and broke the law.

I used to walk to Thrifty's to buy skin bleach. I would pour it all over my body, hoping it would turn my skin white. But all it did was burn. I bleached my hair, too—to the point where it fell out, which is why I still don't have hair to this day. All because I wanted to be white.

My father forbade me from dating black girls and told me that the only way to get ahead in life was with a white woman on your arm. He also told me stories about how it was for him growing up black, and watching people get lynched. Because I didn't want that for myself, I didn't want to be black.

I used to go out of my way to avoid other black people. I didn't want anyone thinking I was associating with the likes of a black person, because that would mean that I accepted them; and because I couldn't accept myself, there was no way I could accept another black person. My self-hatred for being black ran deep.

And then I met this guru—an amazing healer named Mike—who helped me confront my issues around being black. Mike taught me that just because black stereotypes were programmed into the mass consciousness in a certain way didn't mean that I had to sign on to that version of black, or that I had to *be* that version of black.

That perspective had a profound impact on me and allowed me to root into a deeper understanding of who I was beyond the labels and conditions the world was trying to place upon me. I realized that I was something greater—something more complex, and unique, and mysterious. That's when I started to realize how beautiful it was for me to be black; and I started to realize that what was happening to black people on the planet had nothing to do with me. It was what was happening to this construct called "black people," and that I could be black, and I could love being black, but that I didn't have to sign on to that construct, or to the indoctrination that sustains it.

THE IDENTITY THING

Identity is a cage. Straight up. Identity is a way of putting people into boxes and categories that completely invalidate nuance, and complexity, and individual experience, while attempting to homogenize people based on shallow stereotypes and random classifications. Identity cages close a whole lot of doors and shut down a whole lot of opportunities and experiences, while keeping the bobbleheads feeling safe, and like they belong, and are a part of something.

This current phase in human evolution, which I call the Age of Narcissism, has given way to a collective identity crisis that has massive chunks of the population pledging allegiance to labels like *queer, black, cis, Jew, Capricorn, crippled, Puerto Rican,* and what have you. People seem to think these identity constructs are all so different when, in fact, they are exactly the same. They are all a means of architecting a sense of self, and worth, and purpose based upon labels the matrix uses to divide and control us.

The thing is, labels aren't free. Labels come with baggage. Labels carry all these implied traits and tendencies that we're supposed to take on as soon as we identify with them. Like, the second someone comes out of the closet, and identifies themselves as "gay," they have to put a rainbow sticker on their car, and vote Democrat, and listen to show tunes, and wear crop tops, and do crunches—unless they're taking the Bear route, in which case they have to have a potbelly and grow a beard. Labels imply that there's a formula people have to follow for being gay, or black, or Muslim, or whatever, instead of just being gay, or black, or Muslim in whatever way works best for them.

IDENTITY DIVIDES

These formulas are boxes, just as identities are boxes. When we put ourselves in a box, and we identify with the box, and we say we are this thing that the box stands for, then we automatically separate ourselves from everyone else who isn't in the box, and who isn't also everything the box supposedly stands for, which is completely absurd in the first place. The identity thing is just another way that humans do the matrix's bidding for it, because identity is just another construct we use to separate ourselves from each other.

Now, with the Blackout, we are seeing identity politics dividing people in really extreme, discordant, and violent ways. The extent to which the identity thing is currently playing itself out in our culture is a reflection of the larger masculine/feminine imbalance plaguing our planet, where, instead of seeking to understand and connect with those who hold beliefs different from ours, we separate ourselves from them, and scorn them, and shame them, and make them our enemies. It's unfortunate, given that these identity constructs are bullshit anyway.

KNOW THYSELF IN EVOLUTION

People confuse their identity constructs with the Self, and then they misunderstand the construct of the Self as though it is fixed, or constant. As though I declare myself this one thing, and so I am always this one thing, and I will always be this one thing, and that is my identity, and this is who I am; this is my Self. This idea is a distortion. The idea of a static identity goes against the whole of life, which is always moving, and is always in flow.

Nothing is fixed or static in this reality, *especially* the Self. It's why I always laugh when people try to define themselves by saying, *I'm the kind of person who* _____, as though the behavior they are describing logically equates to an identity construct. It's crazy how illogical people are! When we define ourselves as *the kind of person who* wears pink socks, then we limit ourselves from wearing different colored socks, because according to our "logic," as the type of person who wears pink socks, wearing purple socks would make us an entirely different kind of person. This would require a whole existential identity crisis to process, instead of just a simple wardrobe adjustment. Why handcuff our behavior to an identity? Why put yourself in a box? Boxes are for bobbleheads. Not for lit love beings living poprocks lives on a planet of peace and prosperity for all.

Contrary to popular belief/nonsense, the Self is not a fixed location on a map, or a static state that we can point to with a label, or a box that we check off when we are applying for a passport. The Self is an ever-evolving, ever-unfolding evolutionary process. The Hermetic axiom *Know thyself* is not what people think it is, because there is no constant, singular Self. To know ourselves doesn't mean to attach ourselves to a fixed identity by declaring: *I am* this *type of person*, or: *I am* that *type of person*. It means to be aware of how one is evolving and developing in an ever-changing quantum reality that is constantly offering new data, new input, new experiences, and new reflections, which—as long as we're not stuck in any stubborn idea of who we are, or who we are not—we can allow to shape us however we want.

AWARENESS

If we are to live free of labels and boxes, and know ourselves authentically in evolution, then we must sharpen our awareness. Without the crutch of an identity construct, and the formula and the rules that go along with it, the only way to actually know ourselves is to be *aware* of ourselves—to be present, and open, and loving, and accepting and to always turn our lens of observation toward ourselves.

Awareness is a very important shamanic tool. When we focus our awareness on something, we observe what is. That's it. We don't analyze it, we don't judge it, we don't try to make it better or different; we just observe. It is both very simple and very powerful, because when we observe what is, we are flooded with truth. When we observe something, and we allow it to show itself to us, we are doing that which everything in life wants us to do—we are connecting with it.

Have you ever noticed what happens when you allow people to talk about themselves, and you don't chime in with how what they're saying relates to you, and you're not thinking about yourself, but you're just focusing your awareness entirely on them? And have you noticed how the more you just listen, and simply observe, the more they will reveal? How they will tell you things they've never told any other living being in their whole lives? And how they will tell you things they didn't even realize they thought or believed themselves? That's because you gave them your awareness.

Shamans aren't special, per se. It's just that we have learned how to sharpen our awareness, and how to expand our awareness, and how to sustain our awareness, because shamans know that it is our awareness that allows the doors of possibility to open, and to multiply. Shamans know that everything in our reality wants communion, and so we train ourselves to expand our awareness, and to focus our awareness, so that we can be receptive to not only the data that is available, but also to the intelligence that is being transmitted. The reason I can connect with a tumor in a client's spleen, and then communicate with the spleen to discern what the source of the imbalance is, and what the spleen is needing to heal itself, is not because I am special, or because I have magic powers. It is because I have sharpened my awareness to the point where I can pick up on subtle communications that most people aren't aware of.

What makes a bobblehead a bobblehead is lack of awareness. The bobblehead is checked out. Bobbleheads are so occupied with maintaining their online personae, and keeping up with whatever's on trend, or on fleek, or whatever else their peer group is telling them matters, that they are oblivious to the discord threatening our world, as well as to what's really going on inside themselves. This is by design. This is why the system puts celebrity breakups on magazine covers and fluoride in municipal drinking water. Both perform the same function—to flood the brain with toxins, and disconnect people from their awareness, so that they will be easier to control.

The only way to combat this problem is to check back in; and that, my love, means getting aware.

Spirit Hack: Shamanic Awareness

This is an ancient spirit hack my ancestors taught me to strengthen my shamanic abilities. You want to practice this spirit hack as often as you can, as it will allow you to cultivate an expanded awareness and to start to perceive things you wouldn't normally see.

Ideally, you want to practice this spirit hack on an empty stomach, when the body is in fasting mode and isn't occupied with the tasks of digesting and assimilating. The lighter you are, the more you will be able to perceive.

- Place your hand out in front of your face.

It doesn't have to be your hand. You can do this with any object. But, for the sake of consistency, let's use your hand as our working example.

- Observe it.

Now, when I say *observe it,* I mean focus the entirety of your awareness upon your hand. Not with your eyes. Not with your cognitive understanding of what a hand is, or what a hand should be. Just focus your awareness on your hand. You are not trying to figure it out. You are allowing your hand to present itself to you from a place of relaxation and allowing.

- Ask your hand to reveal itself to you. Say out loud: *Hand, show me you.*

Notice what sensations arise as you invite your hand into a deeper communion. These sensations are how your hand—and your entire body—communicates with you.

- Speak each observation aloud as it registers.

You might notice tingling on one side or the other, so you would say: *I feel tingling on the right side of my palm.*

You might notice a dull throbbing in your knuckles, so you would say: *I feel a dull throbbing sensation in my knuckles.*

You might notice a weightiness in your palm, so you would say: *I feel a weightiness in my palm.*

You might notice a tremor in your pinky finger, so you would say: *I feel a tremor in my pinky finger.*

You might notice a blue light encircling your thumb, so you would say: *I see a blue light encircling my thumb.*

You might notice none of these things; and you will probably notice completely different things. There is no wrong, and there is no right. You are simply observing.

- Expand your awareness and focus even more deeply on the hand in front of you. Say: *Hand, show me more.*

If you are trying to describe what your hand looks like, or if you are trying to figure it out, you are not observing it. You are analyzing it, which means you are trying to control your experience with your mind. Don't try to control it. Let it just be; allow the sensations to emerge. Continue to speak the sensations aloud as you observe them.

- When you feel complete, finish by offering gratitude to your hand for the exchange in saying: *Thank you, hand.*

Spirit Hacking Tip

When we are spirit hacking, we always speak aloud what we are sensing as a way to acknowledge the communication taking place, and as a way to strengthen the bridge between our physical body and our spiritual body. This applies to things we see, feel, hear, taste, and smell, as well as to whatever extrasensory perceptions reveal themselves to us.

Sometimes people feel silly talking to their hand, or a tree, or a spirit, out loud. It doesn't really make a whole lot of sense to me, but that's because I grew up in a family of shamans, where talking to unseen entities was just what folks did. Regardless, in shamanism, we know that everything is infused with light intelligence, and we don't waste a single

second worrying about what anyone else might think if they hear us talking to that intelligence. That's just vanity. That's just ego. That's just
weak-willed, bobblehead, sheep-think. You gotta get over that stuff if you
wanna ride the lit train.

The key to awareness is training the mind to observe without judgment.
Objective, open-ended observation allows us to gather way more data from
that which we are observing than the act of observing with preconceived no-
tions. When we observe with judgment, we are not seeing objectively; rather,
we are seeing in such a way as to confirm our beliefs. Most humans perceive
the world through the lens of judgment, which is both arrogant and pointless, because they're not seeing with a genuine desire to know what is; they're
just looking to prove that they're right. Shamans aren't hung up on being
right, or confirming the status quo. We're okay with the not-knowing. In fact,
we're great with it; because it's the not-knowing that allows us to observe
from a place of receptivity, which creates a field of unconditional acceptance
in which the object of our observation can reveal itself of its own accord.

To level-up our will, and grow our emotional intelligence, and ring in
a poprocks Giant Age here on Earth requires us to make a quantum leap in
our awareness faculties. We can't get to where we're going, unless we know
where we're at now. Awareness is the tool that allows us to figure that out.

YOUR POWER IS NOT WAITING TO BE FOUND ON THE SIDE OF A MILK CARTON

The reason we are in the Blackout, and the world is the way it is, is because
most human beings on the planet feel disempowered—like they have no
ability to effect change, or to make a positive impact at any level whatsoever.

My mission—the whole reason why I incarnated, and died, and came
back again, and healed my body and my brain, and studied with mystics

and teachers and elders all over this world, and so many other worlds—is to help humanity step into their power. Let's be clear, this isn't because humanity's power is lost, or broken, or missing. It is because their power is something they've forgotten to keep their awareness on. A lot of people talk about their power as though it is lost, or missing, or like they have to take it back from someone who stole it. No; their power is there. Their power is always there. That's not the issue. The issue is that their awareness, and their devotion, are not on their power.

When you decide to align with your will, and to walk your authentic path as God intended, the darkness is going to take issue with that. Big time. The darkness can't have you all empowered 'n' shit—walking tall and confident, knowing yourself, and knowing your value, and having a positive impact on the world. No way. So, the darkness is going to throw all kinds of obstacles in your way to throw you off, and get you to change your mind, and go back to being a sheep. It's going to do anything it can to distract you, and to challenge you, and to keep you from moving forward and manifesting what you want. It's going to tell you that you can't have it, and that you're not qualified, and that you're not good enough. It's going to use the grand glamour to steer you off track. It's going to do whatever it can to keep you where it wants you, which is stuck in the system, and stuck in the status quo, and stuck in your disempowerment. And that's where your will comes in to say: *Step off, darkness. I'm running the show.*

SELF-EMPOWERMENT

The will is the mechanism that allows us to take charge of our vessels and steer our own ships. We empower ourselves by actively authoring our own lives, and we can only do this when the will is strong. A strong will is what supports us in pivoting, and shifting energy, and changing direction, and creating new pathways, and opening new doors, and forging new ground. This is self-empowerment, and it isn't something you can buy, or you can borrow, or you can wear, or you can fake. Self-empowerment is an aspect of recognizing one's Self and believing in one's Self. Self-empowerment comes from within.

THE OUTCAST FEAR

There is a myth circulating among New Age communities that people are afraid of their power. This is false. People are not afraid of their power. People are only afraid of their power as it relates to how they think other people are going to perceive them in their power. What people are really afraid of is that other people won't be comfortable with their power. What they're really afraid of is not being loved, and not being liked.

Human beings' number one fear is of being an outcast. The idea that we are going to be exiled, alienated, ostracized, or abandoned rocks people to the very core of their being. Outcast terror is the biggest fear humans harbor.

That the vast majority of humans compromise themselves because of this fear is indicative of our emotional intelligence deficiency. An emotionally intelligent person knows that there is no such thing as being abandoned, and no such thing as being alienated, because if someone doesn't want you in their life, then they're not meant to be in your life. If someone doesn't want to be in your life, it doesn't mean that you're wrong, or that you're bad, it just means that your energetic signatures are no longer vibrating at a coherent frequency. And that's fine. Their choice to leave your life will free up space for more resonant people to come in. But because people aren't operating with emotional intelligence, or a healthy sense of Self, they compromise themselves in order to stay in discordant relationships, and to fit in.

ARE YOU A SPIRITUAL FREEDOM FIGHTER, OR ARE YOU A SLAVE?

I came to terms a long time ago with the fact that some people just aren't going to like me. I ruffle people's feathers. As far as I'm concerned, if you're not ruffling feathers, then something's off. Then, you're just people-pleasing. I'm not here to people-please. I'm here to people-push. I'm here to push people's limits, and to push people's buttons. I'm here to make people uncomfortable, and to get them to look at what's going on inside of them so they can get realer.

Sure, sometimes I get bothered by people not liking me, but never to the point where I'm willing to sacrifice my truth. That's the difference between being a spiritual freedom fighter and being a slave. It's really simple. I'm willing to bet your love, and I'm willing to bet your approval, and I'm willing to bet your choice to like me, or not, on my freedom. I'm willing to throw it all on the table, because I have nothing to lose. You don't like me? Okay, I can deal with that. I can deal with the fact that you won't like me; and I can deal with the fact that you won't love me; but what I can't deal with is being a slave, which means I'm willing to sacrifice your approval for my freedom.

When I was a kid, my dad did everything in his power to keep me away from shamanism. He beat me; he bribed me; he kept my mother away from me. And every time he opened his mouth to forbid me from studying shamanism, and from practicing shamanism, he added another bar to the prison he was attempting to forge for me—a prison he built with his words, and his constructs, and his limitations, and his indoctrination. The only way for me to escape my father's prison was to defy him, and to defy all those principles he was using to try and program me. And, let me tell you, defying those programmed principles was scary shit, because it meant I was going against my tribe, and it brought up all this fear around being an outcast. But my will was strong, and my devotion to love, and my devotion to Spirit were greater than the fear. And there is a not a single moment, when I look back upon my life, where I regret having stayed true to myself and defying my father like I did. In fact, my defiance is the only reason I'm still here, inside this biological space suit, talking to you right now, because my defiance was what kept me true to myself, and what kept me true to everything I stand for, which is love.

HACKING THE MATRIX

I hear so many people talking about fighting the system, and smashing the patriarchy, and whatever other nonsense they're using to justify their rage, and their issues, and their urge to smash things. Raging against the machine is all well and good if you want to waste your energy, and create drama and conflict, and get bruised, and banged up, and whatever. But it's not an effective means of creating change. Not by a long shot.

So, what do we do?

For starters, we don't fight. We don't smash the matrix, and we don't fight the matrix, and we don't try to convince the matrix that it needs to be kinder, or gentler, or different. We become aware of the matrix, and of how the matrix is affecting our lives, and then we make the matrix work for us.

The more we hone our awareness, and the more we strengthen our wills, and the more we get empowered, the more we start to understand that even though we may be operating inside the matrix, we are not *of* the matrix. This awareness is so liberating. Because, let's get real. Unless you move to some off-grid shack in the middle of nowhere, and grow your own food, and make your own clothes, and barter, and what have you, you're still going to be dealing with the matrix on some level or another. Leaving the matrix entirely isn't really an option. But empowering yourself to be impervious to the matrix, while using the construct to grow, and to evolve, and to manifest a Giant Age here on Earth, well, that's what getting lit is all about.

4

WORD YOURSELF UP

Self-love isn't valued in this culture. We are not taught to love ourselves in school. Self-love is not modeled in our media. *I* certainly didn't get any insight into it growing up in my father's house. And when we do love ourselves, we are judged as being stuck-up by our peers, because we're not doing what the rest of the herd is doing, which is hating themselves and complaining.

Sarcasm, on the other hand, is very much valued in this culture. Self-deprecation ranks high as social currency. It goes over well at parties, and on Tinder profiles. I can't tell you how often I see people walk into a social setting where they don't know anyone, and they choose to put themselves down as a way to ingratiate themselves into the group. Then everyone else jumps on board with all the ways that they're deficient, and that they suck; and then all of a sudden, everyone's going back and forth, and bonding over all this negativity. It's like, *Great, you just traded your confidence and your self-esteem to fit in, and to feel like you belong, while the darkness gets to keep growing fatter, and stronger. Way to go.*

SELF-LOVE ISN'T SEPARATION

Humans confuse confidence with conceit. They are stuck in the dualistic distortion that wants you to think that because I love myself, then I am somehow in opposition to you. That it means I must think I'm better than you, or that you are inferior to me. This is false. This is just human insecurity being projected out onto the person who is reflecting it. But because most people are not operating from emotional intelligence, they identify with the thought form, and the separation frequency it generates, which has them thinking that any person who loves himself or herself is an egomaniac.

Arrogance, narcissism, and conceit seep into our consciousness when we place our love for ourselves above our love for the other—when we jockey for position, while putting others down. That's not self-love. That's insecurity. That's separation.

Self-love isn't about separation, or comparison, or hierarchy. It has nothing to do with anyone else. Self-love is only about our relationship to and with ourselves. It's about sharing time with ourselves, and learning ourselves, and nurturing ourselves. And it's about being kind, and compassionate, and generous, and accepting with every single aspect of ourselves, even the ones we wish were different.

SELFISH IS THE NEW SELF-LOVE

People call me selfless for sharing my shamanic teachings, and for my global activism and philanthropy. But my work is actually fueled by selfishness. There is nothing selfless about it. Because I am a shaman, and because my sensorium is so strong, I feel the suffering of the world, and the pain of all people; and let me tell you—humanity is hurting. So, no. I don't fly all over the world to work with clients, and consult with government leaders, and teach workshops, and offer healings because I am noble, or because I am saintly. I do these things so that I can alleviate my own suffering. I do these things because every time I help one of my brothers or sisters by putting their power back in their own hands, that's one less person's pain and suffering for me to feel; and that's one more person who is awake, and who can create positive change in the world, and who can inspire other people to take their power back, and to awaken, and to create more positive change in the world. I do all these things so that I can sleep better at night, because I am selfish.

Selfishness carries such a negative stigma in our culture, because selfishness gets conflated with entitlement, wherein we put our needs and our preferences above the needs and preferences of others. That's not what I'm talking about. I'm not talking about hierarchy, or competition, or rank. To me, being selfish means connecting with myself and making sure that my needs are being met, and that I am being taken care of, and that I have time to get to know me, and to find out what I like, and what works, and what moves me to be who I am. It's not about doing these things while dropping the ball on being of service to others. It's about doing these things so that I can authentically be of service to others. Selfishness is necessary for authenticity. How else are we going to learn these things about ourselves, if we don't take the time, and put in the effort to figure them out? How are we going to be of service to others, if we don't know how to be of service to ourselves?

The truth is that self-love can only be achieved through selfishness. We cannot give to ourselves unless we have a full cup to pour from; and we certainly can't even begin to think about giving to anyone else if we ourselves are running on empty.

FILL YOUR OWN CUP

Healthy relationships are created from the inside first. I have so many clients who come to me complaining about all the things they're not getting from their spouse, or their friends, or their family, or their coworkers, while their soul is telling me that they aren't giving these things to themselves. As if it's anyone else's responsibility to fulfill our needs for us. *Please.* When we carry around these expectations that it's other people's responsibility to make us feel good, or to make us feel loved, or to make us feel worthy, our relationships become transactional and codependent, and we get resentful. If you're wanting people to honor your time, and your gifts, then you need to honor your time, and you need to honor your gifts. If you're yearning to feel loved, and to feel good, and to feel beautiful, and worthy, and amazing, then you need to start loving on yourself, and making yourself feel good, and beautiful, and worthy, and amazing.

Lack consciousness isn't just about the numbers in our bank account, or the material possessions we don't have. Lack consciousness is also about the energies and emotions we are wanting to experience, but that we are not giving to ourselves—energies like kindness, and laughter, and affection, and relaxation, and play. When we love ourselves, we learn to give ourselves these energies and these experiences, instead of burdening the people in our lives with the responsibility of doing it for us.

Sustainable Self-Love

When we outsource love, and we depend on others for it, then love can be taken from us. Love can be lost. Love can be abandoned. Love can be lacking. But when we ourselves are generating love from within, then it flows infinitely, always.

Seeking outside of ourselves for love is not sustainable. It doesn't even work, because if we don't love ourselves in the first place, then the love that others shower upon us just falls through the cracks in our consciousness, and passes right through our spirit. To be abundant is to be plentiful in the nature of Spirit, which means to be able to give and receive sustainable love. This can only happen when we learn to love ourselves. When we talk about sustainability as a society, we tend to focus on buildings, and energy, and agriculture. But the Blackout is inviting us to expand our understanding of sustainability, and to apply the concept to the living nature of human beings, which includes our emotions, our self-esteem, and our connection with Spirit.

When we find ourselves frustrated, agitated, and grumpy, it's usually because we've dropped the ball on filling up our own vessel. It means we're depleted. It means we're not getting enough rest, massage, meditation, sex, nature, or whatever other activities and experiences we've pinpointed as the self-care practices that allow us to supply our own storehouse of wellness so that we can stay lit. Don't kid yourself. This planet is intense, and the matrix places a lot of demands on us. We all need to supplement the basics—food, water, shelter—to fortify and nourish ourselves, so that we're not leaking our emotions onto others, or expecting them to anticipate our needs and take care of us.

I'm not blissed-out 24-7. I have my moments. But when I get bitchy, and snappy, and irritable, and I start taking it out on the people around me, it always means that I need to amp up my self-love. It means I've given to others too much, and given to myself too little, and that my vessel is empty. It means I need to give myself those things that will fill me back up—like getting a mani/pedi, or playing with my action figures, or taking a beach day. It's not anyone else's responsibility to nurture me. It's my responsibility to nurture myself.

Spirit Hack: Shamanic Infusion
for Self-Love

Shamanic infusions are a great way to flood the body with amazing, high-vibrational energy through the breath. The breath is a powerful tool in many ancient spiritual traditions, including traditional Hawaiian shamanism.

Hawaiian shamans call upon the air spirits to bring certain energies into their bodies by way of the breath. You can use shamanic infusions to bring in any energy you want, but for this one, we're going to use self-love. This spirit hack is a great way to develop mental, emotional, and spiritual immunity, because self-love is what allows us to move through the world unaffected by external events or circumstances.

Ultimately, you can practice shamanic infusions lying down. But when you're first starting out, you want to be sitting upright, so that you can be sure to stay awake. As well, you definitely want to practice this one with bare feet, and your legs uncrossed. Crossing the legs locks up the flow of energy. Be sure to remove any belts or watches, as well, so as to minimize restrictions.

- Sitting comfortably in a chair, with your feet touching the ground, become aware of your breath.

- Speak these words in your mind while inhaling deeply: *I breathe self-love into my body.*

- As you exhale, feel the love circulating throughout your body. You can direct the love into your limbs, and into your digits. You can direct it into your belly, and into your brain, and into any parts of you needing a little extra love, or you can simply allow the love to permeate your body of its own accord.

- Inhale, repeating the words in your mind: *I breathe more self-love into my body.*

- Again, exhale, feeling the love permeate your every cell.

Repeat for 10–15 rounds, or until you feel full of self-love.

While shamanic infusions aren't a replacement for self-care, they can definitely help when we are depleted, and our vessels are running low. Use this spirit hack as often as you like, especially when you're feeling like you could use a jolt of self-love.

SELF-LOVE ISN'T A SPA DAY

Don't misunderstand me. It's not as if you can treat yourself like shit on a daily basis, but because you get a facial and a hot stone massage once a month, you're good; you've got your self-love dialed. It doesn't work like that. Self-love isn't just about sensual indulgences, or spa treatments. Self-love is about how we relate with ourselves every minute of every day through the thoughts we allow into our minds, and through the words coming out of our mouths.

INCORRECT THINKING

People have a bad habit of thinking against themselves. They wake up criticizing themselves, and cursing themselves, and thinking all these negative thoughts about themselves, and then they allow this to continue throughout the day, all the way up until they go to sleep at night. *I messed up. I'm doing it wrong. I'm such a loser. I hate my thighs.* You name it. As if that wasn't crazy enough, people say these things out loud. Things like: *I'm an idiot. I can't. I don't know. I'm broke. I was bad today because I ate a cupcake.* I mean, people actually say things like this about themselves all the time. These kinds of aspersions are regular, all day/every day thoughts and statements that accompany most people's lives, and the people who are casting them aren't even thinking twice about all the ways they're defaming their own characters.

THE CHILD INSIDE US ALL

Most human beings think God is some bearded guy on a cloud who rewards the good, and punishes the bad, just like Santa Claus, minus the reindeer and the elves. But that's not what God is—not by any stretch of the imagination. God is that little child inside you—that little girl, or that little boy who exists inside each and every one of us as pure innocence and unconditional love. That child is your soul. And the soul that I have inside me is the same soul you have inside you, because there is but one God, despite God's many forms. The soul expresses through your individual form as you, just as the soul expresses through my individual form as me. Our unique forms allow the soul to express differently, and to play out its incarnation differently, but at its most fundamental level, it is the same soul.

When we speak about ourselves in cruel, defamatory ways, we are directing our words to that innocent child who lives inside us. There is no difference between saying those words to a small child who is sitting right in front of our faces, and saying them about ourselves. Just because you can't see the child inside you, doesn't mean that child isn't there; and it certainly doesn't mean your words are harmless. Your every word is being registered by your little child inside you. Imagine what people would think if they saw you telling a five-year-old that he was stupid, or that she was ugly, or that she ruined everything, or that you hate his guts, and imagine how those words would affect that child. That is exactly what your words are doing to your child inside you.

SOUL TALK

Managing such heightened levels of sensitivity and awareness was very, very difficult for me as a kid, and especially as a teenager. Though my father knew what was going on with me, and understood firsthand what I was dealing with, he refused to talk to me about it, or acknowledge it on any level.

It would have been so easy for him to have said, "Hey, you're not crazy." That gesture would have gone a long way in supporting me, and allowing me to feel safe, and sane, and held in my journey. But because my father rejected shamanism so strongly, he ignored my experiences, and he pretended not to notice what I was going through. So I became convinced that my father didn't love me, and—without that unconditional parental love tethering me to this plane of existence—I decided I didn't want to be here anymore.

I was sixteen when I tried to kill myself. I took a whole bunch of Lithium, which a psychiatrist who had diagnosed me as bipolar and schizophrenic had prescribed. Because that's what the Western medical model does—they pathologize things they don't understand (like being a shaman), and then give you pills to take to mask the symptoms. My sister found me passed out on the stairs, and I woke up in the hospital, where they pumped my stomach, and made me drink ipecac, so I would throw up all the pills.

Afterward, I spent some time in the mental ward. When I got out, my friend Anthony took me to an animal shelter to get a dog. A little golden retriever jumped on the fence to get my attention, and spoke to me telepathically.

I'm going to help you to see yourself, he said.

My dad refused to let me keep the dog. I begged him, and I pleaded with him, and then Anthony chimed in and suggested it would be good for me to have something to anchor me to this reality, and to give me a reason to want to be here. So, with an eye roll and a huff, my dad gave in and let me keep the dog. I named him Dexter.

I used to take Dexter to the beach to do rituals with me. One time I was meeting with a Native American shaman—a Lakota elder. He took one look at Dexter and said, "That dog is your spirit animal, man. He talks to you. That dog tells you things."

It was true. I learned a lot from Dexter.

One day we were playing together in my room, and Dexter looked like he was crying.

"Why are you crying?" I asked him.

I am not crying, Dexter told me, telepathically. *You are the one who is crying. I am showing you what you are doing to yourself.*

When I asked what he meant, Dexter explained that it was the little boy inside me who was crying, and that the reason he was crying was I was saying mean things to him. Dexter explained that human beings are constantly beating up on themselves with their words and their thoughts. He explained that humans are lifted by love, and that humans are inspired by love, and that it was time for me to start speaking to my little boy with love.

At first, it felt weird, and I didn't really know what to say.

"Uh, little boy?" I asked. "Is there a little boy in there?"

Yes, I heard a little boy's voice say.

Tell him, Dexter said, as I took in the fact that I was talking to a small child inside my person.

"I love you," I said to the little boy.

You do? the little boy's voice asked.

"Yes, I do," I said.

This went on for a while—that every time I told my little boy I loved him, he'd ask me: *You do? Really?*

"Yes," I kept reassuring him. "I love you. I really love you."

After a while, he began to trust me, and to rest in that love, because he could feel that it was true. And then I expanded on the practice and started telling my little boy what exactly I loved about him—his kindness, his care, his sensitivity, his generosity, his tenderness, his intelligence, his playfulness, his compassion.

That practice, which I call *soul talk,* is what brought me back from that suicidal place. Soul talk had such a profound, transformative effect on me that I didn't just come back, I came back with a force. I came back with a mission. That practice got me so lit about being me that I stopped eating meat. I started volunteering at a battered women's shelter; and I threw myself into women's empowerment activism in really big, hands-on ways. It only took a few times before that way of communicating to myself became normal. Now, I talk to myself like this all the time, and I've even made it a daily practice. Every morning, I take the time to talk to my soul, and to tell that little boy inside me all the ways that he is amazing, and, of course, to tell him that *I love him, I love him, I love him.*

Spirit Hack: Soul Talk

You want to do this spirit hack first thing in the morning, as in: before you talk to your partner, before you wake up your kids, before you check your email, before you drink your coffee, and before you meditate. Soul talk sets up your relationship with yourself for your day, which is why it's so important that you do it immediately upon waking—before anyone has a chance to knock you off your center, or convince you that you are anything less than magnificent and amazing.

When you do soul talk, you are creating your path, because you are speaking to your little girl, or your little boy, which means that you are talking to God. God creates the realities we speak from our mouths and from our minds, which is why when you are doing this spirit hack (and always), you want to speak from a place of love, and from the place of that which you want to become. Remember, when you are doing soul talk, you are speaking directly to your soul.

For this spirit hack, place one or both hands on your heart while holding yourself in a field of unconditional love. Speak lovingly to yourself—in the second person, while describing the qualities that you appreciate about yourself, as well as the ones you want to develop and manifest in yourself, knowing that whatever you say to that little child inside you, you will become, and you will amplify. Here are a few examples of some things you can say:

> I love how beautiful you are.
>
> I love your intelligence.
>
> I love your playfulness.
>
> I love how free you are.
>
> I love how easily and gracefully you handle stress.
>
> I love your giving and loving nature.
>
> I love what a wonderful friend you are.
>
> I love your kindness and compassion.
>
> I love your sense of humor.
>
> I love how you're always thinking the highest for yourself and the highest for others.

Really, there is no limit to the wonderful things you can say about yourself to your soul. Play. Be creative. Have fun showering yourself with love and appreciation, and speaking your ideal self into form.

SPEAK NO SABOTAGE

A lot of the time, the ways that humans think against themselves aren't as obvious as self-defamatory thoughts and words. Quite often our self-abuse plays out as self-sabotage. For instance, a friend of mine was really stressed out when he was launching his business, and when I asked him why he was working so hard, he said, "Start-ups take time; and we're doing everything we can so that we don't fail."

But what my friend didn't realize was that he had already failed. He had already cursed himself by naming the possibility of failure. You see, if we are taking action to avoid "failing," then we are pretty much guaranteed to fail, because we are framing our efforts around the idea of failure. It doesn't matter whether we want to fail, or not, but just giving the energy of failure life by speaking it empowers the energy of failure.

"Why not just do everything you're doing so that you succeed?" I asked my friend. "Why not line up your ducks for the *success* you're choosing, instead of the *failure* you're afraid of?"

"Holy shit!" he exclaimed. "I never thought about it like that."

YOU'RE EITHER A TAP OR A DRAIN

We are far more than simple two-legged mammals biding the illusion of linear time on a spinning rock. We are quantum creators living in a multidimensional reality of infinite possibility. Every time we open our mouths to speak, or touch a screen to type, or fire a neuron to think, we are either creating or destroying. Like I always say, you're either a tap or a drain.

Words are powerful, powerful tools of creation. When we speak, we align our words with our will, which fuels those words into form. The act of thinking, and the act of speaking, are creative acts, because our words function as a magic wand that God has given us to wield our will into the world.

God creates based on our words, taking each and every one as instructions as to how we want our realities to shape themselves. Every word we speak is a seed of creation, without exception. People have God so wrong. They think God is occupied judging, and counting sins, and tracking how many times we said his name in vain, and then sending scourges to punish us. All God does is listen to what we say, and listen to what we think, and then manifest our words into form. God is occupied only with creating.

This is why it is so important that we are mindful of our words and our thoughts, because it is a law of the universe that God creates whatever we say, and God doesn't just create the good stuff. God isn't stuck in any delusions of duality, so God doesn't do *good* and *bad,* or *right* and *wrong.* Those are human constructs. God gave us free will so that we could figure out our evolution for ourselves, which means that everything we say, and everything we think, *becomes.*

THE HEALING POWER OF WORDS

After I died, I was in the hospital for a long time. I was paralyzed. I had brain damage. My organs had failed, and my lungs had collapsed. My body was a mess. As I lay there, by myself, hooked up to all these machines, completely unable to move or talk, all I had were my thoughts. And because I'd just died, and I was scared, and I barely knew where I was, I was thinking things like: *Am I going to be okay? What if I can't ever breathe on my own again? Am I going to be hooked up to these machines for the rest of my life?*

And while I was lying there, worrying, the spirits came to me and explained that everything I create, and everything I experience, is based upon how I talk to myself; and that in order for me to breathe again, I needed to imagine myself breathing, and I needed to tell myself that I could breathe. The spirits told me to speak what I wanted to happen, not what I didn't want to happen.

I wrangled hold of my thoughts and started telling myself over and over again: *I am breathing. I am breathing on my own. And it is easy for me. I am breathing on my own, and it is happening quickly. I am breathing. It is happening overnight. It is getting easier and easier for me to breathe. I am breathing strong, and I am breathing well. I am breathing. I am breathing.* Sure enough, a voice came to me that night and instructed me how to breathe, and taught me how to guide the oxygen so that my lungs could handle it. By morning, I was breathing on my own, and taken off life support.

The spirits came to me again when I was sent home from the hospital in a wheelchair, told I was never going to walk again. The spirits told me to will myself to walk with my words.

I love and appreciate my legs so much, I would tell myself. *I love how my legs are getting stronger and stronger. I love how well my brain is communicating with my legs. I am excited by all the accelerated healing that is taking place in my body.* Soon enough, I wasn't just walking, I was dancing again.

I used this practice to heal the blood clots in my organs, and the damage to my brain, and all of the damage my body incurred when I died. I healed my entire physiology with my words and thoughts.

HOW NOT TO PRAY

The spirits were very clear: if I wanted to breathe again, and walk again, and use my hands again, I was not to align my thoughts with fear, or doubt, or worst-case scenarios. The spirits explained that I had to align my thoughts with the reality that I wanted, and then speak to that reality, and to that reality only. Because whatever we say, we are giving God permission to make possible for us. Remember, God doesn't judge. God creates. God creates whatever it is that we tell God to create through our words and our thoughts. If I had let my mind run wild with all the negative possibilities that could have played out in that hospital, I would have been giving God the impression that I was choosing those realities. If I had spoken about healing my body with doubt, or if I had prayed about my body from fear, then I would probably still be in that wheelchair today, if I'd ever made it off life support at all.

Most people pray incorrectly. They pray out of fear, and they pray out of doubt, hoping to convince some punishing Universal Force to deem them worthy enough to grant them their wish. This is pointless. We must pray with the knowledge that whatever we are asking for already *is*—that it is already done, and that our prayer has already been answered. Notice how when I spoke to my lungs, and when I spoke to my legs, I spoke about the healing that *was already* taking place. I wasn't *hoping* to be able to breathe, and I wasn't asking God to have mercy on me, and to pretty please, allow me to breathe again someday in the future. I claimed that reality for myself right then and there. I wasn't asking, and I wasn't hoping, and I wasn't begging, and I definitely wasn't doubting. I was saying: *this is how it is*. And that is why I succeeded. But most people don't pray with that certainty, or that conviction. Most people pray from insecurity. We can thank the darkness for that one. It's the darkness that got humans all mixed up about how to pray, and tricked them into filtering their desires through fear, because God operates from the field of pure love, which means that God doesn't get the messages that are being filtered through fear. Think about it—how is a lower density frequency like fear going to get itself off the ground, and up into the higher realms where God can receive it? Here's a hint: it won't.

The real way to pray is to express your gratitude for what is happening in the present tense, as if it is already done, as in: *Thank you for the healing that you are doing on my body right now*; or *I am so grateful for this accelerated repair to my cells*; or *I feel so wonderful in my healthy body, and am so excited to be opening up to higher levels of consciousness as I continue to raise my vibration*. We pray with the knowledge that we are worthy of what we are praying for; and we pray with gratitude, from a place of confidence, knowing that as we speak our prayers aloud, they are already being fulfilled.

People misunderstand how creation works. They'll take these sections of the Bible and all these other so-called spiritual books so literally, when they're actually meant as metaphors and parables; but then they don't believe the parts that really are meant to be taken literally, like: *Knock and the door shall open*, and *Ask, and ye shall receive*. It doesn't say: *Knock, and be worthy, and the door shall open*. It doesn't say: *Ask, and if you haven't committed any sins, then you'll receive*. But, because the system doesn't want you to know that it can be easy, and that it's actually meant to be easy, and that we really can realize our greatest dreams, and live a Giant Age here on Earth, people are being programmed to think against themselves. And so instead of thinking about everything they want, and about how amazing it can actually be, they are thinking in fear, and they are thinking in worry, and they are thinking in lack, and they are thinking in separation—all of which are creating the very malfunction in thinking that is the reason why humans are suffering in the first place.

LOVE GOD, LOVE THYSELF

Self-love is the act of acknowledging ourselves through creation. It means we recognize our value as a by-product of our existence. It's so funny that self-love gets confused with arrogance, when it's really such a humble act. Self-love is the understanding that we matter because we *are*—not because we are rich, or famous, or talented, or beautiful, or successful. It's exactly the opposite. Self-love means loving ourselves simply because we exist.

When we truly love ourselves, we understand what it means to love God, because we are in touch with the divinity that animates all beings, and all life. This is why people who love themselves are holy, because people who love themselves recognize that there is no separation between individual beings, and that there is no separation from God. They see the whole world as holy. People who love themselves know that loving themselves is loving God, and that loving themselves is an act of worship, and that loving themselves is prayer.

Loving ourselves comes along with the understanding that every time we say something to ourselves, we are saying it to God. So, if I tell myself I'm an idiot, I'm calling God an idiot, because I am God's creation. Anytime we put ourselves down, we are putting creation down, we are putting down the very fiber of life.

When we judge, and we condemn, we are challenging God's creation in saying *I can only love and accept that which I understand from my limited perspective,* which means we don't actually love God, because God is not limited to one form, or to one perspective, and God's love isn't ever conditional. So, self-love means being able to love God's creation in all its forms, which includes you. Obvs.

Spirit Hack: Self-Love Altar

An altar is a power source that exists in all cultures and most spiritual traditions. Altars are a way of focusing our energy and our devotion upon something. The more you pay attention to your altar—by lighting candles, and making offerings, and keeping it tidy—the more you are building your momentum of power.

A lot of people build altars to gurus they've never met, and to spiritual people they put on pedestals and worship like golden calves. These kinds of altars are fine as long as they bring us joy, but they're not necessarily all that potent. A lot of the time, these altars are superficial, and function as a means of telling other people how holy we are, rather than as an authentic focal point for divine worship and reverence.

The purpose of creating a self-love altar is to honor the consciousness of self-love as divine love—to acknowledge that the more you love yourself, the more you love creation. This is the energy I want you to call forth in yourself as you go about making your self-love altar.

Things to include on your self-love altar:

- an image of yourself that you love, and that inspires you

- money for prosperity

- a stone for strength

- a candle to burn for energy and protection

- a message that reads *As I see myself, I see God* (or a similar idea that resonates with you)

Your goal is to create an altar that inspires you, and uplifts you, and reminds you of your divinity every time you gaze upon it.

Be sure to keep your altar tidy, and to make offerings of fresh flowers and regular dashes of attention. The more energy you give to your altar, the stronger your self-love momentum will build.

THE MATRIX LOVES YOUR SELF-HATRED

The matrix has a vested interest in our self-hatred, because if we loved ourselves, then there would be no internal void. There would be nothing to entice us to look outside of ourselves for love, and nothing for us to achieve to earn love from others, and nothing for us to buy to impress others, and the whole system would basically screech to a halt. But the darkness can't have that, which is why the matrix is constructed to keep humans from loving themselves.

In order for us to create a Giant Age on Earth, we must transform the structures and the constructs that are not aligned with love, and that are not sustainable. This means overhauling the legal system, the educational system, the financial system, the medical system, and all the rest of it. To do this, we must come together with our fellow humans and brainstorm, and share ideas and knowledge and solutions, while figuring out what needs to be changed, and what that change looks like, and how to go about implementing that change. This collective conversation is crucial if we are to make it through the Blackout. But humans are not focused on sharing this conversation, and humans are not devoted to creating and implementing change. Instead we are misdirecting our devotion and our attention on pop stars and rappers, singing about bitches, and broads, and Benzes, and Benjamins, and heartbreak.

WORDS GOT SKILLZ

Are you aware of the words reverberating through your system when you sing along to your favorite songs? Are you hearing the lyrics you are repeating over, and over, and over again? The ones that claim *I'm nothing without your love,* or that *I'd rather die than live without you,* or that *Money is a hassle,* or that *Bitches be frontin',* or that *My ride is better than your ride,* or that *Your kicks are wack,* or whatever else musicians are singing about these days?

Most people think that words are just symbols we use in order to communicate. But words are way more multidimensional than people realize. Words are coded with frequencies that program our subconscious minds, and entrain our various systems to match their vibratory resonance. Every word has its own energetic frequency that unlocks its own set of codes. Those codes affect our physical bodies, our emotional bodies, our psychological bodies, and our spiritual bodies. When we sing along to music that has us affirming lack, or hierarchy, or materialism, the frequencies of those lyrics are entraining our systems to vibrate at the frequencies of lack, hierarchy, and materialism, while programming our minds with whatever other limiting bullshit the Barbie doll with the mic is going on and on about.

BRAIN STING

The matrix uses media to control our minds. You drive to the grocery store, and you're bombarded by billboards on the side of the road that are designed to agitate the mind, and trigger feelings of lack and self-doubt. You turn on the radio, and you're flooded with aggravated stimulation, and news of war, and strife, and fear, and discord. According to newscasters, only terrible things ever happen on planet Earth. Good news doesn't make for effective indoctrination, and it certainly doesn't make for hefty advertising revenue. So you flip to a Top 40 station, because you figure the music will calm your spirit, except that's where the brain sting comes in.

Remember how I told you that when I died, the spirits explained to me that all human suffering comes from incorrect thinking? All of it. The matrix uses music to program the population by hacking into their brains and creating malfunctions in people's thinking. Popular music is crafted to get people to act in opposition to their character, and in opposition to themselves. The news and the politicians like to tell us about all these wars happening on foreign soil, in parts of the world where there's terror, and tyranny, and oppression, and oil, but the real war is the brain sting coming through our screens. The media onslaught that is bombarding us all day, every day, is the real war.

MUSIC IS MANTRA

When we listen to music, our body, our brain, our psyche, and our energetic fields all entrain themselves to the frequencies the song is emitting. This includes the melodies, and the harmonies, and the sounds the instruments make; and it also includes the lyrics, which act as mantras that program the subconscious mind.

Mantra refers to words or phrases that are uttered in rhythmic repetition to entrain the mind with specific frequencies, like love, or peace, or abundance. The repetition allows the frequencies of the words to align the subconscious mind to these energies, so that we can embody them and radiate them out into the world. Generally when people think of mantras, they think of Sanskrit chants praising Lord Krishna or the goddess Lakshmi—chants that are meant to uplift and optimize the human spirit. The matrix utilizes pop music lyrics to enslave the human spirit using the same principle as mantra, by repeating words and phrases over and over and over again to program the subconscious mind, and to entrain the brain to the frequencies encoded in the words. Instead of repeating words and phrases about love, and light, and abundance, and connection, the music industry writes lyrics that are deliberately meant to disempower people, so that they will be easier to control. That's why you've got pretty pop stars singing about how worthless they are now that their man is gone, and how life has lost all meaning since they broke up, and how they might as well just kill themselves. And it's why you've got hip-hop artists rapping about the numbers in their bank account, and the tags on their designer shirts, and the colleagues they're in competition with and want to murder.

These songs are tools of the system, and the lyrics are designed to manipulate us. Think about it. That new tune you love has a slick beat, and a bumpin' bass line, which means that whenever it comes on the radio—which is several times a day—you sing along, repeating the chorus over and over and over again, because choruses are repetitive like that. Repetition is how we program the subconscious mind. This means that—from a shamanic perspective—when we listen to songs that degrade the human spirit, and that degrade other people, and that tell us we're worthless unless we get more bling, we are effectively cursing ourselves, because we are programming our subconscious minds to work against us, and to disempower us. And what's even crazier is that the system has set itself up so that—yet again—we do it to ourselves.

We don't have this kind of manipulation in tribal culture. The chants, and songs, and spirituals my ancestors used to sing were about uplifting, and empowering, and guiding oneself through difficult times. Personally, I don't listen to pop music. I listen mostly to country music. But not everyone likes country music, so what are people supposed to be listening to? I leave that decision to you, my love. As a quantum creator, you have to honestly evaluate whether the songs you are listening to are transmitting information you truly want to hear repeated over and over and over again, and that you truly want to have looping through your consciousness. Because every time you loop something through your consciousness, it becomes a little bit more engrained, and a little bit more engrained, and a little bit more engrained. You have to decide for yourself what kinds of energies and information you want to allow into your consciousness.

Spirit Hack: Dodging Brain Sting

It's one thing to be mindful of the songs we listen to in our homes, or in our cars, or on our computers. It's another thing when we are out in the world, where the matrix is pulling the strings. So often I'll find myself in a store, or at an event, or even at the gas station, or the bank, and some song comes on with a whole bunch of lyrics I really don't want sinking into my brain. When this happens, I use this simple spirit hack to protect the sanctity of my consciousness.

- While tapping the back of your neck with the palm of your hand, say aloud: "Generate a barrier so that my mind does not take these words into my being as fact."

- Take a deep inhalation, and then blow it out with a loud "Whoo!"

Duly protected, there's no need to worry about the frequencies of brain sting infecting your consciousness. Still, there's no need to push your luck by singing along or anything.

EMOTIONAL STING

The music industry is using brain sting to deliberately disempower people as a means of control. The system uses music, and television, and movies, and video games as carriers to disseminate corrupt coding. But make no mistake, the system is writing the code. The system is writing the lyrics. This is all by design.

While brain sting is transmitted through music, emotional sting comes in through scary movies and aggravated stimulation. Emotional sting wreaks havoc on the nervous system and the emotional body by spiking the heart rate and the cortisol levels, and sending a surge of fight-or-flight hormones through the body, which are really, really damaging to the biological space suit. Duly whacked-out by the hormones flooding the system, the psyche undergoes just as much damage, as it holds on to the anxiety the various chemical responses are generating, and stores it in the amygdala, where it leaks into the emotional body and creates all kinds of fears, phobias, traumas, sleep disruptions, and behavioral changes.

Scary movies are created by the system to hold us back, which is why, these days, every new release is about some sort of zombie, vampire, evil alien, AI apocalypse. It's no coincidence that we are smack dab in the middle of the Blackout, and suddenly, horror movies are all the rage again. These films plant atrocious images in the subconscious mind, where they seed the consciousness with all sorts of horrible things we would never consider on our own. Once these images have been programmed into our imaginations, they become actual potentialities that humans can more easily manifest, because they've been imprinted onto our consciousness as possibilities that can actually happen. If we continue to focus our energy and our devotion onto these types of situations and circumstances, then we will create more and more of these situations and circumstances in our waking reality. That's why I never watch scary movies. You literally couldn't pay me to program those frequencies into my mind, because I have no interest in destroying my nervous system and attracting those events or situations into my life, thank you very much.

AS YOU SPEAK IT, SO IT IS

But, it's not like we are just these passive victims the matrix is bombarding with incorrect thoughts. People willingly limit themselves all day, every day, by writing their own corrupt codes. It happens all the time. I was doing a podcast interview, and just before we started recording, the interviewer said to me, "I really hope people are going to like this, and are going to get it."

And I was like, *Ugh*. Because "hope" and the future tense are encoded with doubt and uncertainty.

I replied, "How about *People are loving everything we're saying; and this podcast is activating transformational experiences that are opening them, and awakening them, and inspiring them to go deeper into their self-love practices?*"

I mean, if we're going to set intentions, then let's set some poprocks intentions, right?

Here's the thing: curses are real. They're called complaining. They're called worrying. They're called doubting yourself, and limiting yourself, and sabotaging yourself, and putting yourself down. For example, I never tell my clients to "try" a spirit hack. I always tell them to "do" the spirit hack. When I tell someone to "try" something, I am cursing them with the experience of not completing. The word "try" is encoded with the frequency of doubt; and therefore, "try" functions to program our consciousness with the possibility of failure.

FROM WORK *TO* LOVE

So often I do events with spiritual teachers, and they're always talking about "doing the work," and "working on ourselves." It's really annoying. "Work" is a matrix word. The word "work" is coded with resistance frequencies, because we live in a world where we must work to survive. "Work" implies that we have to do something we don't really want to do, and triggers the idea of slavery in the human vessel. It's really messed up, because we have all these gurus constantly referring to "the work" we have to do to get enlightened, because the matrix has programmed this resistance into their New Age vocabulary. It's no wonder people cling to their slumber. The idea that we have to *work* in order to transform doesn't make the evolutionary process sound all that appealing, does it?

Instead of saying that I'm *working* on myself, I say that I'm *loving* on myself. We are not *working* on our issues, we are *lovingly accepting the energies that we are moving through*. That's a good one, because it communicates that we have already decided that we are moving through it, which means that movement is already happening, which means we are accelerating the process.

People who are not conscious of their words curse themselves all day long and craft lives for themselves that they don't really like, by saying things such as:

"I'm so bad with money."

Got it, Spirit says. *I'll keep those financial troubles coming.*

"There are no single guys."

Cool, Spirit says. *You love being alone. No available men for you.*

"This is going to be really hard."

Gotcha, Spirit says. *Let's make this endeavor extra challenging.*

"I don't know what's going to happen to me."

You want to be in limbo, Spirit says. *Great. Limbo it is!*

When we speak, the frequencies of the words reverberate from our mouths, unlocking the codes embedded therein. So when we say *Life is hard,* we are activating the coding that corresponds to the word "hard." Those frequencies are then projected out into the universe, where they link up with everything else that is vibrating at the frequency of "hard," and then the ego goes about organizing our reality to affirm this statement, and to make sure our life is full of difficult experiences, so that we can be right.

This is why we must be extremely mindful of our words—every one of them. When we speak words that are not in alignment with the realities we want to be living, we must rewrite those words, and respeak those words *immediately,* before they have time to take root, and program the subconscious mind, and materialize in our reality.

So instead of declaring how bad I am with money, I would say: "I'm getting better and better at managing my money."

And instead of complaining about there being no single guys, I would say: "I love how I'm meeting more and more aligned and available men, every day."

And instead of cursing myself into a state of purgatory, I would say: "I am so excited to see what exciting, amazing, harmonious opportunities Spirit has in store for me."

It is very important that when you hear yourself speaking against yourself, you restate the idea in a more positive light, immediately. Remember, everything you are experiencing in the present moment is the result of the thoughts, words, and actions you've spoken and done in the past. So if we want our realities to change, then we have to speak that change into our present moment experience, which means describing things the way we want them to be, instead of in the ways we are tired of them being. Do not be shy about correcting yourself in front of other people. Your alignment and the quality of your consciousness are far more important than what anyone else may or may not think about you leveling up out loud, like the lit leader you are.

THE EGO

As soon as we enter the Earth experience, the mind starts creating an attachment to this reality through an identity that is known as the *ego*. The more identity constructs we take on, the stronger, bigger, and more stubborn the ego grows. People get really hung up on this ridiculous idea of "killing" the ego, as if that were possible. We have to have an ego to live on this planet. We cannot survive without an ego. The ego was built into our system as a way for us to attach to this reality, so that we will choose to stay in these freaking bodies. If we didn't have an ego, there would be nothing keeping us here in this dense, third-dimensional plane. We're too powerful. We are way more powerful than these biological space suits we're walking around in. So we created the ego as a means of attaching to this reality construct. The ego gets a bad rap because some people's egos are based in lower densities, which are characterized by fear, and judgment, and hierarchy. But plenty of people choose to evolve their egos such that they are rooted in love, and devotion, and service. The ego isn't bad; it's just misunderstood, which is why the ego is not properly engaged, or evolved.

The ego is simply an affirmation device. Its purpose is to organize your reality to match your beliefs. That means that if you are holding on to a belief that says *Men suck,* the ego will make sure to organize your reality so that men treat you like shit, so you can be right. That's because the ego is the thing that actually makes your reality real for you, as a creator. I call it *the great paperweight.* Its job is to make you believe in the world you want to see. Remember, we live in a quantum reality. There are infinite realities; and everyone's reality is unique to them. So if you choose to believe that life is hard, the ego will make sure it aligns your reality to be full of challenges; just as if your beliefs are aligned with love, the ego will create a loving reality for you.

CREATE TO REPLAY

When we complain about our lives, or the state of the world, or anything, we only empower the issues we are complaining about. When someone says, "It's terrible how the ocean is so polluted," they're not helping to heal the ocean, they're just adding more pollution to it. They are sending instructions to every possible universal creative force, commanding them to be sure to keep the oceans nice and polluted. They are doing what I call *create to replay,* which means the more we talk about something, the more we experience it. If we really want to help clean up the oceans, then we would communicate this same idea in saying, "The oceans are getting less and less polluted every day," or "It's exciting to see so many positive changes happening on the planet now that Earth is cleansing itself." This sends a new set of instructions to those creative forces, which is what sets into motion the act of Earth cleansing itself.

SPEAK LOVE

It is so important for us to be aware of the codes we are speaking into the world of form, because we are literally creating reality with our every word. Whether we know it or not, and whether we like it or not, this is universal law. When we speak from love, our words create a loving reality. When we are not speaking from love, our words create realities comprised of fear, limitation, and separation, which all empower the darkness. This is why we are in the Blackout, and this is why the Blackout continues to intensify, because it seems like all people want to talk about is what's wrong, and whose fault it is, and how oppressed they are, and why everything is terrible. All that this complaining is actually doing is creating more of those energies, and more of those realities. At this stage of the Blackout, we really need a zero-tolerance policy when it comes to complaining. What we need to be talking about is what's wonderful about the world, and how it can be better, and what it looks like to live on a balanced, thriving, abundant, poprocks planet Earth.

5

DREAM GREATER

Because we live in a quantum energy field, every possibility you could possibly imagine, and all the possibilities you haven't yet imagined, exist. And the whole reason you incarnated here on Earth was so that you could experience as many of these possibilities as you want. Unfortunately, humans play small. Even though we are children of God, and we are imbued with the same creative powers as God, the vast majority of us don't take advantage of these powers. It's a wasted opportunity, because we are not here to play small. We are here to get lit, and to live our most amazing, magnificent dreams while making the world giant.

The primary issue is that people aren't doing what lights them up, and keeps them on blaze. People don't think they even have the right to figure out what lights them up, and keeps them on blaze, let alone actually do it. We are not welcomed to this planet by friendly, supportive spirits who explain upon our arrival that we are quantum creators in an infinitely loving and abundant universe, here to experience whatever we choose. Instead we are born inside a sterile box, under artificial lights, and taken out of our mother's womb by hands that are wrapped in latex, and all too often attached to the arms of a man (as if men should be birthing babies, but that's a whole other thing for a whole other book). When we are old enough, we are placed in an institution that stifles us with rules, and tells us to sit still, and to shut up, and to raise our hands to ask the questions we are discouraged from asking in the first place, and to then regurgitate all this indoctrinated nonsense they're shoving down our throats so we can get into a good college, and take out thousands and thousands of dollars' worth of loans, to go to yet another institution that exists to indoctrinate us some more, so we can tack a bunch of letters after our name, to get a job that will suck our time, our life force, and our creativity, in exchange for just enough money to survive, plus two weeks' vacation per year. And if we dare to deviate from this formula, we will be poor, and we will be cast out, and we will live in a tent in an alley until we die penniless and alone in a ditch somewhere.

Because the system programs us to believe that we have no choice but to live out this formula that is hammered into our consciousness from the get-go, people don't put any effort into figuring out what it is they really want. They don't believe they are allowed to figure out what it is they really want. *Who am I to live my dreams, and shine bright?* the darkness whispers in our ears. And because we think that voice belongs to us, we believe it, and we give our power away to the programming that tells us we're not worthy. And then because we don't have some great, grand authority's permission to be lit, and to be happy, and to live poprocks lives, we don't.

POPROCKS IS EASY

The lies that hold the system together are so flimsy, they're like dandelion fluff just waiting to be blown away. Because if humans were to understand how powerful they are, and how boundless they are, and how effortlessly God has set it up for us to manifest everything we could possibly dream of, the matrix would crumble. It's another reason why people aren't living magnificent lives filled with amazing experiences and beautiful adventures— because they are programmed to think it's hard, and that it requires time, and effort, and blood, and sweat, and adversity.

People are indoctrinated to think they have to overcome great odds and massive obstacles to earn the right to live a good life, and to have nice things. The media relentlessly instills this program in us—the one that alleges that we must earn comfort and enjoyment through suffering. Human beings place a high value on pain and hardship, and utilize these energies as a means of justifying wealth and pleasure. It's like, *I went through all these terrible things, so now I deserve to enjoy my infrared sauna, and my Kangen water filter, and my marriage.* It's a trap. It's a trap that we set up for ourselves to legitimize the belief that we have to go through something in order to get something, instead of just choosing to open a door to a dream and walking right through it with ease and joy.

The reason people aren't creating poprocks lives for themselves isn't because creating a poprocks life is hard. God wouldn't have made us creators if creating was something that was hard for us to do. The reason people aren't creating poprocks lives for themselves is because people don't understand how to manifest. Again, it's not because manifestation is hard; it's because everything we were taught about time is wrong.

LEAP YEARS AREN'T A THING

The system deliberately distorts our relationship to time to keep us from stepping into our power as creators. Days, weeks, months, and years are all arbitrary constructs the matrix created to trap us inside the program that has us perpetually associating with this thing called "time" that there never seems to be enough of (unless we're bored, in which case it's endless). These distorted ideas of time create parallel constructs in our cells, which are therefore programmed with the same distortions, meaning the body believes it has to age and die. But seriously—think about how janky it is. Some months have thirty days. Some have thirty-one. And then there's the February situation, which makes no sense on any level whatsoever. December isn't the tenth month, and October isn't the eighth month, but according to the dictionary, "dec" means ten, and "oct" means eight, so what the fuck? The whole thing is so ass-backward, and yet humans give their power, their authority, and their lives to this completely illogical construct. I mean, shouldn't a system that measures time be—at the very least—consistent, or rational, or easy to follow, if not all three?

THERE IS NO SUCH THING AS *NOW*

One of the most basic principles of shamanism is that life is always in flux. Everything is constantly moving. Your cells are moving. Your blood is moving. Your bile is moving. Your thoughts are moving. The wind is moving. The ocean is moving. The planet itself is moving. Everything is moving, moving, moving. That's why Eckhart Tolle's whole *The Power of Now* thing is such bullshit. There is no *now*. How do you get into a *now*? By focusing on it? By staring at it really intensely? What does that even mean? The *now* becomes the past as soon as we try to identify it. The act of acknowledging the so-called *now*, and stepping into the matrix's programmed perspective of time, means we have ceased to be present. Because the *now* isn't static, and the *now* isn't fixed. The *now* is always in motion. It's why, whenever I hear these spiritual people going on and on about *now this,* and *now that,* I'm like, *What the hell are you talking about? Your* now *just became the past, and your past just created your new future, so where is this imaginary pit stop called* now *that you think your meditation app is going to take you to?*

TIME ISN'T LINEAR

The extent to which we misunderstand time is the biggest roadblock humans face when it comes to manifestation. The primary issue is that people think time is linear. The matrix programs humans to think of time as a straight line that leads them from the past to the present and into the future, which is why the system is structured around institutional benchmarks and experiences meant to maintain the illusion of a linear trajectory. This is why we are rewarded with parties, presents, ceremonies, celebrations, and positive feedback from our friends and family when we "achieve" certain milestones that affirm this so-called progression (i.e., birthdays, graduations, weddings, anniversaries, retirements). The illusion of linear time was created as a way to make sure that humans stay in line, and follow the rules, and keep to the system's prefab formulas. The problem is that when we operate from the distorted perspective of linear time, we cut ourselves off from the quantum realm of limitless possibility.

THE QUANTUM FIELD OF EXPERIENCE

If you want to know your future, you don't need to consult a psychic, or an oracle, or a Tarot reader. All you need to do is pay attention to what you are doing now. The future isn't this mysterious, preexisting construct that is waiting to surprise us once we catch up to it. The future is a synthesis of everything we are thinking, doing, saying, and being now.

The quantum field of experience always exists, and is always available to us, but we can only access it when we truly understand that there is no future. What most people refer to as "the future" is just an extension of the present moment, which is always moving. If I were to speak to you right now, the words would leap into the past before your brain had a chance to register them. And that past would immediately lead to the creation of my next experience, which will create the next, and the next, just as that past would immediately create your next sequence of experiences. The future is comprised of tendrils like this, and each tendril represents a certain series of choices; and all these choices are quantum, which means that each one leads to its own array of different experiences. There is no single future path that leads us to some grand destiny human beings seem to think they're moving toward. There is no one destiny. Life does not unfold by chance. It is built upon the choices we make. Every choice leads us along one of those tendrils, and at any given time, we can change direction, and leap on over to another tendril—another pathway, another dimensional reality— by shifting our perspective and changing the way we think. Those operating in the quantum field of experience understand that the future does not exist until we create it. That awareness allows us to recognize the creative opportunities that are available in each and every moment, which allows us to manifest from a platform of expanded possibilities.

DREAM GOOD. LIVE GOOD. FEEL LOTS.

Shamans say that a person who lived a good life was a good dreamer, meaning they created a lot of options for themselves. A good dreamer avails themselves to all the possibilities that are held within the quantum field of experience, and knows that the way to access these possibilities is to allow their feeling state to permeate their being. Everything that exists in the spirit world is a flow—like a river, or a stream. Nothing is static, or fixed, or permanent. So when a good dreamer decides they want to experience joy, they invoke the feeling of joy in their body, which allows them to magnetize a dimensional river that flows at the frequency of joy. Then they jump in, and wade in the joy stream for a little while, and see where it takes them, and what doors it opens. Then the energies shift, because everything is always in flux, and now maybe our dreamer is wanting to experience some affection. So they call forth the feeling experience of affection, and then they get to see what happens in the stream of that flow, and what possibilities open up for them in the waters of affection. Then, when they feel ready, they step out of the river of affection to immerse themselves in the stream of inspiration, or in the stream of magic, or in the stream of play, or in the stream of stillness. It all exists, and we can jump into any stream at any time when we are operating in the quantum field of experience, and allowing ourselves to be fluid.

Spirit Hack: Past Tense Your Future

Most people manifest by speaking their desires into the future. They talk about all the wonderful things they are going to have, and all the wonderful things they are going to do, and all the wonderful things they are going to create. What they don't understand is that every time we say we are "going to" do something, we move that energy farther and farther away from us, into that procrastination construct called *the future*. When we speak in the future tense, we delay our manifestations.

Speaking in the past tense is a powerful spirit hack because it allows us to bypass the influence of the past, and to create from a fresh place, quickly. When we speak our future into the present, we clear the slate, so to speak, in declaring a new now, and a new trajectory. This means we speak about the things we are manifesting as though they have already happened. So, instead of saying: "I am excited that my book is going to help uplift and empower millions and millions of people," I say: "I am so excited that my book is helping millions and millions of people to uplift and empower themselves." When we speak about things that haven't yet unfolded as though they already have, we trick our subconscious mind into accepting our future projections as real. Remember: the mind is bound to the ego, which exists to make us right. In speaking our manifestations in the past, the mind goes about organizing reality to affirm the story we are telling, which means grabbing hold of the experience we are talking about, and carrying it into the future, so that we can experience it as the present unfolds, and be right.

If we want to manifest in the future, we speak in the past tense, as though we are looking back and reflecting upon the experience that has already happened. Like that time I said, "I love how these beautiful, amazing people just called me out of the blue to join them on their boat, and how we had the best time ever sailing around the Mediterranean, and swimming in the sea, and eating delicious food." And within a few days, I got a call from my friend Jeremy, asking me if I wanted to join him and his family for a sailing trip around the Greek islands.

WE CREATE OUR FUTURE

Humans must realize that the future is entirely of our making. It has no autonomy, and no agency, and no agenda. The future is waiting on us to direct it, and to build it, and to shape it, and to nuance it. We decide how it's going to look, and how it's going to grow, and how it's going to prosper. The future is a composite of our actions, our behaviors, and our beliefs. There is no X factor. The future is entirely what we make it. So when we, as a collective, choose to align our thoughts, behaviors, and beliefs toward a loving, nurturing, peaceful, prosperous, sustainable future, then that is how the future will align, as long as the majority of people are directing their consciousness toward that vision. Unfortunately, humans are not currently directing their consciousness toward that vision, because humans are too busy being entertained.

GIVE THEM BREAD AND CIRCUSES

We are programmed to believe we have to work to survive, even though our survival should be a given, and our work should be an authentic contribution to the upliftment of the species. The system imposes all sorts of have-tos upon us. We have to pay rent. We have to pay bills. We have to buy things. We have to insure things. We have to sign paperwork. We have to remember passwords, and update user agreements, and authenticate our identities. People feel overwhelmed, and people feel trapped, and people feel depressed. And because they don't want to deal with the pressure and the have-tos, they look to external things to make them feel better. They turn to entertainment.

Julius Caesar pacified the poor, disenfranchised Romans by giving them "bread and circuses." It was the key to wrangling political power during a time of extreme strife: give the people cheap food and plenty of entertainment to distract them from their disempowerment, and their status quo. Little has changed over the course of history, as the system continues to pacify the masses by using the very same strategy. So what if people are drowning in debt, and doubt, and depression, and disease? Just throw them a glamour bone, and keep them entertained, and they'll pretty much let you do whatever you want, because the darkness has co-opted their attention.

ATTENTION CREATES REALITY

Our attention is the glue that holds reality in place. The only thing that renders something real is the act of us putting our attention on it, and interpreting it as real. This entire dimensional construct is held together by our attention—by what the consensus of consciousness is focusing on, and devoting themselves to, and is therefore asking God to create. The act of directing our attention is like casting our vote for how we want our world to look.

For example, let's say someone is diagnosed with cancer, and they say, "I'm going to fight this cancer. I am going to beat this cancer. I am not going to let this cancer kill me." It doesn't really matter what they do, or how many treatments they undergo, I can tell you right now, they are creating an experience for themselves where that cancer is going to be unlikely to beat. The act of focusing so much of their attention on *fighting cancer*, and on *resisting cancer* only strengthens the cancer, and empowers the cancer, because it's all about *cancer, cancer, cancer.*

We are quantum creators, directing God with our every thought, and our every word. So when we direct our attention toward "fighting" cancer, we are reliant upon cancer to stick around to give us something to fight, and something to do. But when we remove our attention from the cancer and instead we commit to "thriving in a healthy body," and to "living a long, active life," we are directing our sacred attention toward the health we are calling in, and the healing we are experiencing, instead of on the disease we want to transmute, which allows the universe to amplify our health accordingly.

DISTRACTION

The problem is that people misuse their attention. And people disrespect their attention. They don't honor their attention as their primary reality filter. They aren't mindful of how they are focusing their attention, and of where they are directing their attention, and of what constructs and situations they are fueling with their attention, because they don't see their attention as a sacred instrument of creation. They don't understand how to use their attention to better their lives, and so they do not safeguard their attention. They just react, and let their attention be pulled by any random thing—by news, by gossip, by cellulite, by consumption, by cat videos, by political farce, by anything and everything the matrix throws out to deliberately wrangle our attention away from us, and to steal our creative vigor, and to strengthen and fortify the system, and all the status quo it perpetuates.

The matrix targets our attention through distraction. When we allow ourselves to be swept up in the glamour of distraction, we cast our vote for the reality that distraction is creating. That means that if you are focusing your attention on all the atrocities they're telling you about on the news, or on all the shoes you can't afford that your favorite reality star has in her walk-in closet, or on all the ways the patriarchy is disempowering you because of your skin color and your genitals and your sexual preferences, then those are the realities you are choosing to empower, and those are the experiences you are choosing to affirm, and to create more of. But let's be clear—it is a choice. It is always a choice. Most people think they have to accept the reality construct they are living in. That's because they haven't studied shamanism, and they don't know that the box only stays the box because we keep putting our attention on the box. They don't know that the box dissolves the moment we take our attention off it, because they don't know that their attention creates their reality.

ABOUT THAT DREAM . . .

The reason why people aren't creating poprocks realities for themselves is because human beings haven't learned how to dream. When Martin Luther King Jr. spoke the words *I have a dream*, he was talking about dreaming a new reality into being. He was talking about dreaming greater than how most people were dreaming at the time. Dr. King is one of my greatest and closest mentors. He visits me often in the spirit world and guides me as to how to use my thoughts to shape myself; and he always reminds me of his dream. Part of the reason that I chose to come back after I died was to forward Dr. King's dream, and to dream it greater.

Dr. King's initial dream was to create racial equality for all people. Dr. King succeeded in shifting people's consciousness to see that a greater dream was possible, and the collective took a quantum leap into a new reality where black people were no longer segregated. But the system couldn't allow culture to evolve in this way, or it would collapse, so it manipulated people into forgetting about the greater dream. You see, the dream was not fulfilled. The dream was to continue. The dream was not just "to transform the jangling discords of our nation into a beautiful symphony of brotherhood"; it was to transform the entire world.

But because a reality marked by global peace doesn't serve the darkness, the system created a whole bunch of distractions that distorted Dr. King's dream into a kind of glamour that made it seem like black people were free, while putting them right back into slavery—a different kind of slavery, decorated with gold rims, a whole lotta bling, and a killer weave, but just as oppressive. The system accomplished this by bringing in the spirit of narcissism to distract us from Dr. King's dream, and to distort Dr. King's dream, by changing it from the dream of being equal to the dream of being a superstar. This is why we now have so many people focusing their attention on all these celebrity athletes and entertainers, instead of on their own dreams, and on their own lives, let alone on establishing global equality here on Earth.

THE SPIRIT OF NARCISSISM

The spirit of narcissism exists to get people to believe that they are nothing unless they become something. What the system does is target the vacuous void that generates the false belief that we need to achieve something in order to be loved, and then it supersizes it by bringing in the spirit of narcissism, and tricking people into thinking that unless they achieve a certain level of acknowledgment, or appreciation, or value—meaning, unless they become famous—they will not be fulfilled. This is how the matrix lured people away from Dr. King's dream and redirected their attention onto that carrot, and onto that cage, while allowing the racism to seep back in and to spread like a virus, even though that virus had been vanquished, and was releasing, and being transmuted into love.

I refer to this phase of the Blackout as the Age of Narcissism, wherein humans are trying to understand themselves through the identities they mistakenly believe they are, while attempting to adapt to the social construct that says: *I value myself based on how many* Likes *I get on social media*. It's not necessarily a bad thing. Narcissism is allowing people to see themselves, and to learn about themselves. But most people are stuck in the shallows, and are distracted by the glamour, and by how cool they look, and by their *Likes,* and their matches, and their virtual popularity, instead of digging deeper into themselves to figure out who they are—like, who the fuck they really, truly, actually are—and why they are operating the way they are operating.

TO THINE OWN SELF BE TRUE

People need to let go of the distractions that keep them from focusing on themselves. That means letting go of entertainment. That takes courage, because people are scared of what they might find, and they are afraid that they don't have the tools to deal with what they'll find, which is why I'm sharing these spirit hacks and these shamanic tools with you now. We can't dream greater dreams until we understand why we are dreaming our current dreams. We can't level-up our lives until we figure out why we are living the lives we are living now. *To thine own self be true,* wrote Shakespeare. But the only way to be true to ourselves is for us to figure out what's motivating us to make the choices we are making in the first place, even when those choices aren't ones we're particularly proud of.

My friend was reading *Star* magazine while we were getting mani/pedis. When I asked her why she was reading that particular publication, she said it was because she wanted to know what such-and-such celebrities were up to.

"Are you friends with them?" I asked, genuinely perplexed.

"No," she said. "It's a guilty pleasure."

"What makes it a guilty pleasure?" I asked, even more confused, because clearly my friend and I had very different ideas about what *pleasure* actually means. "Is it a guilty pleasure because you get to look at all the things these people have that you don't have, so you can feel even worse about your life than you already do? Do you mean guilty pleasure, or do you really mean *self-abuse*?"

And then my friend got upset and put the magazine down, which was an empty gesture, because she was just doing it to get my approval, not because she had actually figured out why she was putting her attention on celebrity gossip, and what medicine was in it for her.

WHAT'S THE MEDICINE?

In shamanism, everything has medicine to share. If a snake bites you, then your spirit was calling for snake medicine. If your house floods, then you were clearly needing water medicine in your life—a lot of water medicine, but water medicine, nonetheless. When events like this happen, we can't integrate the lessons until we understand the medicine these experiences are giving us. So if our attention is focused on things that are not aligned with our devotion—like doubt, or sugar, or debt, or criticism—then we need to discern what medicine is there for us in those unhealthy choices before we can authentically shift our attention away from them.

From a spiritual perspective, if our attention is on anything, it is because spirit wants our attention on that thing. Not necessarily because spirit wants us to keep our attention on that thing, but because spirit wants us to use that thing to learn about ourselves. We can't shift our attention from the poison until we know what medicine the poison is giving us. That's why it was pointless when my friend put down the magazine. That wasn't growth; that was just her trying to control the situation. So, she wants to read about celebrity gossip. That's where her attention was pulled. Okay, that's real. That's what's happening. The next step would be for her to figure out *why* her attention is being pulled to *Star* magazine before she can authentically shift her attention onto more productive things, like talking to her shaman friend who happened to be sitting in the chair right next to her.

Kissing the Dragon

When I was in my early twenties and still figuring out whether I wanted to be a shaman, or a model, or a dancer (as though I actually had a choice in the matter), I used to drink like crazy. I would spend my days training in shamanism, and doing readings, and healings, and divinations for people, and then I'd rehearse with my hip-hop troupe, and then I'd get wasted while playing video games with my buddies, and then we'd head to the Castro to shoot paintballs at the gay guys coming out of the clubs, because I didn't just have a drinking problem, I was also homophobic.

You see, my father—who was very African, and very Haitian—taught me that homosexuality was wrong, and that men who shared love and intimacy with other men were weak, and weren't real men. These ideas, which had been engrained in me throughout my entire life, proved threatening on a very deep level, because—as it turns out—I, myself, am sexually attracted to both men and women. But because I was afraid of being rejected by my father, and because I was afraid of losing his love, I dealt with these feelings by repressing them and by acting out against the men who had the courage to be themselves.

The thing is, that pain I was inflicting upon those men was actually my own pain. It was the pain I felt toward myself for not living my truth. You see, when human beings act out with hate, or intolerance, or violence, or aggression toward others, we are really acting those things out toward ourselves, because we are not in harmony with ourselves, and because we are in judgment of ourselves, and because we want to attack ourselves. The reason people act out all these egregious behaviors toward one another is because they are afraid of their own reflections, and because they are afraid of what lies deep within themselves, and of that which they don't understand about themselves. My personal experience of homophobia gifted me a deep understanding of conflict—both global and interpersonal—as well as a pronounced ability to see both sides of a situation, which, ultimately, prepared me to be the great peacemaker and mediator I am today. Was it wrong how I treated those men? Absolutely, it was wrong. But sometimes in life we must take steps into the darkness to move us higher into the light.

But this isn't actually a story about homophobia. This is a story about alcohol abuse. This is a story about how, after yet another night spent drinking, and harassing the gay guys coming out of the clubs, I woke up on someone's lawn with my hand down my pants (which were on backward), and with vomit on my shirt, and a whole family staring down at me, looking none too pleased.

I went home humiliated and decided to figure out why I was devoting my attention to alcohol. I arranged a bunch of liquor bottles around my room, so I could face the very thing that I was afraid to confront—that alcohol had made me its bitch. In shamanism, we call it *kissing the dragon*. I sat down on my bed, surrounded by all the bottles, and blasted Metallica, and dug into the emotions that were making me drink.

Why is my attention on alcohol? I asked myself. *Why is my attention on inebriating myself?*

I wasn't asking from a place of judgment. I was asking from a place of genuine curiosity, from a place of really wanting to know what my attention was trying to teach me. What I realized was that the reason I kept putting my attention on alcohol was to mask the pain of the abuse I still hadn't dealt with—the physical abuse I endured from my father, and the sexual abuse inflicted upon me by my male babysitter. That realization allowed me to see that alcohol wasn't actually the problem, and that the alcohol was Spirit's way of drawing my attention toward the actual problem, which was the hurt that I needed to heal, and needed to integrate.

It was the act of getting real with myself, and examining why my attention kept getting pulled toward alcohol, that allowed me to authentically remove my attention from alcohol for good. And, you know what? I haven't had one drink since that day. Haven't even been tempted. But if I'd skipped that step, and I'd just said, *I'm never drinking again,* without digging into *why* I was dreaming the alcoholic's dream, I would definitely still be drinking myself stupid.

DREAM GREATER

After we figure out why we are dreaming our current dream, and we extract the medicine from our current reality construct, then we can go about dreaming a greater dream. We can't level-up our realities until we go about dreaming better ones, because we can't step out of something and into nothing. That's just basic physics. If we are talking about quantum leaping, which we are, then there has to be an actual location we are leaping to. We have to know where we're going, if we are to get there. We have to dream greater.

When I was surrounded by all those alcohol bottles in my room, listening to Metallica, and examining my alcoholic's dream, I didn't stop when I figured out why I was dreaming it. I dreamed a greater dream—many greater dreams. If I'd just dreamed that I went a day without drinking, or a week without drinking, that wouldn't have been an expansive enough leap to really change my dimensional orientation. When we are dreaming greater, we have to stretch ourselves, and we have to dream many dreams beyond our current dream to really transform our reality in a giant way.

So I dreamed beyond that which I currently was. I dreamed beyond the drinking, and beyond the blacking out, and beyond the inconveniencing other people. I dreamed about staying sober at a party and being in touch with my feelings, and my sensorium, and being able to hold a conversation without slurring my words. I dreamed about what it would be like to take that hurt that I was holding on to, and allow it to open me, and to empower me; and then I dreamed about being able to help others to do the same. I dreamed about living out my grandmother's wishes, and about going out into the world, and touching other people's lives in big, meaningful ways. I dreamed so much bigger than my then reality, that when I was done dreaming, and I sat up, and saw all those bottles surrounding me, it was a total disconnect. I had followed my bigger dream so far away from the realm in which I was drinking, that when I came back to that dimensional construct, our vibrations were no longer a match, and alcohol had no traction for me— like, literally, none.

I get a lot of clients who come to me because they say they want their lives to be different, but when it comes to figuring out what those different lives actually look like, and what those different lives actually consist of, they've got nothing. I may be a powerful shaman, but I can't go dreaming someone else's dreams into existence for them. If we ourselves don't take the responsibility and the initiative to dream greater dreams for ourselves in our own minds, then nothing's going to change.

So now we have all these activists claiming they want to change the world by marching against the current reality, and by protesting against the current reality, and by railing against the current reality. But all they're actually doing is expanding the reality they're so against by giving it all this attention. If they really want to change the world, what they need to do is put down their signs and get to dreaming greater.

Spirit Hack: Dream Greater

Dreaming greater is a practice that allows us to expand our lives beyond their current manifestations. The more we do it, the better we get at it. It helps to start off dreaming something material until you get the hang of it, at which point you can step it up and start dreaming the conceptual.

For this spirit hack, you want to wear light, minimal clothing. Ideally, you will practice this technique in nature, or at a park, or even with some kind of plant nearby, because nature expands our ability to perceive.

THE WARMUP: OBSERVE GREATER

- Observe your hand.

Focus your awareness upon your hand. You are not analyzing, or intellectualizing, or judging. You are simply observing what is.

- Now, observe greater than your hand.

Observe something greater than your current experience. Allow your observation to extend beyond this third-dimensional reality without letting your mind go crazy trying to figure out what that means intellectually.

There are no rules as to how this unfolds. You might observe your hand entwined in the hand of the partner you are magnetizing toward you. You might observe an object in your hand, or a bracelet encircling your wrist, or even a VIP wristband, or some holy thread. The background behind your hand might change from solid ground to a crystal-clear ocean, or to powder-white sand, or to an opulent marble floor, or to lush jungle soil, or to cosmic, geometrical patterns in the vast expanse of the great void. Don't try to force or control the dream, just allow yourself to dream greater than your hand, trusting that the dream will follow the intention.

- Speak your observations aloud as they present themselves to you.

Here are a few examples of what you might say, depending upon what you see: "I see a gold ring encircling my finger," or "I see a key in the palm of my hand," or "I see an eagle's talon," or "I see a child's hand in mine."

- Keep dreaming greater. Once you've honed in on the greater dream, speak it aloud, and then dream greater again. And again. And again.

SHOWTIME: DREAM GREATER

Now that you've dreamed your hand greater, you are ready to dream something more abstract.

- Pull up a negative thought—the first one that comes to mind.

- Observe it.

Notice where it comes from and how it's shaping your life. For example, let's say you pulled up the thought *No one likes me.* Now, think back to the first time you had that thought.

It was in elementary school, when I was picked last for dodgeball.

And how is this thought shaping your life, now?

It's isolating me, and giving me social anxiety, and keeping me from participating in events and experiences I want to be having.

- Dream greater.

A dream greater than *No one likes me* would be to see yourself being liked. So, you would say aloud: "Lots of people like me" while seeing yourself surrounded by people who are excited to be connecting with you, or whatever greater dream presented itself to you. You don't want to force the dream, and you don't want to control the dream, and you don't want to manipulate the dream. All you're doing is instructing your subconscious mind to dream greater. What your subconscious mind actually comes up with will be entirely unique to you, and will most likely surprise you. These are simply examples of what could arise.

- Keep dreaming greater.

Now, dream even greater. So, maybe you will imagine yourself being showered with cards and flowers and balloons on Valentine's Day. Now, dream greater, which means you might see yourself cracking up a whole table full of people at a dinner party, or dancing in a conga line at a wedding.

Keep dreaming greater, and keep speaking your greater dreams out loud. You'll know you're done when you try to go back to the original thought—the one that tried to convince you that no one likes you—and it's not there anymore, because you've dreamed so great that the initial negative program has been completely deleted from your consciousness.

THAT TIME MY CLIENT DREAMED GREATER

I had a workaholic Wall Street exec client who thought the only way to make it in the world was to fight, and scream, and hustle, and stress out. When he came to see me, he had an ulcer, a drinking problem, and multiple lawsuits against him. I explained that he wasn't dreaming correctly, and that this dream he was having where he had to thrash, and kick, and fight to be seen, and to get respect, and to make money was not supporting him; and that this dream was actually a nightmare.

My client's greater dream was to make a lot of money while living a peaceful, harmonious life, but he didn't believe he had the capacity to dream that dream into reality. He didn't believe it was possible. I explained to him that the only reason we were sharing that moment, and that session, was because he had dreamed me into his life. That meant that some part of his mind already had the capacity to dream beyond what he was experiencing; all he needed to do was to ask that part of him that dreamed me into his life to dream even more expansive possibilities for him to manifest.

Soon after our session, my client went to a bookstore where a book about a vision quest literally fell off a shelf and onto his feet. He read the book and dreamed his own vision quest. He ended up training with a tribe of Lakota elders and did a four-day vision quest, which inspired a whole new set of dreams and changed his entire life. He ended up leaving Wall Street, becoming a deeply spiritual person, and starting an environmental hedge fund devoted to making the world better and more sustainable.

MONEY IS SO NOT EVIL

Some people get really triggered when they hear others say that money is a priority for them, or that their greater dream involves making a lot of money, because people are indoctrinated to think that money is evil.

The system programs the masses to associate money with people who steal it, stockpile it, and misuse it, so that the masses will reject money and sell their souls to suffer in survival mode, instead of jumping on the lit train, and creating abundant, prosperous lives for themselves.

Money is not evil. Money is just energy. And because money is a construct of the matrix we happen to be living in, thriving in abundant prosperity is a brilliant way to make the matrix work for us.

SHAMANIC ECONOMICS

Money is the energy of exchange. Currency is how that energy manifests in physical form. Abundance is the accumulation of currency (or of anything, really). And prosperity is the flow of the exchange. Just like the current of a river, currency likes to move. Prosperity means that money is doing what it's supposed to be doing, by moving through the community and enriching people's lives accordingly. Money is a wonderful energy, because money allows us to do things, and to have experiences, and to give to others, and to live the way we choose to live, instead of scraping to get by and thinking we have to live in just survival mode.

People who are operating in lack consciousness think that money is hard to come by, and that they have to work really hard to get it, and that they have to compromise their values to get it, and that they have to hurt other people to get it. Except money never asked us to do any of those things; and money doesn't want us to do any of those things. All money wants us to do is to get in alignment, and to call currency into our lives, and to allow it to move and flow, and get us lit.

Spirit Hack: Shamanic Infusion for Currency

As I explained in chapter three, shamanic infusions are a great way to attune our energy to the frequencies we choose to draw into our lives through the breath. This spirit hack is a powerful meditation to draw currency into your life.

Now, let's be clear: it's not like you're going to do ten rounds of currency infusion, and a million dollars is going to drop into your lap from the sky. It doesn't work like that. But what this spirit hack does do is align your energetic frequency with the vibration of currency, which allows you to release and transmute any blocks or imbalances that have been restricting the flow of currency in your life.

- Sit quietly in a comfortable meditation posture.

- Say these words in your mind as you inhale deeply: *I pull currency into my being with full allowance.*

- Now, trace the symbol of the dollar sign in the air with your finger, exhaling sharply through your mouth with each finger stroke. Imagine the dollar sign is electric blue, which happens to be a power color in shamanism.

- Repeat the cycle several times while feeling the currency expanding into your body with each inhale, and seeing the blue dollar sign expand outward into the world with each exhale.

Because this spirit hack illuminates blocks and imbalances in our prosperity flow, pay attention to what comes up for you around finances in the days following your infusion practice, and journal any and all relevant experiences, including thoughts, dreams, and financial exchanges.

I gave this spirit hack to a client who was a graphic designer and had a backlog of money owed to him from clients who hadn't paid him, and within about a week of incorporating this spirit hack into his daily practice, checks that had been owed to him for months started rolling in. Shamanic infusions are powerful stuff.

POVERTY ISN'T SPIRITUAL

Spiritual people are abundant. That is how they can be of service to the whole—because they have a surplus to share. The matrix programs people to think that being spiritual means rejecting comfort, and possessions, and nice things to steer people away from cultivating an authentic relationship with Spirit. But it's a bunch of bullshit. Spiritual people are definitely not poor, because if you don't have anything to give, then you're not going to be very good at being spiritual.

I've gotten flak from people for what I charge for my sessions, as though shamans shouldn't be financially compensated for their services. It's as though people think that money is dirty, and that money tarnishes my spiritual offerings, or something.

I had a big celebrity country music singer come to my house in the Hollywood Hills for a session. He eyed my car, and my pool, and my garden. Then he came into the guesthouse I used as my healing studio and told me he was having second thoughts about working with me, because my lifestyle was inappropriate, and because charging for spiritual work was wrong. Then he told me that I should be living minimally, off other people's charity, while offering my sessions, and my workshops, and my teachings for free.

"I see," I said. "And how do you expect me to eat, and to take care of myself, and to be of service to my clients who so often need me to jump on an airplane, and fly across the globe to help them, if you don't think I am deserving of income?"

And Mr. Country Music Superstar said that I should offer my services on a donation basis, and that the quality of my spiritual sessions should determine whether or not people are inspired to give, which would determine whether I fly, or eat, or whatever, because—according to him—charging for shamanic healing sessions isn't spiritual. And he said all this with a totally straight face after he'd rolled up into my driveway in a Porsche, and—according to *Us* magazine—had just paid $2.4 million for his latest home, but he had the nerve to tell me I should be begging for alms on the side of the road in tattered rags and bare feet. As though making music isn't just as spiritual. As though his fans should decide after his concerts whether or not he deserves to be paid for his performance. As though money isn't spiritual. As though wealth and freedom aren't spiritual. As though God wants us to be poor. That's all darkness nonsense the matrix programs us to think. And it's bullshit. God wants abundance for all beings, spiritual people included.

That Time I Thought That Money Wasn't Spiritual

Years ago, when I had just started offering shamanic healings to people, I drove to Northern California from LA to work with a very sick woman who was part of an extremely wealthy and influential family of multibillionaires. I stayed with her for three days and worked with her almost the entire time. As I was packing my things, she asked me what she owed me for the long weekend. I told her that I worked on a donation basis, and that she was free to offer me whatever she liked for the three days of shamanic healing and rituals, plus the drive up from LA.

As we exchanged good-byes, she said, "That was amazing. You helped me so much. I feel a thousand times better. Thank you for everything. Here you go, sweetheart," and handed me an envelope.

When I got in the car, I opened the envelope to find twenty-five dollars inside it. It was so laughable, I actually laughed. And then I got sad, and then I got mad, because twenty-five dollars didn't cover even one of the multiple tanks of gas it took me to even get to Palo Alto, let alone drive back to LA. It wasn't until I got to San Luis Obispo that the lesson she was teaching me finally sank in, and I was overtaken—yet again—by laughter.

You see, because I hadn't died yet, and I still hadn't committed myself fully to my path as a shaman, I wasn't convinced that it was actually okay to charge people for my healings; and I was half-assing it. That attitude filtered into my sessions in such a way that it allowed others to devalue my healings and my teachings to the same extent that I was. I spent that drive back to LA delving deep inside myself, looking at all the judgments I was holding about not being deserving of compensation for my skills and my offerings. The laughter erupted when I finally got it—when I realized that if I don't honor my worth, then no one else is going to honor my worth, and that if I don't honor the value of my spiritual offerings, then no one else is going to honor the value of my spiritual offerings.

That experience taught me that it's not about waiting for some external authority to tell me that my offerings are worthy of compensation; it's about me honoring them from the get-go. It's about me declaring my own authority, and my own self-worth, and claiming for myself that what I am offering has value and is worthy of financial remuneration.

IT'S ALL ABOUT FLOW

Everything we have in our lives came to us from someone else. This is how life works. The tomatoes topping your pizza were picked by other humans. The canvas you paint on was stretched by someone else, over a frame that was made from wood chopped by yet another person. All the money in your bank account was given to you by other people. We pour into one another, just as nature pours into us. The river doesn't hold back its water from the plants on the shore because it's afraid there might be a drought coming. Nature pours into itself and into us, just as humans are meant to pour into one another. While it's true that the more we give, the more we receive, because we are strengthening that energetic channel, the point of giving is not to get, rather it is to support the universal flow of energy in service to a thriving, poprocks planet that sustains us all.

Spirit Hack: Gratitude Offerings

Gratitude offerings are a great way to drop us into the giving stream, and to honor the energy of universal flow, while allowing us to cultivate gratitude and humility in our lives.

An offering is any form of energy directed toward someone without an agenda, for no reason other than to be generous, and to give. When we give gratitude offerings, we are acknowledging the abundance this world has to offer, and we are acknowledging the universal flow that sustains life on this planet.

I recommend doing gratitude offerings at least once a month. You can offer anything you'd like to whomever you'd like. My general rule of thumb when it comes to gratitude offerings is that when it occurs to me to move some energy, and to give, whoever pops into my mind first is the person I give to.

Here are some ideas for gratitude offerings:

- Bless a tree.
- Weed a garden.

- Give a flower to a stranger.

- Burn a candle for the spirits.

- Send well wishes to your ancestors.

- Mail an envelope full of coins or cash to a friend without a note or a return address.

- Perform a dance for someone.

- Give someone a healing.

- Carry someone's groceries.

- Babysit a friend's kid.

- Help someone with a project.

- Bless the stranger you hear sneeze.

Again, be creative. Be generous. You are giving for giving's sake, which is a beautiful thing. Even if it's simply offering a french fry to the stranger sitting next to you, know that by giving, you are participating in the universal flow that sustains us all.

LIVE LIT; MANIFEST GIANT

Now that you get how easy God has set it up for you to manifest, why would you ever play small? Why wouldn't you want to experience luxury, and comfort, and beauty? Why wouldn't you want to eat the cleanest, yummiest, highest vibrational organic food? Why wouldn't you want to travel all over the world to be able to connect with people from different cultures, and learn from them, and be enriched by them? Why would you deprive yourself of these experiences? These are wonderful experiences to have and to share. Why not experience everything you could possibly want to experience while you are on this planet? You *can*. That's why you came here. To manifest your dreams into physical form, and to get giant.

HOW TO MANIFEST LIKE A MOTHERFUCKING SHAMAN

You can't be wishy-washy when you're manifesting. You have to be bold, and you have to be engaged, and you have to be specific. You can't just say, *I'm going to manifest a new job* and leave it at that, and think you've just created a new career path for yourself. You have to guide the energy. Everything in shamanism is about guiding energy; and to guide energy, we must be conscious, and we must be deliberate, and we must be crystal clear about what it is we are calling into material form.

When we throw out some vague, half-baked idea that we haven't really felt into, or filled out, the universe doesn't know what to do with it. There are too many blanks to fill in. There's not enough information to give the manifestation any traction. Now, if you say, *I'm manifesting a high-level administration position in a lovely office where I get paid really well to work with creatives who are devoted to changing the world; and I'm going to learn a lot, and get promoted quickly; and I'm going to start February first, or sooner*—now, that's a manifestation Spirit can work with.

Deadlines are important because they create a container for the energies to manifest within. Deadlines are a healthy masculine energetic that allows us to direct the energy and to activate corresponding future tendrils. Remember, there are infinite quantum futures. So it's helpful to clarify for Spirit which future you're actually talking about—your *five years from now* future, your *one year from now* future, or your *next week* future. Plus, dates and times render your manifestation a proclamation, which lends a certain weight in this dimensional construct.

Spirit Hack: Manifesting Giant

Despite the hype, and the hashtags, and *The Secret,* most people aren't actually manifesting correctly, which is why a lot of people aren't manifesting, period. They read Abraham-Hicks, or they watch some manifestation coach's vlog, and then they cut up a bunch of magazines for their vision boards, but they omit basic steps in the manifestation process, and their shit doesn't materialize. That's when they decide that manifestation is dumb, and that manifestation doesn't work; and they go back to stifling their dreams and zoning out on Netflix.

If you want to get good at manifesting, you must follow these four steps.

1. KNOW YOU CAN HAVE IT.

Everything you have in your life is because some part of your being knows that you can have it. That knowingness comes from your understanding of your own value, and your own worth. What you believe you're worth, and what you believe you deserve, and thus what you allow yourself to have, are all the same.

When you are manifesting, this knowingness must be foolproof. Do not take your attention off the knowingness to entertain doubt, or to tell yourself stories that affirm why you don't deserve what you are calling in. Ground yourself in the knowingness.

2. GET CLEAR.

Feel into your vision. Fill in as many details as possible. Nuance the specifics. Attach deadlines. Don't hold back. Be bold. Dream big. Stretch yourself. There are no limits.

3. SPEAK YOUR MANIFESTATION OUT LOUD.

When you speak your manifestations aloud, the sound transports the manifestation from the spirit world into the physical world, which activates your emotional response, which allows you the feeling experiences of having realized your manifestation. By speaking your dreams and visions out loud, you are bringing your word into being.

4. LET IT GO.

This is where most people take a wrong turn. After we speak our manifestations out loud, we must let them go. What we do not do is repeat our manifestations over and over again. A lot of manifestation gurus have people speak their affirmations out loud, and then repeat them over, and over, and over, several times a day. That approach defeats the whole purpose, because when you repeat something over and over, it means you didn't believe it the first time, and therefore your will is not fully connected to it. Repeating your dream only affirms your disbelief. That's why when you're manifesting giant, you speak your manifestation once. *Done.* You don't need to say it again. You don't need to talk about it anymore. Because you know it's happening.

WHAT DOES A POPROCKS REALITY LOOK LIKE TO YOU?

The future is entirely in our hands, and we get to dream it however we want. The single most powerful way for us to change the world is to take back our attention from the matrix—to pull it away from the distraction, and the entertainment, and the glamour, and the all of it, and to redirect it toward the greater dream; and to focus it—single-pointedly, and wholeheartedly, and consistently—upon dreaming the Giant Age now.

6

TAKE RESPONSIBILITY

If it's so easy to manifest, I can hear your beautiful, stubborn mind protesting through the quantum field, *then why are so many people in lack?*

Because, my dear, we still share a universe with dark matter, which means that darkness is still a thing here on Earth, and—as you already know—the darkness is all about lack and limitation. But, guess what? You are here to remedy that. That's right. You see, you are not just here to get lit, and to manifest joy, health, prosperity, a poprocks life, and a Giant Age, you are also here to ascend the darkness.

ASCEND THE *HUH*?

As we discussed a few chapters back, the darkness is the part of this dimensional reality that is held in density. That density exists to illuminate the possibilities that are not held in the field of love. Remember, we live in a quantum reality of infinite possibility, which means that *all* possibilities exist, including those that are not aligned with love. A lot of people misunderstand these possibilities as being somehow separate from God, and thus misunderstand the darkness itself as being separate from God, and the oneness of all that is. This is false.

The oneness is infinite and eternal, and is thus held in a field of consciousness that expands far beyond the limitations of human perception and understanding. God is not of us. And while God imbued humans with free will, which gives us creative powers similar to God's own creative powers, our creative capacity is not the same. Free will is the ability for humans to choose from whatever possibilities exist. God *is* all the possibilities that exist. God is not a box, and God is not a fixed destination. God is eternal expansion; and within that expansion, we humans have sovereign agency in which to create. This means that we can create forms that are aligned with love, and we can create forms that are not aligned with love. But that creation is still held within the oneness that is all possibility, which is God.

The density that comprises the darkness—when utilized intelligently—creates the friction necessary to fuel our evolution. As I've already explained, Earth is not a planet of perfection, but a planet of refinement. We choose to incarnate on this planet to learn, and to grow. The density that the darkness holds—when utilized intelligently—is actually a tool for human evolution. The more we allow ourselves to open and accept *all* realms of possibility, the more our minds will grow and expand into higher levels of consciousness. This means allowing ourselves to perceive the density that comprises the darkness without judgment, and without aversion, and without opposition. This is how we expand our consciousness.

But because God imbued humans with free will to create whatever it is we choose, humans have chosen to utilize that density to create structures and belief systems that limit our ability to expand our consciousness. We do this by reacting to the density, and by judging it as an obstruction, instead of perceiving it as a neutral energy that we can transmute and transform. This judgment is what has humans stuck in duality, wherein we mistakenly perceive these options as diametrically opposing forces, which keeps us trapped in a perpetual quantum entanglement of right versus wrong, and good versus bad, instead of simply perceiving these different energy forms as options with which we can choose to align our energies, or not.

Further complicating the problem with this orientation is the human tendency to attach all types of rules, and labels, and identities to each dualistic field they choose to align themselves with, and categorize others according to which field they choose. These identity constructs keep humans trapped inside the limitations they have imposed upon those dualistic fields. And so instead of learning from these denser energies, and understanding these denser energies, and utilizing these denser energies as teaching tools to develop our creative capacities in an infinitely expanding universe, humans judge these denser energies as wrong, and as bad, and as worse, and then align themselves in opposition to them by way of rules, and labels, and identities, to make themselves feel virtuous, which—ultimately—blocks them from experiencing the oneness that is.

THE DARKNESS HAS NO FANGS

On a physical level, the darkness is a realm that houses everything that is not aligned with love. For a lot of people, the darkness conjures up all sorts of dramatic visions of demons with pitchforks, and monsters with claws and stinky breath. But that's not what darkness is. Not by a long shot.

Religion has programmed people to associate the darkness with scary, horrific forms and imagery, so that we will fear the darkness, and judge the darkness, instead of engaging the darkness. Remember, religion is a tool of the matrix that exists to keep humans from developing their own authentic relationship with Spirit, and to keep us tethered to the energetic frequencies of lack, limitation, fear, and discord—all of which fuel the darkness. These images and these stories function to perpetuate these energies to feed the dark realm, while manipulating people to think the darkness is something to be avoided at all costs.

The truth is, darkness has no form in and of itself. Darkness simply puts on the costumes that humans project onto it and appears in dreams, visions, over-the-shoulder glimpses, and spirit world sojourns, based upon whatever fears and images we are harboring in our own imaginations (which are the fears and images the matrix programmed humans with in the first place). It's another reason why I don't watch scary movies. Because I don't need the darkness showing up in my room in the shape of a blood-sucking zombie, or a fire-breathing demon, thank you very much.

DARKNESS IS . . .

So, if darkness isn't the monsters, or the vampires, or the goblins we have been indoctrinated to believe it is, then how does darkness show up in this reality? Great question, love. The way darkness shows up in this reality is as that disembodied voice in your head that whispers, *You can't* or *You're not good enough* or *Everyone will laugh at you*. While not necessarily demonic, that little voice is insidious and incredibly destructive, because it exists to disempower us, and to isolate us, and to keep us from realizing our potential and our purpose; and, we let it.

As a human being incarnate on planet Earth, you've probably experienced this type of interaction with the darkness at least a dozen times today, if not a dozen times already this *hour*. The darkness creeps into our minds as a negative thought. The more we focus on that negative thought, the more access we give the darkness to our being. Focusing our attention on the negative thoughts the darkness generates is pretty much the same thing as opening your door to darkness, and inviting it in for coffee and scones, and saying, *Hey, Darkness. Come shit all over my internal landscape, and fuck up my vibratory field. Would you like almond milk in your macchiato, or hemp?*

But who would we even be talking to? Whose voice is it that wants us to think such terrible things about ourselves? Well, this might be a little hard to swallow, but—believe me—it's the straight-up truth: the voices in our heads are underworld spirits. They are the voices of our brothers and sisters who are stuck in the darkness, and who need our help getting back to the light.

THE UNDERWORLD SITUATION

The underworld is a specific realm of darkness—much like a city, or a region—that sustains itself on human discord. Again, despite all fairy tales to the contrary, the underworld is not populated by ghouls, or demons, or monsters. The beings who populate the underworld are human beings who've walked before us, and who got stuck holding on to certain energies they couldn't forgive themselves for back when they were incarnate. You see, when we die, we are shown everything we've ever done in our life, and all the ways that our choices, and our actions, and our behaviors affected everyone around us, and the world at large. Only if we are able to let it all go with unconditional love and acceptance are we free to move on to other dimensional experiences, or to new Earthly incarnations, or to whatever we choose. But if we allow ourselves to get stuck in judgment and opposition to the darkness that we ourselves acted out while we were here on Earth, and if we can't let go, then we are sent to the underworld, which is a specific realm of the darkness that we, as incarnate humans, have a responsibility to clean up.

The underworld is dependent upon human discord to feed its inhabitants, which is why it goes to such great lengths to generate fear, and lack, and limitation among human beings on Earth. The way it works is that the underground spirits—who look and act as human as you and I do—utilize certain neurological algorithms to tap into the consciousness of human beings whose own unintegrated trauma matches the frequencies of the issues the spirits themselves are still holding on to. Let's say you have trust issues with male authority figures because of an incident you had with a priest when you were a child. If you haven't healed that trauma, and integrated the lessons from that trauma, then you would very likely attract an underground spirit who incurred a similar trauma, and who was dealing with similar trust issues, which inspired him to enact certain behaviors or actions in his own lifetime that he couldn't forgive himself for when he passed on.

You see, the spirits need fear to survive. They cannot feed on light, because light is pure love. So, the spirits infiltrate the minds of the people here on Earth and corrupt them with fear, and lack, and doubt, and separation, and whatever other unresolved stuff the spirits attached to us need to work through. This is why people are in lack, and this is why people are in fear, and this is why people play small—because they listen to the negative thoughts the spirits are generating in their heads, and they buy into them and give their power away to them.

HUMANS LIKE THEIR UNDERGROUND SPIRITS, THOUGH

The truth is that most humans don't want to be in their power. In this way, darkness is like that low-vibe friend who's a bad influence on you, because they enable you to play small, and to keep sabotaging yourself so that you continue to generate the energies that feed it. Darkness is that codependent energy sucker who's rooting for your disempowerment.

Most humans are afraid of aligning themselves with the light, because it means accepting our responsibility as creators. Humans already feel so much survival pressure from the stress of bills, and bureaucracy, and insurance premiums, and kids, and credit card debt, and mortgages, and cholesterol levels, and all of it. The survival program the matrix imposes saps a lot of energy that could be put into focusing on who we are, and on what we want to create. But because most humans are struggling to juggle so many have-tos, they don't have the bandwidth to deal with creating new realities. And so the idea of having some kind of creative power becomes overwhelming, because we can't come into that power unless we know our true selves. And to know our true selves would mean having the time, and the energy, and the support to learn about our true selves, and to develop our true selves, inside a system that does everything it can to dissuade us from knowing our true selves.

In this way, the setup creates a codependent, symbiotic relationship between humans and their underworld spirits, wherein humans get to keep themselves stagnant, while making excuses, dodging responsibility, and playing small, while the darkness gets to feed on their discord and their misery. And so it is that we have all these bobbleheads walking around on autopilot, giving their power away to the spirits in their heads, when what they really need to be doing is taking them to the light.

THE DARKNESS DOESN'T HATE YOU

The darkness is devoted to maintaining its dimensional realm, because as long as darkness can sustain its realm, the beings in the darkness are safe. Remember, the darkness is not evil. Evil is a judgment based on humans' duality hang-ups. The darkness has no nefarious agenda, and the underworld spirits aren't messing with humans to be mean. People are so narcissistic. It's like saying that human beings are evil for killing cows and goats for food; or like accusing people of being mean to daisies and cilantro when we cut their stems. It's absurd. The darkness is not enslaving human beings and feeding off their fear because it hates us. The darkness is just doing what the darkness needs to do to survive. It's not all about humans, all the time, in every dimensional plane of existence. I mean, really.

The thing is, the darkness created this intricate structure, and the darkness goes through all these elaborate measures to create discord on Earth— all so it can serve the beings in its dimension. It's almost endearing, because the darkness goes to all this trouble to take care of its own. The thing is, the beings the darkness is bending over backward to feed don't actually belong in that realm. The underworld spirits belong with the light.

DARKNESS NEEDS LIGHT

The underworld is like a kind of purgatory. It's a way station for stuck souls. But it's not the kind of realm that any being would consider "home." It's kind of like when your flight is delayed, and so you sleep on the floor of the airport, and you wash your armpits in the airport bathroom, and you drink juice at the airport café. Sure, you're living at the airport while you're there, but it's not your home. It's not your realm. So while it's admirable that the darkness shows up so full force to provide a safe space for its spirits, its efforts are misplaced, because those spirits don't belong there. Those spirits have their own stories to play out, which means that what they really need to do is to get out of the darkness, and into the light, so they can get on with fulfilling their own journeys.

That's where we come in. The spirits can't get out of the underworld of their own accord. They need an embodied vessel to escort them to the light. That's you. You are that which clarifies their redemption for them. Human beings are the ones Spirit has entrusted with the task of taking the spirits from the darkness to the light. It's another reason the spirits berate us with negative thoughts after glomming onto our matching trauma frequencies. They're trying to get our attention, so that we will realize that they are with us, and do something about it. We're like cosmic custodians, here to clean up the darkness, and to bring it home to the light.

TRAUMA

U nresolved trauma is like a magnet for spirits. The trauma itself resonates at a frequency that attracts spirits whose own unresolved issues are a vibrational match, and who will then guide our life events to affirm the trauma and the beliefs it creates. So if there is an underlying trauma that is creating the unconscious belief that says *I want to be angry at the world,* then I need reasons to be angry at the world so that I can give myself permission to be angry at the world. That trauma will then go about magnetizing a spirit from the underworld to connect me with people who betray me, and events that piss me off, while whispering in my ear about how infuriating everything is so that I will have plenty of reasons to be angry at the world.

Trauma is trapped energy that has not been properly released from the physical or emotional body. The mind holds on to the energy because it is waiting for something to meet the trauma with love, and to tell it that it's going to be okay. Trauma is a portal to emotions from our past that are trying to get our attention so that we can acknowledge them, and embrace them, and move forward. But when people don't step through that portal, and don't acknowledge or embrace those trapped energies themselves, but instead wait for some imaginary savior to come do it for them, the energies calcify in the body and create a belief that says that something went wrong, and that it could happen again, which distorts future decisions while schizing out the nervous system, and programming reality accordingly. And it also attracts underworld spirits.

DISCERN THY SKETCHERS

A ny thought that is not pure love is not coming from you; it's coming from the darkness. That means that anytime you hear a negative thought in your head, you can be sure it's a spirit, and you can be sure it's coming from the darkness. This is why the voices in your head—which I call *sketchers*—need to be discerned immediately. Most people hear a voice in their head, and they just go with it. They don't put in any effort to discern who the voice belongs to, or where the voice is coming from. So they let themselves be manipulated by these thoughts, which run wild and distort the psyche, instead of having the wherewithal to realize, *Oh, this isn't even me. This is a spirit,* and then dealing with the spirit accordingly.

It is important to discern the thoughts in our head as quickly as possible. This means that when we hear a negative thought, we must invoke the feminine factor, and check in with our emotional body, and take note of how the voice makes us feel. *Do I feel lifted? Do I feel nurtured? Do I feel honored? Do I feel respected? Do I feel empowered? Do I feel good?* And if we get a bunch of *nos*, then we know we're dealing with an underworld spirit, at which point you want to ask it point-blank, "Are you from the underworld, spirit?" And if you get a yes, that's when you know that it's time to transport it to the light.

AVK (AUDIO, VISUAL, KINETIC)

There are three ways that people can receive spirit communication: through sounds, through images, and through feelings. Some people are auditory, some people are visual, and some people are kinesthetic. The sensory option that is the easiest/strongest for you is the one that your spirit will allow.

For people who allow themselves to hear spirits, the voice that they hear sounds like their own voice. Just like how the darkness takes on the forms that we already hold in our imagination, the spirits take on our own voices so that we will listen to them.

Feelers get specific feelings in certain parts of their body, and they learn from experience what those feelings in those particular places mean. Visual people get images in their mind's eye, or upon objects, or reflective surfaces, like glass, or mirrors.

I have a client who isn't very adept at hearing, or feeling. She's visual. She came to see me for guidance when she cut her mother-in-law out of her life. I led her through a mediation in which she saw an image of two people hugging, which she took to mean that she should mend the relationship.

You can tell which sense people are most comfortable using by the way they speak. Kinesthetic people will say things like: "I feel you" or "I feel that _____." Auditory people will say: "I hear you" or "It sounds like _____." While visual people will say: "I see your point." I can always tell which sense my clients are going to be most comfortable with by the words they use.

That Time My Friend Didn't Discern the Voice in His Head

A lot of people think the idea of talking to the spirits masquerading as the voices in their head sounds crazy. But let me tell you, the true crazies are the ones who aren't questioning their own thoughts and engaging their spirits. Those are the ones you really have to watch out for, because those are the ones who are losing their minds.

My friend Stephen decided he was going to move to the middle of some forest in the Pacific Northwest and live off the grid, surrounded by nature. This thought just occurred to him out of the blue (*Hello, underworld spirit*), and he didn't think to question it. When he called to tell me his plan, I knew it was a bad idea.

"Why don't you at least take some botany classes?" I suggested. "Or, some horticulture classes?"

People think discerning their spirits is all shaman mumbo jumbo, but really, it's very practical. Like, how did Stephen think he was going to survive in the middle of nature with no skills whatsoever? As it turns out, Stephen never took the classes I suggested, and Stephen never paused to interrogate the voice that was telling him to move to a cabin with no electricity in the middle of the forest, which is why Stephen died from eating water hemlock.

Spirit Hack: Get Thee to the Light, Spirit

Given the intensity and the acceleration of the Blackout, we have to start taking action, and we have to start doing our part to put the planet back into balance. This means cleaning up the underworld spirit situation, and escorting our brothers and sisters back to the light where they belong.

You want to do this spirit hack standing up, because underworld spirits like to put you to sleep. So be sure you're standing in a strong, powerful stance, with your arms crossed over your chest, so that the darkness can't fuck with you.

STEP 1: INTERROGATE THE SKETCHERS.

- Ask the voice, "Where are you from, spirit?"

First off, you want to be questioning any voice in your head that isn't coming from love and isn't lifting your spirit. This means asking it point-blank if it's from the darkness.

- Utilize your AVK sensory tool to receive the spirit's reply, then grill it for self-knowledge.

Once you get confirmation that you're dealing with an underworld spirit, then you want to take advantage of your proximity, and gather more information, so that you can get clarity as to why it's in your field.

Some questions you can ask the underworld spirit include:

"How are you serving me, spirit?"

"Spirit, what benefits are you offering me?"

"Spirit, why have I held on to you for as long as I have?"

So, let's say you hear a thought that says, *You're doing it wrong.*

You want to challenge that voice, and ask it: "Who are you to tell me that I do everything wrong? Where do you come from?"

And the spirit will say something like, *I am the voice that keeps you small. I am from the darkness.*

So now you have confirmation that it's an underworld spirit. Cool. Next, you can ask the spirit something along the lines of: "What do I get out of being small?" and then follow that pathway of inquiry to get clarity as to where and why you are hiding in your life.

What you don't want to do is get nasty with the spirit. You might have some emotions come up around the issues the spirit is playing out with you, but you definitely don't want to take them out on the spirit, or let the emotions knock you off your center—which is unconditional love and acceptance. If you are engaging a spirit through the lens of judgment, you're not going to get any real clarity as to why it's in your life; and you're definitely not going to be able to send it to the light.

In Case of TSD
(Temporary Spirit Deafness)

If you don't hear the spirit respond to your questions, it's because you're afraid to hear the answers. The spirits never withhold information.

My uncle taught me this spirit hack when I was a kid, when my own fear of the darkness was keeping me from hearing the spirits. It's a two-step process, and it always does the trick.

1. Clap your hands five times while saying aloud each time:

   "I am not afraid to confront the darkness."

Clapping is a traditional shamanic technique to break up blocks, fear, and stagnation. Make sure you smack both palms together with strength and conviction. The noise it makes should be sharp and loud.

2. Next, say out loud to yourself: "I know you're afraid,
    but I'm here with you. I'm not going to abandon you. You
    are completely safe with me. I love you. You can let the
    darkness speak. You are completely protected. You are
    so powerful. You can hear the darkness, and you can
    hear the spirits, and it is easy for you."

I used this spirit hack on this macho Mexican guy who came to
one of my classes with his wife. He told me flat out that he didn't
believe in any of my shamanic mumbo jumbo. I sat him in a chair in
front of the class and led him through these steps, and within two
minutes, he had these big, fat tears rolling down his face, while he
chatted up his guides like they were long-lost friends. The whole
class was crying. The guy now follows me on Instagram and comments all the time. He's a full-on believer.

STEP 2: SEND THOSE SUCKERS TO THE LIGHT!

After you're finished interrogating the spirit, now you're ready to take it
to the light and get some radical closure on this disempowering thought
invader that's been messing with you for God knows how long.

- Say: "Spirit, I am taking you into the light, to a place of unconditional love and comfort and acceptance and freedom."

- Then ask: "How do you feel now that you're in the light, spirit?"

It's important to get confirmation from the spirit after you've trans-
ported it to the light, so that you know your efforts were successful, and
that the spirit is out of your field for good. Plus, confirmation is helpful and
encouraging when we are practicing our shamanic skills.

- Once the spirit confirms that it's in the light, ask: "Do you have any
  wisdom to share with me now that you are in the light, spirit?"

Because, guess what? Now that the spirit is in the light, it is speaking from the consciousness of light intelligence. When we transport a spirit to the light, that spirit goes from being a nuisance to being a great helper. Remember, you and that spirit were energetically enmeshed for some time, and you are the one who released it from the darkness and facilitated its return to the light. Now, that spirit's got your back. As soon as it is reunited with the light, that spirit becomes a part of your spirit force, supporting you from the light realm as a lasting ally you can call on whenever you need.

- Offer the spirit your gratitude, and a fond farewell.

After you receive the spirit's wisdom and teachings, you thank the spirit, and you say good-bye to the spirit, because it's good manners, and you weren't raised in a barn.

Your Spirit Force Is a Thing. A Very Good Thing.

I bring spirits to the light all the time. I once dealt with a spirit that was generating a lot of self-hatred. After I interrogated it, and brought it to the light, I asked if it had any wisdom to offer me. The spirit taught me that the more that I love, the more love I have to give; and that the more I embrace people with love, the more powerful I become. And by *powerful*, I don't mean power that is based on having agency over others. I mean power that is sourced from my devotion to being a servant of love and healing for humanity, and power that is sourced from my devotion to helping shift humanity into a new consciousness by choosing to take my love to greater heights, and expanding my capacity to hold, and give, and share, and emanate love. That spirit gave me a whole different perspective on love that allowed me to transcend my parental programming, which was *Love is pain,* or *Love is when someone buys you something,* and to be able to love for the sake of loving, for the sake of loving, for the sake of loving; and to know, with every fiber of my being, that through my love, transformation arises.

LOVE-AND-LIGHT, MY ASS

I meet a lot of New Age types who claim they're all about love-and-light because it sounds cool, and it's on trend. Except, they're pretty much just talking out of their asses. These are the people who won't deign to entertain the notion of bringing an underworld spirit to the light, because it's too dark, or it's too low vibe, or it doesn't fit into the love-and-light brand as according to how social media tells them love-and-light is supposed to look and be hashtagged. These people have no idea what the hell they're talking about.

You can't claim to be all about love-and-light if you can't stand in the face of darkness. Light consciousness is not swayed by underworld spirits, or by negative emotions, or by any perceived lack of love. Light consciousness is the consciousness that loves infinitely, in constant form, unconditionally, and without expiration dates. The light does not run from darkness, the light does not yield to duality, and the light does not give in to the lie of separation. The light holds its position, and keeps holding its position, until the darkness taps out, and surrenders, and harmonizes its vibration to the only truth there is—light.

A lot of people in the New Age spiritual scene are blinded by their misunderstanding of love-and-light and therefore won't acknowledge anything that contradicts their perspective, which is *Darkness doesn't exist if I pretend it doesn't exist*. This denial is what got us into the Blackout in the first place, and this denial is going to be the end of the species unless we get to engaging the darkness, and quickly.

That Time I Learned to Meet the Darkness with Love

When I was fourteen years old, the darkness showed up in my room as a bunch of demons. Because I had given those images validity in my consciousness, the darkness projected those images back to me, and—voilà, demons. I called forth a blade on the astral plane and began fighting them with it. To the outside observer, it just looked like I was lying in my bed, having an intense dream. But on the astral plane, I was at war.

Then, an angel appeared. She looked like a regular human, but I wasn't buying it.

"Is that what you really look like?" I asked, still clutching my blade.

The angel immediately transformed into her true form. She was very tall, and very thin, like an ET made of white fire, with lights beaming from the inside out. Her wings looked like they were made of opalescent jellyfish liquid. She didn't have visible eyes all over her body, but it felt like she did, because her whole body was a sensory apparatus, and it was clear she could see everything.

The angel told me that I had forgotten the truth of why I had come to Earth, and that she wanted to show me something. Suddenly I was riding a white horse in a scene straight out of *Braveheart*. I was leading an army of people from all races, and all cultures, and all ages, who I knew were of the light. Across from us, in this massive green meadow, was another army, comprised of killers, and rapists, and witches, and evil sorcerers, and all kinds of wretched-looking beings from the darkness.

I led the army of light as we charged across the grass, weapons in hand. A powerful old wizard appeared in front of me, laughing in my face.

"The child of light!" he yelled. "HA! You are so foolish."

The wizard smacked his staff to the ground, as a serpent made of fire slithered up from the earth, flew into the air, shot across the field, and went straight through the center of my body, leaving a big, burnt hole in the middle of my chest. It hurt like a motherfucker. And as I lay there on the ground, coughing up blood, I looked up to see the army of light collapsing all around me as they were being killed by the darkness.

I heard a voice say: "Again!"

Suddenly, I was back on the horse, readying my light army to charge, once again. I instructed my army to put down their weapons and told them that, instead, we were going to fight with our fists, and with our magic.

As we charged across the grass, a woman with pale white skin and fiery, red eyes appeared in front of me. She sneered and laughed, waving her hands in the air and conjuring all these mystical symbols, which caused my entire body to erupt in massive boils, which were bursting with blood and all sorts of nastiness.

"This is the child of light who has come to wake up the people?" she cackled as I lay there bleeding, and my army of light collapsing around me. "This is the child of light who has come to help them remember the truth?"

And then I heard that same voice say: "Again!"

Again, I was back on my horse.

"What are you doing, child of light?" asked the uniformed general who suddenly appeared over my shoulder.

Again, I addressed the army of light as we prepared to charge across the meadow, where the beings of darkness were taunting us.

"We cannot fight with our fists," I yelled over the hollers, cackles, and screams coming from the dark army. "We cannot fight with magic! We cannot fight with weapons! There is only one thing left for us to do!"

I instructed the army of light to think of someone they love. Then I told them to take one another's hands, and to walk with me across the grass to greet our brothers and sisters. I told them to hold that thought of love in their consciousness, and to beam it toward the dark army with unwavering devotion, regardless of what weapons or magic they tried to use against us.

Hand in hand, we walked across the field, beaming love straight from our hearts as the beings of the darkness ran toward us with knives, and daggers, and magical weapons. As the light hit each one of them, the beings emerged from the other side in human form, dressed in white. Their faces lit up, as they remembered themselves, and they remembered each other, their cheeks wet with tears of joy, as they were reunited with the people they had once known.

In the midst of this joyful reunion, a grouping of massive stones etched with circles emerged from out of the ground, in geometric formation, like Stonehenge. An ancient Druidic woman named Helga stood in the center of the rocks. She called me to her, placed a gold medallion around my neck, and told me to look up. As I lifted my chin to the sky, I saw dozens of angels floating above us in a circle.

"Do you understand what must be done, child of light?" she asked.

"Yes," I said.

"You can never fight darkness with anger," she said, affirming the lesson I had just learned. "You must always meet darkness with love."

That was the last time the underground spirits appeared to me as demons. Now they appear to me as people, as my fellow brothers and sisters, and I always, always meet them—and all darkness—with love.

ENGAGE THE DARKNESS

Shamanism is all about engaging. When we happen upon something we don't understand, we don't judge, we don't contract, we don't attack, we don't shove our heads in the sand, and we definitely don't run away; we engage. We say, *Oh, hey there, voice of doom and gloom. Who are you? Oh, you're a sketcher. Got it. Why are you here? How are you serving me? What's your medicine? Okeydokey. Off to the light you go, dear one.* And then we take the wisdom, and we let it propel us on our poprocks paths. . . .

Our refusal to engage our collective shadow has made us an arrogant culture, blindly devoted to consumption and profit, and oblivious to the magnitude of suffering and discord we create in the process. This distorted perspective is greatly limiting the spectrum of evolution available to us at a time when humanity needs to be expanding their capacity to evolve. We are not being honest about our waste, our corruption, or our addiction to oil, and to sugar, and to screens, and to doubt. And we are not being honest about how we are disrespecting our planet, our bodies, and our fellow beings.

The Blackout marks a turning point where human beings have no choice but to take responsibility for the darkness we are perpetuating here on Earth—the darkness we hide from, and blame everyone else for, and victimize ourselves, too.

BVP

Human beings are currently under full-fledged assault by the victim program. The matrix is flooding the masses with false ideas about the virtues of victimhood, and false ideas about the value of victimhood with astounding intensity, thereby turning victimhood into a competitive sport, with people literally fighting for the title of *Biggest Victim on the Planet.* The program is like a virus that spreads rapidly and ferociously through gossip and filtering—gossip, meaning the lens through which facts are distorted to individuals through conversations with other people; and filtering, meaning the lens through which the events taking place are being distorted to the masses by the media.

The system uses the media to program the people, and to control their minds. Our trusted news organizations manipulate the information they are disseminating to deliberately disempower the populace. They no longer tell stories objectively in such a way as to allow the public to engage their critical thinking, and to draw their own conclusions. The media tells people what they are supposed to think, and how they are supposed to feel, while angling their stories through the system's agenda, which is to profit, and to divide, and to control. The media filters objective facts through fear, lack, duality, and negativity, and through the tired old formula that pits an evil aggressor against an innocent victim.

The vast majority of Hollywood movies indoctrinate people into thinking that those who suffer the most, and endure the greatest hardship, are the ones who rise to the top. This programming only exacerbates the disconnect humans are already experiencing when it comes to elevating themselves spiritually, mentally, and emotionally—by choice—because the system doesn't teach us how, and the system doesn't encourage us to try, and the system offers no models or myths that would inspire us to follow suit. The media doesn't traffic in stories about conscious evolution, or deliberate transformation, because the people choosing this kind of growth for themselves don't make for marketable influencers in a culture that prays at the feet of victimhood. So we conflate our elevation with pain and suffering, because we are beholden to the false belief that adversity is the path to fulfillment. Ugh.

But it's not just media and entertainment that are propagating the victim program. Organized religion is not only doing its part to squelch the masses, but getting them pumped to disempower themselves, as well. Look at the whole Jesus narrative, which is, like, the worst public relations campaign in the history of public relations campaigns. Millions and millions of people worship this image of a man in his underpants, nailed to a cross, bleeding from his skull and his hands and his feet, while being tortured to death on the worst day of his otherwise magnificent life. Like, that image is representative of this man's legacy? Seriously? And these devotees have the nerve to hang that image in their homes, and to wear that image around their necks, when it's this massive, pulsing testament to victimhood? It's no wonder we live in a culture where people are fighting to win the BVP trophy when that's the best picture they could come up with for the freakin' messiah. I mean, really.

EVERYONE SUFFERS

Look, as much as I love being prosperous and abundant, and manifesting wonderful things and experiences, the reality is that we didn't come to Earth to be pampered in luxury every minute of every day. We came to Earth to actually *do* something—to lift and to shift, and to create, and to transform the system, which happens to be riddled with darkness. Which means that when we incarnate, we agree to take on obstacles, and challenges, and loss, and trauma, and pain, and humiliation—all so that we can learn about ourselves, and grow, and teach, and lead.

Everyone suffers—until we learn how not to, that is. But no one incarnates on planet Earth, and gets a free pass that allows them to skip out on the trauma, and the sadness, and the terror, and the pain. That's all part of the ride. Just because someone has a particular skin tone, or a particular body part, or a particular belief structure, or a particular net worth, doesn't mean they are immune to the human condition, and to the wheel of suffering we all incarnate into.

Right now we have people on the planet who are claiming that their suffering is greater than anyone else's suffering, and that their suffering is more valid than anyone else's suffering; and it's ridiculous. There are no levels to suffering. Suffering is suffering. Each person's perception of suffering is based upon their own experience of pain, and their own relationship to pain. Some people have endured a lot of pain and therefore have developed a high tolerance for pain, and do not suffer through the sort of experience that would inspire suffering in other people. So to offer such a person pity for what you perceive as suffering is misdirected, as well as useless. Because what value does pity have, except to allow the person offering it to feel superior to the person he pities, which isn't really very empowering at all, now is it? People hear my story, and say: "Oh my God, I can't imagine how much you've suffered." But to me, it wasn't suffering. It was an opportunity to become Shaman Durek—to learn about the human condition, and human resilience, and to become a steward of human nature, and to help people to develop into superhuman versions of themselves. I don't see it as suffering at all. I see it as a necessary part of my authentic path.

ACCEPTANCE

People who are operating in victim consciousness are seeking sympathy and external validation for the parts of themselves they are not willing to love and accept themselves. Because they are not willing to bring love and acceptance into the fold of their own lives, they choose to position themselves as victims to rationalize the hurt and the trauma they are not dealing with. It's unfortunate that our society has been set up to reward such a disempowering orientation, especially when the external validation our victim stories beget does nothing to quell the pain we are attempting to mask. Trauma is not transmuted by pity. The only way to transmute trauma is through acceptance.

Healing occurs when we accept reality as it is, and when we acknowledge that everything happens for the greater good of our being—that our trauma is leading us somewhere. Maybe it will lead us to stand more firmly in our power. Maybe it will lead us to take more responsibility for our lives and our relationships. Maybe it will lead us to communicate more clearly and more compassionately. It could mean a multitude of things. But we will never find out where our suffering is meant to lead us if we don't accept that it happened, and that it happened for our benefit, which means being willing to step out of the identity construct of *being a person who got hurt.*

FROM VICTIMHOOD TO VICTORY

Look, under no circumstances do I condone any behavior that causes any harm to any being whatsoever. However, we live in an ever-shifting, anything-can-happen-at-any-moment kind of world, populated by a handful of people who are sick, and who are traumatized, and who are looking for a victim to share the pain they feel inside.

When life configures itself in such a way that we do experience trauma, or that we are victims of abuse, or pain, or misfortune, we must not dwell in the place of suffering, or self-pity, or *Woe is me*. We must not stay in victimhood. We must acknowledge that yes, I was a victim. Take me, for example. Yes, I was molested by my babysitter as a child. Yes, I was abused by my father, and my stepmother. Yes, all these things happened, and, yes, I was a victim. But I chose not to stay a victim. I chose to use my experiences as fuel to amplify me from victimhood to victory. We must all utilize our every experience to propel us into greater iterations of ourselves, and into success and empowerment—not just for us, as individuals, but for humanity.

Gandhi was a victim. Nelson Mandela was a victim. Martin Luther King Jr. was a victim. But they didn't sit there and dwell in their victimhood. If they had, they would never have impacted society and the world the way they did. They didn't cling to their victimhood. They moved on, and they turned their experiences into material to learn from, and to grow from, and to empower themselves with.

You see, the deeper you delve into the shamanic path, the more you realize that all the hurt you have experienced—all the mistakes, misfires, and miscalculations, and all the stumbles, and fumbles, and faceplants—have all been absolutely, unequivocally necessary for your evolution. When we remove the judgment from our past, and we embrace it in its entirety with love, our traumas and our hurts become the source of great power, wisdom, courage, strength, and love.

That Time My Client Got Stabbed, and— Ultimately—Saw It as a Blessing

I had a client named Jane who was stabbed coming off the subway in New York City. For as long as she could remember, Jane's biggest fear was getting stabbed, so I wasn't all that surprised when she was. Her recovery was long and arduous. She was in the hospital for months, and left with one less kidney and a serious chip on her shoulder. When I asked Jane if she could accept what had happened to her, and if she could be grateful for what her assailant had done to her, she said no. She said she would never accept what had happened, and that she would never forgive the man who stabbed her, let alone extend any gratitude his way.

I explained to Jane that until she found her way to gratitude, she wouldn't learn the lesson that Spirit had sent to help her in her evolution. Jane's immediate response was to ask if I thought it was okay for children to be raped and murdered. It's funny how many people leap to this hypothetical when I invite them to thank their perceived aggressors. It's like standard-issue victim consciousness pushback at this point.

I replied that no, I do not think it is okay for people to harm children, but that the fact remains that we must utilize our every life experience to elevate ourselves to higher levels of consciousness. I told Jane that yes, it was horrible that she had lost her kidney; and that yes, it was horrible that she had to spend all that time in the hospital, and in pain, and in recovery. But none of those terrible things changed the fact that in order for her spirit to reveal the hidden reason as to why the stabbing had to happen, she had to find a way to be grateful for it, and she had to find a way to extend that gratitude to her attacker.

It took some time, but Jane came back about six months later with a very different perspective. You see, she had found her way not only to gratitude but also to jujitsu. Jane's experience in self-defense classes stirred something deep inside her that she had never felt before. As a kindergarten teacher, Jane had thought her path was in educating children. It turned out that her passion and her purpose were in empowering women to protect themselves, and to empower themselves. Through her willingness to accept the stabbing, and to be grateful to the man who did the stabbing, Jane realized that it wouldn't have even crossed her mind to pursue her true path if the stabbing hadn't happened.

Spirit Hack: Milking the Medicine from Our Suffering

When we cling to our trauma, and to the victim stories we attach to it, all we end up doing is perpetuating our own pain. Pain is that which we experience, while the wound is that which still needs healing. In order to heal a wound, we must open the wound up and allow it to be exposed, so that we can air it out, and allow the light of day, and wisdom, and consciousness to work its healing magic. This spirit hack is a three-step shamanic process that allows us to air out our wounds, and to use our suffering to lift and shift, and to get lit.

For this spirit hack, be sure to set yourself up in a safe space, away from any noise, or interruptions, or other people. This exercise invites you to explore tender territory, so be sure to make yourself comfortable while doing this by sitting somewhere cozy, and comfortable, while wearing loose, warm clothing, and surrounding yourself with comforting items, like a favorite pillow, or blanket, or crystal, and a nice, warm cup of tea.

- Ask yourself: *How did the experience serve me?*

First and foremost, you want to explore why your spirit chose to create these experiences for you, and to examine how this suffering has served your evolution.

Take me, for example. When I look back at the experience of being molested as a kid, in spite of the many ways it distorted my character through alcoholism, and drug addiction, and homophobia, it also heightened my energetic sensitivity in a really practical and applicable way, what with me being a shaman and all. To have been so consistently sexually charged at such a young age activated my sensorium and allowed me to start attuning my energetic sensitivities from a unique perspective/ entry point. At this point in my shamanic undertaking, I can sense frequencies to an extraordinarily subtle degree of energy exchange, just as I can feel the slightest of energetic shifts when frequencies are communicating with one another. That early sexual stimulation is what allowed me to start working with such subtle sensorial energetics all those years ago and has definitely contributed to my shamanic mastery. So, while I don't condone what happened to me, when I look at the experience from a shamanic perspective, I can say that the molestation was a blessing.

- Thank the person who inflicted the suffering.

Thanking the person who caused our pain requires a great deal of humility, and a great deal of compassion—both for the other, as well as for ourselves. It is a way of recognizing that all parties involved shared an energy that needed to play itself out on the physical plane in order for each of you to attain certain levels of information and knowledge that you wouldn't have gleaned without that experience. Thanking the person is a way of acknowledging that your suffering served your spiritual growth, and that your transgressor is your teacher, as well as your medicine.

Note: When we offer our gratitude, it is a simple internal act that we perform in the confines of our own mind. There is no need to reach out to the person directly.

- Ask yourself: *What do I want to do with this gift?*

Now that you know the medicine this suffering holds for you, how are you going to put it to use in empowering yourself? How are you inspired to utilize these gems you've just mined in highest service to yourself, and to humanity?

People get stuck in a victim mentality by continually asking themselves: *Why did this happen to me?* Except *Why* isn't the right question to be asking yourself. *Why* keeps you stuck in victim consciousness; and victim consciousness slows down the process of evolution by creating more aggressors, more attackers, and more pain so that you can be right, and stay hurt, and play small. But this book isn't about playing small. This book is about getting lit, and living large, and manifesting poprocks amazingness while ringing in a Giant Age on Earth, which means the questions you want to be asking yourself are:

> *What can I do now that this has happened to me?*
>
> *How can I use this experience to empower me?*
>
> *What can I learn from this experience?*
>
> *What can I do with this experience?*
>
> *How can I use this experience to better the world?*
>
> *How can I use this experience to create change in my own life?*
>
> *How can I use this to help other people avoid the same pain that I endured?*

"CHILDHOOD PAIN," UGH.

When we hold on to pain, we suffer. But pain and suffering are very different things. Pain is a sensory experience we feel in our physical form—either emotionally, or physically. Suffering is a psychic experience that occurs when we hold on to that pain. Pain is a natural occurrence. Suffering is a choice.

People who hold on to mental and emotional pain that was inflicted in the past are identified with the perspective that something unfair or unjust has been done to them. They cling to the pain either because they are waiting for some sort of grand act of forgiveness, or because they are rationalizing the distorted worldview they've built upon it. But even just the act of calling it our "childhood pain" creates a quantum entanglement in affirming it, and making a proclamation of it. When we name things, we legitimize them as constructs that exist, and as organizing structures in our lives. *Childhood pain* is a generic label we slap on top of stagnant old trauma we haven't dealt with. The real issue we are failing to identify when we rationalize something in our current reality as "childhood pain" is that we are stuck. "Childhood pain" is just a ruse we play out to justify the limitations that we are imposing upon ourselves.

HURT COLLECTORS

I call people who identify with their pain *hurt collectors*. Hurt collectors attach to their suffering and brandish it like a badge of honor. Hurt collectors use their pain as a way to avoid taking responsibility for the areas of their lives they need to be bringing love to. It is also a way of justifying their failings, as in: *The reason I'm not stable, or aligned, or moving forward in my life is because I went through all this pain in my childhood.*

I always think of Helen Keller when I hear people make these kinds of excuses for their lackluster lives. This woman was blind, deaf, and mute, and she transcended the horrible odds against her and figured out a way to make her life work. But you can't pull it off because you're lactose intolerant, and your dad had an affair when you were eight?

Hurt collectors are operating from the perspective that something was done *to* them. The choice to frame oneself as a victim of an experience that was perpetrated *upon them*, instead of as one of any number of players in a neutrally unfolding event that simply *happened*, is what differentiates someone operating in victim consciousness from someone who takes responsibility for their life. The victim narrative blinds the hurt collectors to the larger perspective, and limits them from realizing that every pain they experience is a gift from Spirit meant to open them up to greater depths of truth and wisdom within themselves.

At this phase in the Blackout, a lot of people want to be acknowledged for their hardships, which is why we have so many people sharing their sob stories, and hashtagging their trauma, and telegraphing their pain out to the world, thinking that if people *Like* their suffering, and if people comment on their suffering, and if people respond to their suffering, then their suffering has value. Again, we see people selling themselves down the river in yet another attempt to collect the external validation that they really need to be giving themselves. This is because people are operating from a very limited perspective on suffering, and they don't understand its true value from a spiritual point of view. It is only when we stop seeking external validation for our sad, sad stories that we can genuinely understand that our suffering was a pivotal part of our evolutionary path, and that we can empower ourselves by contextualizing our experiences as *spiritual growth* instead of responding to them and victimizing ourselves by labeling them as childhood pain, or injustice, or suffering.

You see, redemption does not come from telling our victim stories, or from collecting pity from our victim stories. Redemption comes from taking responsibility for them. The moment we take responsibility for our suffering is the moment we realize it had to happen. And that's when the spirits spring to attention, and leap in to support us, because they're like, *Finally! You took responsibility for that thing you've been giving your power away to. Hurray. Now, let's open the door, so you can walk through it, and see why that experience was necessary, and how it served you.* And that's when you get to see that there was a method to the madness all along.

RESPONSE-ABILITY

B ecause people associate the word "responsibility" with the idea of some outside authority imposing itself upon them, they avoid the act of taking responsibility altogether. True responsibility has nothing to do with external agents or hierarchy. True responsibility is the ability to respond with love. The act of taking responsibility means we are responding to whatever the situation is with love. It's very simple.

This means that when life illuminates one of our less favorable qualities, and when we are confronted with a pattern or an aspect of ourselves that isn't serving us, we don't respond with blame, judgment, aggression, defensiveness, or what have you, because all that those reactions do is cut us off from the greater wisdom the experience has to share. We cannot access the method to the madness if we're letting darkness run our emotional body, and thereby judging ourselves, or beating ourselves up. But when we take responsibility for what *is* by rooting ourselves in unconditional love and acceptance, then we are aligned to receive the wisdom the shadow holds for us.

Spirit Hack: Responding with Love

To respond with love means to listen and embrace. It does not mean to judge, or to figure out whether the emotion or the energy deserves our embrace, or is worthy of our embrace. It just means to be fully present with, in a field of unconditional love and acceptance.

Be sure to set yourself up in a safe, private spot while doing this spirit hack. You can do it when you're feeling acute emotional upset—like if you just had a fight with someone, or messed up at work. You also want to do this with emotional upsets that happened in the past but that still trigger you. You're also going to want to have a bowl of water at the ready, as well as a journal, and a pen.

- Call up a belief or a situation that upsets you emotionally. Allow that emotional upset to arise inside you, and allow yourself to feel it.

- Say: "I'm here with you, and I'm here to support you."

- Take a deep breath, then say: "I see that you are upset, and I understand why you are upset."

- Take a deep breath, then say: "I invite wisdom into the situation, so that I can see it more clearly."

Wisdom is energy. When we call upon wisdom, it comes to us immediately. Avail yourself of the wisdom you are calling in.

- Take a deep breath, and say: "I accept the wisdom into this situation."

- Place your left hand over your belly button, and place your right hand over your heart. Take a deep breath, and say: "I am now willing to see this situation through the lens of love."

Remember, your navel is your place of knowing and courage. This positioning allows you to magnetically connect to love, and to perceive through love's lens.

- Take three deep breaths, while still holding your right hand on your heart, and your left hand on your belly button.

- Say: "Now that I see it through the lens of love, this is what I see: _____"; and then speak aloud the wisdom and the clarity that you see.

- After you've spoken aloud all that you see, say: "Now, it's time for me to let it go."

- Take the bowl of water, and hold it up to your face. Say: "I blow all of the energy around this situation into this water."

- Blow into the water.

- Take the bowl, and then dump out the water—preferably in a garden, or a plant, somewhere outside. But if you're in an apartment, the sink is fine.

- Then take your journal, and write about your experience of this spirit hack.

THE SHADOW

The shadow has been so maligned, and is so misunderstood, that people avoid it like it's a plague, which is a shame, given that the shadow is one of our greatest evolutionary tools. People confuse the shadow with the things the shadow holds on to for us—which I call the *junkery*—and then they judge the shadow as bad, or wrong, or scary, when none of this could be further from the truth.

The shadow is called "the shadow" because it is the projection that the light is casting onto our world. The dictionary defines a shadow as *an image cast upon a surface by a body intercepting the light.* This means that the shadowy bits we perceive are not indicative of some evil outside entity, rather they are the projection of light off the *intercepting body,* which is you, and which is me, and which is every human on the planet. If you've got a body, you've got a shadow. And you'd better be able to dance with it, babe.

The shadow is the part of our being that is pure light and that holds on to the things that we are not taking responsibility for. The shadow holds on to our pain, and our fragmentation, and our distorted belief systems. It holds on to our judgments, and our vices, and all the lies we tell ourselves. The shadow is the part of you that knows you judge, and knows you steal from the lost and found at the gym, and knows that you pretend not to see the homeless people panhandling on the subway because you think they're dirty, and beneath you. The shadow holds on to all these parts of us that we don't want illuminated, and that we definitely don't want to look at, much less deal with; and it patiently waits for us to lift, and to shift, and to deal.

THE SHADOW IS OMNISCIENT AF

The shadow isn't just some passive cosmic schlub waiting around for us to get brave enough to look at our junkery. The shadow is a treasure trove of self-knowledge that's totally psyched to dance with us anytime we say the word. The shadow knows everything about you, and can show you everything you need to see, which is why it is so important to develop a conscious relationship with your shadow. Your shadow knows you better than anyone possibly could. When I'm working with a client, and I want to get to the truth of the matter, I always address my questions to the client's shadow, because there's nothing it doesn't know, and it always tells the truth.

Like, I asked a client why he had cancer. He shrugged and said it was genetic; but his shadow told me it was because my client hated his job, and felt confined in his marriage, and because his mental processes were all messed up from the constant self-flagellation, which was activating high levels of inflammation, and degrading his cellular walls, and expressing itself as cancer.

Or, when I asked a client's shadow why she was chain-smoking, and the shadow said it was because she was trying to manage her high sex drive, and that once she found a safe, healthy outlet for that energy, she wouldn't need to smoke anymore. And, you know what? My client started getting Tantric massages and quit smoking altogether.

I talk to my shadow all the time. (Worry not, my love; you will learn how to do this yourself in the next chapter.) My shadow tells me, straight up: *Get off the dating apps.* When I ask the shadow why it's telling me to delete the dating apps, it says it's because I'm on the apps out of fear—fear that I'm not going to meet anyone because I'm so introverted. My shadow says I'm playing out a belief construct that has me using sex as a way to initiate connection, instead of refraining from sex, and drawing in people who are vibrating at more expansive frequencies, and building conscious connections from a more authentic place. My shadow is always weighing in about my life choices. Now, whether I always choose to listen to my shadow is a whole different thing. . . .

SHADOW DANCING

A lot of spiritual/therapeutic traditions, practices, and modalities put a value judgment on the shadow, and orient to it as though it's something we need to transmute or transcend. This is incorrect. From that perspective, the shadow itself is, yet again, conflated with the junkery it's holding on to for us, and is therefore demonized as bad. The bigger issue with this framing is that the shadow isn't actually asking you to transform your hurt, or your discord, or your shoplifting habit. Your shadow is just asking you to take responsibility for them—to own these aspects of your being (and every aspect of your being) with unconditional love and acceptance. The only thing your shadow wants you to do with your junkery is for you to take responsibility for it.

The shadow does not share humans' need to be loved, and to be liked, and to feel safe, because the shadow is the projection of pure light intelligence, which is already safe. This means the shadow doesn't sugarcoat. The shadow tells it like it is, and the shadow doesn't hold back, because the shadow loves you unconditionally, and has no fear of hurting your feelings, or of you being mad at it for saying something you don't want to hear.

Shadow dancers don't fear the truth. We dance with it. When the shadow throws us whammies, we must be able to step, and to sway, and to shimmy with the reflections, no matter how unseemly we judge them to be. We must dance with the truth so that we are able to embrace the truth, and allow it to enrich our lives.

At this stage in the Blackout, it is crucial for people to begin to integrate the shadow into their lives. People need to be developing an authentic, engaged, and deeply curious relationship with their shadow; and they definitely need to be communicating with their shadow on the regular.

Spirit Hack: The Morning Shadow Dance

For starters, you want to check in with your shadow first thing in the morning to set yourself up to be as poprocks as possible for the day ahead. So, grab a pen and a piece of paper.

- Draw a line down the center of the page, and write the questions you want to ask your shadow on the left side of the page. You want to ask your shadow questions like:

  Shadow, what can I do to raise my frequency?

  How should I prioritize my day, Shadow?

  How can I optimize my productivity today, Shadow?

  Shadow, how can I boost my energy today?

  Shadow, how can I optimize my health today?

  Shadow, how can I expand my joy today?

  How can I optimize my connection to other people today, Shadow?

  Where shall I focus my energy and attention today, Shadow?

You always address the shadow—and all energies—by name. We do this as a way of acknowledging that what we are engaging in the spirit realm is real. Also, to be respectful.

- Ask your shadow your questions out loud.

- Using your AVK sensory perception, write down the answers your shadow gives you in the right-hand column of your paper.

Having a physical representation of your shadow's insights gives it greater validity, while helping you strengthen your ability to communicate with your shadow.

- Finish this spirit hack by saying: "Thank you, Shadow. I love you, Shadow."

- Use the insight your shadow gives you to design and organize your day.

Spirit Hack: The Moment-to-Moment Shadow Dance

In addition to checking in with your shadow first thing in the morning, you want to touch base with your shadow as choices and decisions present themselves to you throughout the day, and throughout your life.

For instance, if you're invited to an event that you're not sure you really want to go to, ask your shadow:

- "Will it serve my highest joy, health, and happiness to go to this event tonight, Shadow?"

Or, if you're trying to figure out if you should wake up early to go to yoga, or take a recovery day, you would ask your shadow:

- "Shadow, is it best for me to take a recovery day today?"

Then your shadow might tell you that calling it a "recovery day" won't change the fact that it's actually just you being lazy and wanting to sleep in because you're hungover from wine and carbs, when what your body really needs is to move and to sweat.

Now you have clarity as to what will serve your highest; and you can utilize your free will to honor that highest, or to not honor that highest. It's totally up to you. Choice rocks.

- Remember to finish this spirit hack by saying: "Thank you, Shadow. I love you, Shadow."

Spirit Hack: The *Why the fuck do I keep doing this to myself?* Shadow Dance

Developing a relationship with the shadow allows you to access the insight and wisdom it holds, which you, as a lit leader, can then use to level-up your life. This means getting real about what isn't working in your life, and allowing your shadow to show you how to shift it.

- Again, draw a line down the center of a piece of paper, and write your questions on the left-hand side. You can ask the shadow things like:

  Show me how to increase the joy in my life, Shadow.

  How can I be more effective in my work, Shadow?

  Shadow, why have my last four boyfriends all cheated on me?

  Shadow, what do I need to do to get out of debt?

Basically, you're asking your shadow to give you clarity and advice on the aspects of your life that are proving difficult for you. Be brave, and be honest. The shadow can only take you as far as your honesty. The deeper you are willing to delve into your authenticity, the more the shadow can assist you.

- Ask your shadow your questions.

- Write the shadow's answers on the right-hand side of the page.

- Finish this spirit hack by saying: "Thank you, Shadow. I love you, Shadow. I will take responsibility for all my junkery at some point, and we will be able to merge as one with the light."

EVERYTHING IS A CHOICE

Have-to is a way that people victimize themselves to what they perceive to be their earthly obligations. It is important to remember that we are all operating under free will, which means that everything is a choice. Just because your shadow tells you to get up and do yoga, or tells me to get off the dating apps, doesn't mean we have to make those choices. We might not want to make those choices. We might not be ready to make those choices. If I choose to get off the dating apps just because my shadow tells me to, that's not me authentically lifting and shifting, that's me trying to control the situation, and wanting to appease my shadow. Free will means that I can choose to utilize the shadow's insight if I want to, or I can choose to use the shadow's advice to draw me into a deeper inquiry into the fears and beliefs and experiences that are informing my dating app use, and unravel them at an appropriate pace. I can empower myself through the process of accepting that this is where I'm at, while taking responsibility for the fact that this is where I'm at, knowing that I'm not going to be here forever, because, like my girl Chaka Khan says, everything changes.

A lot of people feel burdened by the have-tos the matrix imposes upon them, but the truth is we always have a choice. You can choose to pay your bills, or you can choose to not pay your bills. If you want electricity, then you probably want to choose to pay that bill, because that's what the exchange is. Same with cell phone service, or waste disposal. But most people don't see it from this perspective. Most people see their bills as some terrible affront that is being perpetrated upon them, instead of recognizing their agency in their choice to participate in the exchange the bill represents.

Framing our agreements and our obligations through the lens of have-to victimizes us to our reality. Have-to is a disempowering energy suck that weakens the spirit. The antidote is free will. Free will gives us back our power. I am not a victim to oral hygiene, and I don't have to brush my teeth twice a day. I choose to brush my teeth twice a day because I value the function of oral hygiene, and I value my teeth for helping me masticate, and for making my smile that much more amazing. So I choose to honor my teeth by choosing to take care of them; and the power that is embedded in that choice is what fuels me to give my pearly whites a thorough brushing, even when it's late, and I'm exhausted and would much rather be asleep in bed.

The act of acknowledging our actions as choices is both energizing and empowering, because the energetic frequencies of choice align us with the truth of our nature as quantum creators.

7

STEP INTO THE UNKNOWN

Our reality here on Earth materializes through the perception of the collective. Everyone has a different perception, so whichever perception the most people believe is how our collective reality manifests itself. Currently, the matrix is programming humans with a mass perception—which is actually a mass delusion—that has people convinced that the biggest problem threatening the planet today is every human being who thinks differently than they do; and that those people are bad, and wrong, and evil, and therefore must be punished. This is why we are witnessing all these mass witch hunts being carried out by unconscious people looking for monsters to persecute. It's kind of like the Christian Crusades, except instead of marching through the village with swords and shields, strapping so-called evildoers onto crosses, and torturing them in the name of God, people are trolling social media feeds, and crucifying each other through slandering, and name-calling, and finger-pointing, and by attacking people's character, and destroying their reputations in the court of public opinion.

These witch hunts are creating a lot of friction among human beings and doing society a great disservice. Why? Because people are not operating with emotional intelligence, they are attacking that which they do not understand, and proclaiming it to be *wrong* and *bad,* instead of engaging that which they do not understand, so as to figure out how it got that way, and thereby to remedy the situation. Humans are not invoking the feminine factor, and therefore humans are not operating with emotional intelligence, and so they are trying to wipe out that which they don't understand from society altogether. It's all just a giant smoke screen to avoid taking responsibility for the fact that each and every one of us is culpable for the calamity and the destruction that is taking place here on Earth by the choices we continue to make, and the darkness we continue to deny.

THE MONSTER ISN'T A THING

The system pits us against one another by manipulating facts to create highly editorialized media content aiming to convince us that the monster is real, and that the monster is to be found among our fellow brothers and sisters. This false framing has people calling out each other's darkness for sport, instead of calling *in* each other's light to help each other evolve into better human beings. It's just another way the matrix gets people to do its bidding for it, because people believe the media's lies, which triggers people's unhealed wounds, which they then project onto the monster-of-the-week by pointing fingers, and calling names, and spewing hate, and stirring up all this discord to feed the very system that's manipulating the whole charade in the first place, while oppressing every single one of us. All it does is deepen the illusion of a divide and keep people in a state of opposition and in a state of agitation, which feeds the underworld. It doesn't matter which side we identify with; the mere act of choosing a side empowers the darkness and the illusion of separation, which makes us every bit as responsible for the discord on this planet as the people whose side we are being programmed to blame and to condemn.

The thing is: all this drama, and all this conflict, and all this discord are just a giant distraction from the truth of the matter, which is that the monster is all of us—well, it's the junkery inside of all of us. The big, bad, scary monster everyone wants to persecute for the state of the world is all those distorted, disregarded fragments that our shadow is holding on to for us. The monster is our rage, and our depression, and our codependence. The monster is every bit of our own darkness that we haven't dealt with, and that we haven't brought to the light.

If we are to meet the challenge of the Blackout, and shift this planet back into alignment, we must realize that there is no monster—that any monster anyone ever perceives in their external reality is simply something they haven't dealt with inside themselves. And that *something* is asking for unconditional love and acceptance, so it can return to light intelligence and serve evolution. I mean, the whole reason we incarnate on this planet is to bring the darkness home to the light, which is why it's so weird to see so many people *not* doing it.

THE SHADOW: TAKE 2

The reason people aren't dealing with their darkness is because—as I've already explained—people are being programmed *not* to engage their shadow. You see, the matrix knows well the power the shadow holds for humans, which is why the system goes to such great lengths to keep us from exploring this sacred portal to the unknown—lest we get ourselves empowered, and get ourselves lit, and set the planet on fire, while bringing on a poprocks Giant Age.

The word *shadow* conjures dark visions and invokes scary connotations for a lot of people, because we have been programmed through the consensus of language to demonize it, as well as anything and everything associated with it. Think about it. If something is *shadowy,* the mind automatically assumes it must be evil, or scary, or bad. Think of all the stories you heard as a kid. *Count Dracula sweeps in from the shadows*; or, *The last place anyone saw the boy was near Shadow Creek*—that sort of thing. The word *shadow* has been imprinted with the frequencies of fear, thereby transmitting those fear frequencies every time it is spoken, or written, or thought, or read. This is how people are programmed to steer clear of the shadows, when it's actually the exact opposite of what they need to be doing.

One of the main reasons the shadow gets a bad rap is because much of the junkery we are not taking responsibility for vibrates at some pretty dense frequencies, and therefore it is uncomfortable to look at, and uncomfortable to deal with. So while the shadow holds on to all these things for us, and waits for us to do what it has been doing for us for ourselves, we vilify the shadow, and we shun the shadow, and we avoid the shadow, and we deny the shadow, and at this point in the Blackout, we really, really, really, really, really need to be engaging the shadow, which is why I'm still talking about it.

REJECT NOT THY JUNKERY

The mind has been programmed by the matrix to compromise in order to be loved and to be liked. To accomplish this, the mind denies otherwise unsavory aspects, tendencies, characteristics, and behaviors that do not conform to the established consensus of what is considered likable or socially acceptable. This programming necessarily narrows the pool of qualities that humans are willing to acknowledge and embrace in themselves and in others. The choice to deny the truth—which is that all aspects are of the light, even the ones we don't like all that much—has caused great suffering to the emotional body. The mind judges the behaviors and beliefs it has been indoctrinated to reject, and then it berates the emotional body for experiencing these behaviors and beliefs, thereby stinging the soul in the process. It's a very damaging cycle, as the act of rejecting or deriding these aspects of ourselves only creates more distortions in our being, because we are at odds with what is. This creates discord in the body and in the mind, thereby contributing to more unsavory behaviors, and to more discord. The only way to correct this cycle is with love.

You have to remember that duality is a sham, and that these shadowy aspects of ourselves that we'd rather not look at are not bad, or wrong, or shameful, or tragic. They just are. But human beings are programmed to demonize the shadow, which is totally ass-backward, given that the shadow is the one that is patiently holding on to this stuff for us, waiting for us to stop pretending it's not there, and to stop distorting our consciousness in the face of the ruse, and to start taking responsibility for our junkery, regardless of how gross we judge it to be.

JUDGMENT

Judgment is another expression of the duality sham—that whole *I'm right, you're wrong / He's bad, she's good* thing humans get caught up in. Judgment is a tool of the darkness that shrouds the truth in human arrogance. Judgment has nothing whatsoever to do with what is so, because judgment is, by its very nature, subjective. Judgment is an opinion.

Judgment limits our perception through bias and agenda. When we are in judgment, we are operating from a place of needing to prove that we are right about a belief we are already holding. When we judge, our allegiance is not to the truth; our allegiance is to being right. It's all well and good for fattening the ego, but it only does us a huge disservice when it comes to engaging the darkness and dancing with the shadows. Remember, it's judgment that keeps the underworld spirits from returning to the light—the judgment they hold toward themselves. Judgment blocks our evolution, which is why humans really need to let go of this useless addiction they have to being right, and start getting neutral.

SHAMANS DON'T JUDGE

It is impossible to gain clarity or insight into the issues the shadow holds for us when we are stuck in judgment, because we have already formulated an opinion. When we are judging, all we are actually "open" to analyzing is whatever data points we can cherry-pick to confirm the biases we are choosing to identify with, which are: *I'm bad; These feelings are wrong;* or *What kind of monster am I?* When we perceive our hurts, habits, vices, tendencies, behaviors, and what have you as "bad," we block ourselves from receiving the lessons and the gifts these energies hold for us.

Let's say, for example, I snap at my assistant. And then I beat myself up for it, and I self-flagellate, and I tell myself that I am a mean person, and that I am an awful person, and that I am a terrible person; and I let myself sink into a funk. If I could pull my head out of my ass long enough to get it together and ask my shadow why I snapped at my assistant, and what's really going on, I literally would not be able to hear a single drop of wisdom the shadow has to share with me. Why? Because I'm stuck in judgment, which means that I'm not neutral, and that I'm not open. So the only data I am actually available to hear is that which confirms my judgment, and confirms the thought-form that tells me that I am a mean person, and that I am an awful person, and that I am a terrible person. There is no opening in my consciousness to receive any alternative perspectives on the matter, which means I am missing out on an opportunity to gather self-knowledge, and to grow, and to shift, and to raise my vibration, and to expand my emotional intelligence, and to become something greater than the mean, awful, terrible person I keep telling myself I am.

When we are confronted with our own junkery—be it a vice, a lie, a jealous thought, a disempowering habit, or an instance of hurting someone we love—we do not judge it. Our judgment only makes the darkness stronger, which means we've already lost. When we are faced with a reflection of our own hurt, and our own indifference, and our own unresolved wounds, we engage those issues. We step into them. We gather the courage and the willingness to go on discovery from a place of authenticity and humility, and we collect the data points, and we connect the dots, and we put the pieces of our own puzzle together so that we can heal, and get lit.

A Shaman's Shadow Dance

I'm going to walk myself through it so you can get the full picture. Let's go back to an earlier example I mentioned and say that my shadow—yet again—tells me to get off the dating apps. When I ask my shadow why, it tells me that the apps are activating my tendency to conflate sex with love and acknowledgment. Okay. It's not, like, the most fun thing to hear about myself—that I confuse sex with love, and that I confuse sex with acknowledgment. But it resonates.

Go on, Shadow, I say.

Because I am open, and curious, and humble, the shadow goes on to tell me that the reason I conflate love with sex is because I grew up without love or affection in my house, or from my family, which is true. My upbringing was very strict, very intense, and very African—completely devoid of tenderness, sensitivity, or nurturing. The only person who offered me those things as a child was the babysitter who molested me; and because I was so starved for affection, I allowed myself to go along with all the twisted shit he wanted to do to me just so I could feel nurtured.

Ouch. And, yeah. It totally makes sense. This data helps connect those dots for me. But what this insight does that's even more amazing, is that it helps me to understand this pattern of allowing myself to go along with intimate situations that aren't aligned for me, and to do things that aren't resonant with me, so I can get the love and the nurturing I've been programmed to associate with sexual stimulation.

Now that all of these realizations have been illuminated, and all these pieces of my own personal puzzle have been illuminated, the medicine is for me to take responsibility. It is to fully embrace the whole damn thing. It is to acknowledge the part of my being that is acting this out, and to love that part of my being, and to accept that part of my being. It is to hold that little boy who grew up starved for love, and starved for affection, and to shower him with all the love and acceptance I have to give. Just as it is to hold this grown man who has made choices outside his character, and to also shower him with unconditional love and acceptance. It is to gather the lessons and the insight, and it is to say—from a place of complete and total neutrality and acceptance: *Okay, that's what happened, and those are the choices I made. How do I want to define love for myself now?*

The beauty of the process is that it allows me to operate with more awareness, which means that there is less of a pull for me to respond in those same unconscious old ways moving forward, which means that I am evolving.

Learning to withhold judgment is a powerful shamanic tool that opens us up to go anywhere we want, and to be able to handle anything that life throws our way. When we are operating free from judgment, we process data more efficiently, which means that we can easily sense imbalance. Therefore, we can easily make whatever adjustments are necessary to restore balance, because we are not caught up in judging the imbalance, or complaining about the imbalance, or giving our power away to the imbalance. We're just taking the journey. We're riding the lit train.

Spirit Hack: Judge Not

This spirit hack trains the mind to operate from a nonjudgmental orientation, and it allows you to get comfortable in the perspective of simply
observing and receiving. The practice weakens the neural pathways that
stimulate judgment, and that leap to label, or attach, while allowing you to
open yourself up to the perceptual pathways that are adept at navigating
the shadows.

You will need a blindfold for this spirit hack, and some time alone in
your room.

STEP 1

- Blindfold yourself.

- With your hands out in front of you, take a walk around your room
  (being careful not to bump into anything, or hurt yourself).

- Touch the objects around you while acknowledging only the feeling of these objects in your hands, without attempting to describe what you are touching with words, or labels, or concepts,
  or images.

While doing this step, you are feeling for the sake of feeling, and having
fun. Allow yourself to perceive with your hands alone, without bringing your
brain into the practice. This spirit hack is about you having a completely
tactile perceptual experience while developing your shamanic powers.

Practice this spirit hack every day for at least a week, resisting the urge
to describe the things you are touching with words, or ideas, or images.
When you are able to touch the objects in your room without giving in to
the urge to describe them, then you are ready to move on to the next step.

STEP 2

- Take a walk around your home (no blindfold this time). Perceive
  the objects—visually—without ascribing words or descriptions
  to them. Allow yourself to perceive the things in your environ-

ment without categorizing them with labels or names that make you think you understand what they actually are, just because at some point in time, someone taught you those labels, and taught you those names, and you believed their associations to be true.

Again, once you can visually catalog the objects in your room without ascribing to them words, labels, or concepts, you are ready to move on to step 3.

STEP 3

Once you've gotten adept at feeling and seeing objects without needing to name or categorize them, you want to do the same thing with your emotions.

- Pay attention to your emotions throughout the day.

- When a feeling is triggered, resist the urge to name the feeling, or to label the feeling. Instead, simply feel the feeling, and describe what the feeling actually feels like.

So, for example, if someone cuts in front of you at the grocery store, you would resist the urge to describe your feelings with an internal statement like: "I feel anger." Instead, you would (silently) describe your actual feeling experience, which could be something like:

- *I feel heat in my face,* or . . .

- *I feel my heartbeat racing,* or . . .

- *I feel tension in my jaw.*

The key is to stay with the kinesthetic experience of what is actually happening in your body, and to avoid the urge to let the mind make up a story about what it thinks the sensation means.

Keep practicing this spirit hack until it becomes your normal way of engaging the world, at which point it's no longer a spirit hack; it's a way of life.

That Time My Client Learned How
Not to Judge

I had a client who was the CEO of a processed chicken meat factory. He had inherited the company from his father, and—when he first came to see me—had no misgivings about running an outfit that slaughtered animals for profit. He was very unhappy in his marriage, and in his life, and he was also very judgmental. He judged his friends, his wife's friends, his family, his employees, his colleagues, his trainer—you name it, he judged it.

I explained to my client that he was judging as a way of distracting himself from what he really needed to be bringing awareness to, but was avoiding. I gave him this exercise. Three months later, he came in for another session, and within the first five minutes, he burst into tears.

"I never knew how hard I was leaning on judgment as a way of avoiding taking responsibility for my true feelings," he sobbed.

My client went on to explain that he'd never thought twice about the fact that his company was slaughtering thousands and thousands of animals a year. He said that after doing this exercise, he stopped judging people, and started observing people, and that through that practice, he started observing himself. He told me that when he did, he started screaming, and he started crying, and that he couldn't stop for a week, and that it was a good thing. He had realized that the company he was running went against the core of his being. The practice had allowed him to see that he was being judgmental as a means of avoiding his truth, and that this path his father had laid out for him by leaving him his company was not for him. Very soon after that, he let go of the business altogether.

THE MAGIC HOUR

The night is a very special time. It is a time to rest, and a time to regenerate, and a time to gather with the tribe, unhampered by the concerns of toil or survival. It is also a time to commune with the unseen, and to learn the teachings of Earth, and the ancestors, and the spirits. All shamans know the power, the potency, and the magic of the night, when the veil is thin, and the divine beckons. That is when we do our deepest work, because the night is a portal to the unknown.

During the day, the sun shines bright and gives off ultraviolet light. This ultraviolet light stirs up the senses, which are occupied tracking colors, and depth, and definition, and all the kinds of things that we don't perceive at night. All this sensory activity stimulates the mind, which becomes hyperactive as it pushes itself to fire stronger and faster, racing to catalog all the details the senses are perceiving.

But at night we are not distracted by these things. When it is dark outside, the brain can rest, because its tasks have been greatly minimized. This allows the brain to open itself to different pathways of thinking and perceiving, and to avail itself to the invisible realms, which is where our power lies. This is why we shamans call the nighttime the magic hour.

THE DEMONIZATION OF THE DARK

Just like our friend the shadow, the night has been purposely misrepresented as scary, and spooky, and creepy, and perilous. This is because the matrix wants us to be afraid of the dark, and afraid of the magic hour, so that we will stick with the program, and follow the rules, and never venture off the path, or out of our cages, and into the great realms of evolution and potential and new pathways of perceiving that await us in the unknown. Duly indoctrinated, humans allow their fear and their judgment to repress the natural impulse to claim their true power, which can only be found by braving the dark of the night, and stepping into the unknown.

No one is born afraid of the dark. The dark is where we find our gifts and our power. We are programmed to be afraid of the dark.

Think back to your childhood. Were you afraid of the dark? Did you let your feet hang over the edge of the bed? Did you take a gigantic leap from the doorway to your bed so that whatever was waiting underneath to grab your ankles couldn't catch you? Has it ever struck you as odd that every human alive has a version of this same childhood experience?

People are afraid of the dark because when we were kids, the smoke spirits came into our rooms at night and programmed us with fear. The smoke spirits represent a defining point in everyone's life when they became afraid of the dark and, therefore, the unknown.

Smoke spirits are invisible operatives sent by the darkness to monitor humans' fears, and to play upon them, so that they can feed the beings in the underworld while deterring us from venturing into the unknown, which is where our power lies. The smoke spirits take on the shapes and forms that have been programmed into our consciousness, and present themselves as such to instill children with fear of the night, and fear of the dark, and fear of the unknown, before heading back to the dark realm to share the intel they collected from our dimension.

(And, for the record, just because you're having a hard time wrapping your mind around the idea of smoke spirits, and you think it sounds insane, doesn't mean it's not true.)

THE UNKNOWN

If we are to evolve and to realize our potential here on Earth, we must interface with that which causes us difficulty within ourselves. Whenever and wherever we experience difficulty in life, we must lean in to it. By leaning in to our challenges, we step into the unknown, trusting that wherever we step, we are going to be poured into by spirit, and we will be fine.

If you want liberation, go to the unknown. The unknown holds the keys to our healing, and the keys to our evolution. The unknown holds the keys to our full potential, and the keys to all the ways we are meant to thrive, and to become superhuman. The unknown holds the keys to every solution to every global threat the species is facing. Basically, the unknown is the shit.

As a child who was exposed to the same programming as all of us, I, too, was visited by the smoke spirits in my room at night; and I, too, was indoctrinated to be afraid of the dark. But at a certain point, I could feel the pull of something waiting for me in all that blackness—something powerful and profound that I did not understand. I grew tired of my fear, and I decided to face that monster hiding under the bed, and to step into the unknown. And that's where I discovered my light, and my strength, and my power. That's where I discovered myself.

KNOW THYSELF IN THE UNKNOWN

The only way to know yourself—like, really know who the fuck you are—is to step into the unknown. The unknown is where we get our power. There is no power to be found in following rules, or trends, or patterns, or formulas. I never got my power from any of that nonsense. My power comes from stepping into the unknown and experiencing myself as a quantum creator, and pulling in new information, and creating amazing offerings, and sharing them with the world.

That power comes from navigating the experiences the unknown gifts us, which are the specific experiences our souls need to evolve. That power makes us unstoppable, because the journeys we take to connect with it teach us to trust, and teach us to listen, and teach us to be fearless. We have only ourselves to count on in the unknown, as we are the only constant. This means that we must go inside ourselves to find all the resources we need to navigate that uncharted territory. But we will never be able to tap into those resources, or to learn those lessons, or to have those experiences, if we are not brave enough to step outside our cozy, comfy, familiar status quos, and get our asses into the unknown.

Spirit Hack: Step into the Unknown

I always tell my clients they need to face the monster hiding under the bed, which means they need to step into the unknown. It is the only way for us to understand that there is no monster, just as it is the only way for us to claim our power, and to change the world for the better.

Stepping into the unknown means saying *I am willing to go to the places in myself that are uncomfortable, and to embrace them with love*.

Stepping into the unknown means saying *Yes* to that which frightens you.

Stepping into the unknown means moving toward the things you want to run away from.

This is a spirit hack to prepare you to step into the unknown. You will need a journal, a pen, and an open mind.

- At nighttime, with the lights on, sit in a chair. Place your bare feet on the ground, your hands palm up on your lap, and your eyes should be open. Ask yourself, out loud: "How far am I willing to travel into the unknown to find my true power?"

- Breathe consciously and deliberately until the answer comes to you. When the answer arrives, write it in your journal.

- Ask yourself, out loud: "What am I willing to let go of to step fully into the unknown?"

- Breathe consciously and deliberately while you wait for the answer. When it comes, write it down in your journal.

- Say out loud: "I am ready to step into the unknown, and it is easy, and fun, and adventurous, and it is going to take my life to the next level."

- Now, turn off all the lights. Return to your chair, with your bare feet on the floor, and your hands palm up on your lap. Say, out loud: "I invite the unknown into my life with love." Repeat this statement out loud ten times.

- Then say: "It is time, and I am ready."

- Turn the lights on, grab your journal, and write down a plan to do something unknown to you.

CONTROL

This is a critical time for humanity, where we are being asked to step into our fear of the unknown, and to embrace it. People are afraid of the unknown because people are taught to fear what they cannot control. You can't control pure potential, and you can't control the unknown. That's intimidating for a lot of people.

As the Blackout progresses, the layers of illusion are thinning, and everything that humans have clung to as a means of security and safety is coming undone. The momentum is thrusting humans into an evolutionary initiation that is demanding that we learn what true safety and true security really are, and that we realize they can only be found inside ourselves.

A lot of people try to control reality as a way to make themselves feel safe. These people construct very limited lives for themselves, with narrow comfort zones they won't venture outside of, and with rigid boundaries they protect by trying to control. Control blinds us by limiting the scope of possibility we can perceive. That's why when I see people who have the control spirit in their psyche, I know immediately that they've missed out on a lot of opportunities.

Safety cannot be found by running around, trying to micromanage our reality construct. Safety comes from knowing the truth of who we are, and knowing the truth of what we stand for. That knowledge is bona fide, genuine, grade A safety, because it's not some external thing that someone gave you. You cultivated that knowledge yourself, which means that no one can ever take it away from you. That's why they say: *as within, so without*. When we know ourselves as safe—authentically and internally safe—then we are safe wherever we go. And it doesn't matter what sort of tests or challenges or initiations the universe throws at us, because our safety has already been established. It's a done deal.

But, just for the record, let's be clear: no one is actually *controlled* by the control spirit. People willingly invite the control spirit into their vessels. Human beings invite the control spirit into their beings because they don't want to take responsibility as quantum creators.

THE VOID

What we shamans call the unknown is what physicists refer to as *the void*—the infinite space of pure potential in which all things are imagined, created, and made manifest. The unknown is where all the magic happens.

Anyone who brings something new to the planet has to go to the unknown to get it. All of civilization's great inventors, and innovators, and visionaries had to break free from the shackles of the matrix to get to the unknown. They had to rebel. They were the outcasts and the black sheep. They faced emotional and mental exile to break free of their programming, and to break free of the status quo, and to step into the unknown, so that they could fulfill their purpose, and enrich the world with their offerings.

People are afraid to take responsibility as quantum creators because, throughout history, everyone who has stepped up to the plate, and taken their position on the front line, has been demonized as an outcast, and as a pariah, and has endured a bunch of conflict before meeting some tragic, bloody end. Look at what happened to Gandhi, and to Martin Luther King Jr., and to JFK, all because they were willing to speak out against the matrix, and to fight for truth and freedom. So people are afraid to speak the truth, and people are afraid to bring attention to themselves, and people are afraid to make waves, and people are afraid to meet their power.

But that reality is shifting. It is no longer about just one person leading the masses, and changing the world; it is about all of us stepping into that place of leadership together. They might be able to take out one person, but they sure as hell can't take out millions of us.

I repeat, child, face the monster.

Spirit Hack: Engage Your Fear

It's not like I'm always 100 percent, totally comfortable in the unknown, and like I never, ever feel afraid. I'm not going to sit here like a hypocrite and pretend that I've transcended the human condition. I get nervous. I feel fear. But I never let fear or nerves stop me. Please. I'm a shaman. I engage that shit.

- Call forth a fear in your mind's eye.

When fear comes up in your life, what you want to do is bring it out from those dark, dusty, cobwebby corners of your mind where it's hiding, and festering, and fucking with you; and you want to shine the light of consciousness on it. This means examining the fear from all angles.

- Ask: "What's the worst thing that can happen if _____?"

Let's say you have a message to share, and you want to expand your platform, but you're afraid to post live videos on your social media feed. Instead of letting that fear stop you, you engage into that fear, and you drop in with your shadow.

So, you ask your shadow, out loud: "Shadow, what's the worst thing that will happen if I do an Instagram Live video?"

- Listen carefully for the answer. If you don't hear an answer, do the spirit hack for TSD, and try again.

- When you do hear the answer, repeat it out loud.

So, let's say the response you hear is: *I'll mess up, and people will make fun of me, and leave rude comments.* Say, out loud: "I'll mess up, and people will make fun of me, and leave rude comments."

- Then ask the question again, based on the response you just got.

So, you would ask: "Shadow, what's the worst thing that will happen if people make fun of me and leave rude comments?"

Again, listen for the answer, repeat it out loud, and ask the question again. You want to keep interrogating your shadow until the inquiry reaches its logical conclusion, and you've hit the end of your worst-case scenarios, and you realize that you are bigger and more powerful than any of them.

This process might not necessarily eradicate the fear entirely, but it gives you a map of the territory, so you can see what you're really dealing with. Because when we acknowledge the truth of what is, we are free.

SAME, SAME, SAME

When we are under the influence of the control spirit, the unknown can't get a toe in the door. How could it? There's no opening. There's no space. When we are controlling, all we are doing is safeguarding our status quo and ensuring the same. That's called being stagnant. That's called being stuck. That's called being in hell; and it's a surefire path to death by boredom if there ever was one, because the status quo narrows our options, and cuts off our access to the quantum field of experience. I mean, why bother even incarnating on this planet, if you're just going to block yourself from your power, and your creative capacity? Human beings are so weird that way.

Most human beings live in a resistance field that has them perpetually seeking safety and security by going through the motions of a repetitive pattern of limited experiences, and doing the same handful of things over, and over, and over again, as though it's Groundhog Day, every single day, except weekends and holidays, which all have their own versions of their own repetition. People living in the resistance field craft lives for themselves that follow a very predictable pattern. They get married because their parents were married. They send their kids to college because they went to college. They sit at the same chair at the dinner table. They shop at the same stores. They eat at the same restaurants. The resistance field is all about same, same, same. And all this same, same, same creates a tremendous amount of tension in physical, emotional, psychological, and mental bodies. In fact, the stress of living in a resistance field is one of the biggest reasons why humanity leans so heavily on drugs and alcohol as a coping mechanism.

But people love their status quo, which is what has them continuing to make choices, and to design their lives so as to solidify their resistance fields, and to make them stronger, and thicker, and higher, and safer, and more isolating. That's how devoted people are to staying inside their comfort zones, and to avoiding the unknown.

It's also how people become wardens of their own prisons. The only shot people have at getting out of that prison is to rebel against themselves. It is to rebel against their indoctrination, and to rebel against their programming, and to put everything on the table, and call it all into question, while stepping out of their comfort zones, and stepping out of their same, same, same, and stepping into the unknown.

AS ABOVE, SO BELOW

The thing with the status quo, aside from being a total snore, is that it limits our perception. You see, this planet is held within a kind of bubble, which is actually very similar to the social media bubbles that reflect back to us the same ideas and beliefs we already hold. Our status quo bubble is such that the collective consensus here on Earth does not acknowledge the existence of other realities besides ours.

When an astronaut is hurtling through outer space to get to Mars to collect dirt samples, he is passing countless other beings, and worlds, and galaxies, and civilizations that he can't see. The reason he can't see them is because he doesn't know what he's looking for. His perception is not attuned to see beyond what it already knows. That's why it's so ridiculous that NASA and these other space programs spend millions and billions of dollars sending all this technology into space when millions of children go to sleep hungry every night. I mean, it's all well and good as far as creating bigger, better machines to go faster and farther into space, so we can collect more and more dirt samples. But if we're talking about discovering extraterrestrial life, or something entirely new, it's pretty pointless. That technology is never going to connect with any of the life that's out there because we are the ones who built that technology, which means that technology is as limited as we are.

It's the same with people who can't see spirits. Some people can see spirits, but most cannot. Most human beings can't even see the spirit that's standing in the very same room, right in front of their face, speaking directly to them, because most human beings haven't honed their perception in such a way that would allow them to sense that layer of reality; so they don't know what to look for.

BOX MENTALITY

The matrix has designed our world to deliberately limit human perception through what I call *box mentality*, which narrows our perception and limits us from recognizing our options. The system programs people with box mentality through infrastructure, and through architecture, in addition to all the rules, and patterns, and formulas it indoctrinates human beings to follow.

The vast majority of urban planning has been calibrated to a masculine energetic frequency, which has created cities, and structures, and an entire world dominated by squares, and rectangles, and straight lines, and sharp angles. We drive in square boxes along streets shaped like rectangles that intersect at sharp angles in massive squares marked with straight lines. We walk on rectangle-shaped sidewalks, forged of square concrete slabs. We enter rectangular buildings through rectangular doors, to sit at rectangular desks, to stare at rectangular screens, to daydream through square windows. Our entire reality construct is molded by square *this* and rectangle *that*.

All these angles confine the brain to perceiving reality through a box. These angles restrict people's neurological functioning such that they think in narrow, defined ways that don't allow for expansion beyond the limited scope the box recognizes and tolerates.

The number of doors, and options, and realities, and possibilities that human beings are cutting themselves off from is truly mind-blowing. It's really frustrating, as a shaman, because I work with so many people who come to me because they feel unfulfilled, and they feel stuck, and they feel trapped, and they feel hopeless. Except the whole time they're talking, their spirits are showing me all these doors and all these possibilities that are available to them, but the person can't see them, because they are blinded by box mentality.

Spirit Hack: The Walkabout

It is very important for people to start stepping away from the herd, and opening their minds, and figuring things out for themselves. This is where the walkabout comes in. A walkabout is a spiritual tool that allows us to dismantle our belief systems, and our mental constructs, and our psychological constructs, and everything we think we know as "real." A walkabout is a journey—a discovery process that leads us to things outside our comfort zone, and outside our known reality.

The Aborigines created walkabouts as a rite of passage. When tribe members reached a certain age, they left the tribe to journey alone into the wilderness, and to embark upon a sacred quest into the unknown to learn about themselves, and to learn about spirit, and to bring that knowledge back to the tribe, so that they could all learn and evolve. While the Aboriginal walkabout can last as long as six months, the modern-day shamanic version isn't nearly as demanding, but it is absolutely just as powerful.

When you're doing a walkabout, you are consciously making choices and engaging behaviors that run contrary to how you would normally operate. This extends to the little things—like taking an alternate route to work, or brushing your teeth with your nondominant hand, or wearing color when you (think you) favor a more neutral palette. It means going somewhere you never thought you would go, or dining alone, when you've only ever been out with other people.

The walkabout also includes bigger things, like attending a ceremony at a place of worship that's unfamiliar to you, or traveling to another country where you don't know the language, or dating someone whose genitals you're pretty sure you're not into.

I have a friend who identifies as straight and has always identified as straight. This friend happens to be someone who has done his fair share of stepping into the unknown, which means that he is in the habit of challenging his own beliefs, and challenging his identity structures. And at some point in his evolutionary process, my friend realized that he needed to have the experience of being intimate with a man if he was to be certain that he truly was straight, and so that he could get a deeper understanding of what it even meant to be straight. And so my friend had sex with a man. It blew his brain open and completely transformed his perspective on male sexuality in a really profound way, even though: P.S. He still identifies as straight.

Now, I'm not suggesting that you go have sex with whomever doesn't fit the gender preference you identify with. The friend I mentioned is an extreme seeker. Just because that was an aligned choice for him doesn't mean that it is an aligned choice for everyone. But what I am suggesting is that you let go of whatever rigid belief systems you are holding on to that have you convinced that something is right, or that something is wrong, as according to whatever you've been taught and programmed, and that you go on a walkabout, and figure that shit out for yourself.

Be sure to keep a journal when you're doing your walkabouts. Write down how you felt, and what came up for you while you were venturing into the unknown. And, if you're at a loss as to where to start, ask yourself what's the one thing you've always wanted to do that you never thought you would have the courage to do. Now, go do that thing.

EXPAND THE SOCIAL SITCH

Our connections with others are based on similarity and familiarity. Sociology tells us that human beings gravitate toward those who look most like them. We are drawn to people who dress the way we do, and who vote the way we do, and who were raised the way we were raised, and who like the things we like, and who don't like the things we don't like. Our connection to other people is based upon what we deem comfortable, based upon that which we already know.

Most people go to parties, and instead of connecting with the people they haven't met before, they rush to find the friends they already know, and then they spend their entire time huddled in these clusters and these cliques, recycling conversations they've already had about stuff they already know. It's such a wasted opportunity, because they have no idea what kind of connections they are missing out on, or what sort of information might be wanting to come through a conversation with a stranger, or how many doors are just waiting to open for them if they would only step outside their comfort zone and connect with someone unfamiliar.

Our collective social insecurity is one of the reasons we have so much conflict on our planet right now. People are not connecting in the realm of the unknown, with an authentic desire to experience something different, or with a willingness to learn something new. People are connecting from box mentality, and from the resistance field, which means their connections are driven by their desire to feel safe, and their devotion to maintaining the status quo. They are only open to relating to that which confirms what they already know and are comfortable with. They are programmed to think that anything that is unfamiliar, and anything that does not mirror their own identity construct, is a threat, which keeps them from opening themselves up to connections that will bring new data, and new information, and new possibilities into their lives.

Science tells us that the more diversity there is among the people we socialize and connect with, the more intelligent we become—as in actual IQ points. Plus, we live longer when we engage with a variety of different kinds of people. Not to mention how much more colorful and expansive those longer lives shape themselves to be when they are enriched by diversity of thought, and belief, and perspective, and expression. This means that when we avoid connecting with people we don't perceive to be like us (because we are afraid to think, or live, or explore, or consider beyond the constructs of our programming), we are literally capping our intelligence and our life spans, while limiting ourselves to status quo conversations, and status quo parties, and status quo existences. Why do we even bother coming to this planet if that's how we're gonna roll? I mean, really. . . .

This fear of other social groups is keeping our species stagnant, and isolated, while limiting our evolution in a big way. The only way to become a well-rounded individual is to open oneself up to a wide variety of possibilities, and a wide variety of inputs. If we are willing to open ourselves only to that which we already know, and that which we judge as safe based on our indoctrination and our limited exposure, then we are confining ourselves to fear-based lives, and we are cutting ourselves off from the quantum field of experience, and we are missing out on the opportunities that would allow us to expand into realms of higher intelligence, and elevation, and consciousness.

RACISM, BIGOTRY, AND INTOLERANCE, OH MY

A racist person doesn't actually hate the culture they position themselves against. They just don't understand it. Rarely is intolerance for other races, cultures, or belief systems based in any thoughtful, critical opposition to said races, cultures, or belief systems. It's based in ignorance, and it's based in fear. Most people who claim they hate another group of people haven't actually had the experience of stepping outside their comfort zones, and engaging the people they say they don't like from a place of openness or genuine curiosity. People who are intolerant of other groups of people are not open to new thoughts, or new ideas, or new beliefs or new cultures, because those things all exist outside of their comfort zones, and outside of what they already know, and therefore those things threaten the safety and the same, same, same of their status quo. So instead of taking responsibility for their shrunken, limited lives, and the stark, barren corners they've painted themselves into, they project their fear, and their boredom, and their disappointment in themselves onto those they deem different, and then they create stories to justify the intolerance they've made up in their heads, and the negative stereotypes the matrix has programmed them to buy into.

Spirit Hack: Burst Your Social Bubble

The next time you find yourself at a social gathering, challenge yourself to connect with someone who appears to be unlike you, and who you can't imagine having anything in common with. Don't just introduce yourself and then rush to get away so you can check it off your spiritual to-do list. Really connect. Engage that person from a place of genuine curiosity, with the intention of making an authentic connection, and opening yourself to something new, and seeing where your courage leads you.

The way you do this is to see each person as their own planet. When you connect with that person, engage them with the understanding that you are not there to change them, and you are not there to impose your views upon them, and you are not there to tell them that they are right, or that they are wrong. You are there only to observe, and to ask questions, and to find out how their world looks, and works, and operates, and what their point of view is. When we let go of our judgments, we realize that the understanding of true tribe, and true community and true connection is found in our willingness to be open to other people's observations, and beliefs, and ideas about life.

Some things you can ask include:

What inspires you?

How do you feel about _____?

What are your thoughts upon _____?

What motivates you?

Where would you like to create change, and why?

What's wonderful in your world?

Never ask *yes* or *no* questions when creating new connections with people. Instead, engage them as though you are a journalist, researching a story about this amazing person, excited to learn as much as you can about them from an objective point of view by asking inviting, open-ended questions.

THE GREAT ADVERTISERS

When you take responsibility for your own junkery, and you claim your power in the unknown, you become one of what I call the *great advertisers*. The great advertisers promote light consciousness and spiritual awakening wherever we go by demonstrating what is possible when we stop running from the monster under the bed, and we face it. The great advertisers do not need to look for monsters among us, or to persecute others for their choices or their beliefs, nor do they need to project their own ills, or the world's ills, onto anyone else, because the great advertisers are taking responsibility for their own ills, and realigning the planet in the process.

Remember, tribe, we do not create change by fighting for it, or by imposing it, or by telling others that they need to get cracking on it. We create change by choosing to be that change, and by modeling that change, and by inspiring others to follow in our footsteps, because we're that lit, and because we're having that much fun.

8

CONNECT

The whole point of embracing the darkness, and stepping into our shadows, is not just to transform ourselves. The point is to transform the world. We heal and we evolve so that we can support our brothers and sisters in doing the same. We empower ourselves, so we can empower others. And that empowerment is what gives us the strength and the courage to speak and to act for those who cannot speak and act for themselves. It's not like we're going to get the world giant by being amazing in isolation, all by ourselves. We have a whole planet to lift and shift. And that means we have to connect—not just with ourselves, but also with each other.

DON'T DITCH YOUR BLOODLINE

It's crazy to see so many people stepping away from their families like it's no big deal. Like it's not going to create any distortions or imbalances in their lives when someone just cuts all ties to their lineage. It's cuckoo. This disconnect, which I see fragmenting so many families, is a huge issue, especially in spiritual communities, where people are running their love-and-light trips and "can't deal" with the emotions their family dynamics trigger, because they ruffle their auras, or schiz out their chakras, or whatever.

People need to stay connected to their bloodline. Period. People need to deal with the issues their family triggers, and they need to see them as opportunities to grow, and to evolve their genetic lineage. Our family junkery is no different from our individual junkery—we don't run away from it. We don't empower the darkness by fragmenting our fractal lines and avoiding the issues that are needing our love and acceptance to transform. We engage that shit. We shake up to wake up, which means we embrace the family shadow, and we use every last one of its reflections, and its challenges, and its uncomfortable dynamics to grow, and to get lit.

Many of the issues people are dealing with aren't even about them. We're so narcissistic. People love to personalize everything. But a lot of what comes up for people in their family dynamics is totally impersonal, and is being triggered so that they can help shift their lineage into a higher and more aligned state of consciousness. When we grow, not only do we evolve ourselves as individuals, but we also evolve our entire family bloodline. You see, you are not here just for you. You are here to be of service to your ancestors—to those who walked before you, and to those who will someday join you, because you all exist in the quantum now, which means your efforts, your love, and your evolution serve the entire fractal line.

A lot of times people have these lingering issues—like, they keep attracting the same relationship pattern over and over again, even though they've been loving on it for years. Or they have this low-grade mystery pain in their body that's pretty much always there, and that they've tried a million things for, and that no doctor or healer can seem to figure out, much less heal. That's bloodline pain. Bloodline pain is held in the RNA, which is where all of our ancestral coding is stored. I see a lot of bloodline pain in my African clients, and in my Middle Eastern clients—in the Muslims, and in the Jews—and in the Native people, and in the cultures and lineages that have been on the planet for a long, long time, and that have deep, deep roots that are grounded in old, old energies, and lots and lots of fractal lines. The most efficient way to change the RNA, and to get relief from these stubborn issues and ailments in our lives, is to connect with our ancestors.

Spirit Hack: Ancestor Altar

I love Día de los Muertos. It's this wonderful Mexican holiday that coincides with our Halloween. People create these beautiful altars and put out delicious food, and desserts, and drinks for their ancestors as a way to honor them when the veil between realms is thin. And so they all get to share the celebration together. It's such a beautiful honoring, and a beautiful remembering.

Creating an altar is a great way to open up your energy to your ancestors, and to begin the journey of cultivating a relationship with them. The altar is an invitation you are extending to your ancestors. It's a way of beckoning them toward you, and inviting them into your life.

Things to include in your ancestor altar:

- pictures of your ancestors

- things your ancestors liked

For example, if your grandmother loved the beach, you would place some sand on your altar. If your father loved golf, you would place a golf tee or a golf ball on the altar.

- an offering bowl

In some cultures, people make offerings of chocolate, or of money, or of spirits to the ancestors. It's helpful to offer your ancestors things that you are wanting more of in your life. So, if you are wanting abundance, you can offer them coins. Or, if you are wanting more beauty and creativity, you can offer a flower.

- a candle

Light the candle when you want to connect with your ancestors' spirits. The more attention you devote to your ancestors, and the more you engage them, the more they will be able to help you in your life.

Note for extenuating ancestor disconnect:

If you don't have any photographs of your ancestors, don't sweat it. You can draw pictures, or you can sculpt figures. It doesn't matter if you're adopted, or you have no idea who any of your ancestors are, or what they look like. You can make it up.

That Time My Student Connected to His Ancestors

I once had a student from Germany named Hans whose life wasn't going very well. He kept making bad business deals, and losing money, and bouncing from one failure to the next. He wondered if he was cursed, because nothing seemed to land for him. I could tell that someone in his bloodline had had similar issues, and I knew that he would benefit from their wisdom. I told Hans to build an altar to ancestors so that they could guide him through this issue.

Hans turned an old wooden table into his ancestor altar. He made offerings once a week—sometimes twice—and asked his ancestors for guidance. That's when his life started to change. He felt protected, and he started making better business decisions. He would go to make a move,

and then he would get a feeling, and he would pause, and think to do it differently, and then make a different choice. Suddenly, doors started opening;
opportunities started to present themselves. Things turned around for Hans
very quickly after that, and—to this day—he makes regular offerings to his
ancestors, and always asks for their guidance before making decisions.

BLOODLINE SPIRITS

Just like the issues coded in our RNA, spirits get passed through the bloodline, too. Spirits are passed down through beliefs. When parents indoctrinate their children with the beliefs that formulate their worldview, they are
simultaneously passing the spirits attached to those beliefs to their children.

So, let's say someone's great-great-great-great-grandmother had money issues that she didn't examine or heal while she was alive. The spirit that was attached to those money issues was passed down through the bloodline, through
the beliefs she taught her children about money and abundance. Every time
she told her children *Money doesn't grow on trees*, or *Money is the root of all
evil*, or *You have to work hard just to make ends meet, but even then, you'll still
be poor*, she was transferring that spirit into their fields of consciousness. And
so that spirit keeps getting passed down through the generations, polluting one
mind after the next with scarcity, and lack, and limiting beliefs about money,
until you have all these fractal lines, and all these familial tributaries where no
one pays retail, or turns on the heat, or splurges on dryer sheets or asparagus;
and everyone is programmed with the same limiting beliefs that money is hard
to come by, and that rich people suck, because their great-great-great-great-
grandmother's scarcity spirit is working through all of them.

It's very efficient the way the darkness works—accessing the bloodline
and holding entire ancestral lineages hostage to limitation. Until an outlier
comes along. Until that one day, several generations down the line, when
a man is reprimanding his son for leaving the light on in the kitchen, and

the man is recycling the same stories that have been passed down through his lineage for centuries—that money doesn't grow on trees, and that money is hard to come by—but, instead of signing on to the indoctrination that's been holding his family back for centuries, the kid rebels against the bloodline curse, and rebels against the spirit of scarcity, and pushes back, and says: "No. I'm not signing on to that story. Your beliefs about money being scarce, and evil, and hard to come by are your beliefs, not mine. And those beliefs are a prison that have kept this family playing small for long enough. I'm choosing a different story, and different beliefs. So, yeah, money actually does come to me easily, and often."

In that moment, that kid isn't defying just his father; he is also facing off with that bloodline spirit that is trying to pull him into that field of limitation and bondage, the same way it's pulled his entire ancestral lineage into that field of limitation and bondage for years, and years, and years. When that kid pushes back on that spirit, and on that story, and that programming, and he claims his sovereignty, that kid heals his entire fractal line. That kid has given his whole lineage their freedom by rebelling against that bloodline spirit, and rebelling against all the toxic, limiting beliefs that came along with it, which opens up new doors and pathways for all of them.

My Fractal Line

My great-grandmother Mamal is my closest guide in the spirit world. She's the one who pulled me back from the dead, and she is always with me. Always. Whenever I go see a psychic, the first thing they all say is that there's this powerful, older woman in the form of a white stork sitting on top of my head.

"Yup." I laugh, because it always cracks me up. "That's my great-grandmother."

Even though I never met Mamal in the material realm because she died before I was born, I talk to my great-grandmother pretty much every day. She first came to me when I was five, and told me I was going to be a powerful shaman.

As I mentioned earlier, Mamal was a great medicine woman in Ghana. She fled Africa in the early 1800s when her tribe was invaded by the Dutch, and her family was put into the slave camps. Mamal escaped by boat, as a stowaway, and ended up in Haiti, where she studied healing and shamanism with the Haitian people. From Haiti, she landed in New Orleans, where she fell in love, got married, and had children, one being my grandmother. My grandmother married a Native American Blackfoot Indian; and together, they had my father.

My grandpa Leon flat out rejected shamanism. He was a God-fearing Seventh Day Adventist who judged the shamanic side of my family as evil, because the spirit that religion had planted in him was all about being perfect with some hateful, punishing God. When the ancestors started showing up in my father's life, and pulling him toward shamanism, my grandfather wasn't having it. And so my grandfather beat my father, and punished my father, and forbade my father from studying shamanism and exploring his roots. That was how my grandfather passed that bloodline spirit down to my father, and in doing so, took away all of my father's power.

When it was my time, and the ancestors came to me, and my father tried to keep me from pursuing my shamanic calling, and tried to pass that spirit onto me, I rebelled. I rebelled big-time—not just because I knew that being a shaman was my truth, but also because there was no way I was going to let the darkness brainwash a third generation of my bloodline with religion and snuff out everything my grandmother and my family's tribe in Africa had worked so hard to build and to root into our lineage.

And, you know what? The moment I stood up to my father, and I rebelled against that bloodline spirit that was trying to come through him, was the moment when my father started to come into his own power. For the first time in his whole life. Because I defied that spirit, I set my fractal line free.

FUCK FORGIVENESS

It's scary to rebel against your family programming, and to defy your parents, and to stand alone in your truth. Being the black sheep in my family exacerbated what was already there—a lot of conflict, and a lot of violence, and a lot of abuse. I loved my father, and I loved my stepmother, and I loved my grandparents, but I don't forgive them. I don't forgive my father for the horrible things he did, and I don't forgive my stepmom for the horrible things she did, and I don't forgive my grandparents for the horrible things they did. I accept what they did. I accept that they did those horrible things to me. And that acceptance is what allows me—and all of us—to be free.

Forgiveness implies that what my family did to me was wrong, or bad, which blocks me from acknowledging that they had their own lessons to learn from those experiences, and blocks all of us from being able to grow from the experiences we shared.

I had a client who was raised by a very abusive, alcoholic mother tell me that she forgave her mother for all the awful things she did to her.

"No, you didn't," I said.

At which point, my client doubled down on her nonsense and insisted that yes, she did forgive her mother, because she went through this whole forgiveness process, and wrote down all her resentments, and burned them during a full moon ritual on the solstice.

And I said, "Honey, you didn't forgive your mother, and you don't forgive your mother. And the more you keep telling this story that you do, the longer you're keeping you and your mother in limbo, and dragging out the suffering for both of you. That fact that you're announcing that you forgave your mother just means you haven't let it go."

My client thought about it for a minute, then burst into tears.

"You're right," she said. "I can't let it go."

People hurt each other, and people do terrible things. That's how life goes. But this idea that forgiveness is the magical key to our healing is bullshit. Forgiveness binds us, and forgiveness limits us, and forgiveness holds us back. Forgiveness is the worst. The moment we invoke the energy of forgiveness, we activate duality, and we activate hierarchy. Forgiveness is a blame construct that implies that someone is right, and that someone else is wrong, which instantly creates separation, and instantly ensnares both people in a quantum entanglement that traps them in the energy field of the initial conflict. Forgiveness is purgatory, and forgiveness warps a lot of shit in a lot of ways.

So what if my client went through the motions of forgiveness? Why would she forgive her mom for what she did, anyway? Forgiveness is a mental trap that keeps us stuck in energetic limbo. It's pointless. But if my client could accept what her mother did, then they would both be free. Acceptance sets us free while allowing us to stay engaged, because when we accept, we are relating in the realms of truth. We are not denying, and we are not pretending, and we are not guilting, and we are not blaming, and we are not victimizing, and we are not judging. We are simply acknowledging. *This happened. This is an energy or an experience that we shared, and that had an impact on everyone involved, and what they choose to do with those energies and those lessons moving forward is up to them.*

It's way more honest and effective than telling someone: "I forgive you." No, thank you. I'd really rather you didn't. Forgiveness is purgatory. Forgiveness is a Chinese finger trap.

ANCESTORS ARE A THING

Loneliness and isolation are contributing to epidemic bouts of depression, opioid addiction, and suicide in America. While it's true that the system is doing its part to separate humans, another reason people are feeling so alone, and so forsaken, is because they have no connection to their ancestors. It's not bad enough that people are walking away from their own living, breathing mothers, fathers, sisters, brothers, aunts, uncles, cousins, and kids because they don't want to deal with the challenges their families trigger, but that people also aren't connecting with their entire ancestral lines, like, on any level whatsoever—well, it's no wonder they're freaking out.

Throughout the ages, everyone was connected to their ancestors. It wasn't until we rolled into the industrial revolution that humans up and ditched their connection to their ancestors. Rationalism gave way to this ridiculous notion that when people die, they are gone forever, which is complete and utter nonsense. Death doesn't mean we cease to exist. Death just means we cease to exist in this biological space suit, in this dimensional plane of reality. But because we have been programmed to believe that death is some sort of final nothingness, people just assume that their ancestors disappeared altogether and have gone about forgetting them; and let me tell you, humans took a wrong turn when we stopped trusting that our ancestors are still with us.

It is extremely arrogant to walk through life thinking that it's all about us, and that we exist all on our own, of our accord—like we were hatched from some isolated pod floating in a vacuum of narcissism that has us completely oblivious to the fact that we wouldn't even be here if it weren't for every grandparent who came before us, and had kids, and raised those kids, and kept those kids alive so that we could be here now. It is so disrespectful not to acknowledge where we came from.

THE ANCESTORS KNOW SOME SHIT

Without a solid connection to our ancestors, we cannot connect with our roots, or with our family history, which puts us in a very precarious position here on planet Earth. Our ancestors are great allies when it comes to navigating the complexities of incarnation, especially as it relates to the Blackout, because—much like the shadow—our ancestors know everything about us. They know what kind of person is going to be best for us to partner up with in our love life. They know which opportunities are going to work out, and which ones are going to fall flat. They're plugged way in.

Our ancestors walked Earth and lived their own lives in their own time. When they died, they learned powerful lessons about the choices they made. Now that they are on the other side, they have a broader perspective. They can see the bigger picture. When we create a bridge to our ancestors, and we invite them to participate in our lives, they support us, and they protect us. They let us know when something is not aligned, or when something is not in our best interests.

But it's not just about what our ancestors can do for us; it's also about what we can do for them. We all have a responsibility to our lineage. The reason our ancestors endured, and the reason our ancestors survived, and the reason our ancestors propagated was not so that their great-great-great-great-grandchildren could enjoy our own isolated existences for our own hedonistic pleasure, but so that we could make things better—for ourselves, and for each other, and for our lineage.

Spirit Hack: Ancestor Bridge

The easiest way to cultivate a relationship with your ancestors is to build a bridge between your world and theirs. When you build a bridge to your ancestors, you are opening up a connection between you and your bloodline, and you are giving your ancestors full-spectrum access to you, so that they can advise you with all the details and aspects of your life in mind.

Having a bridge that connects you with your ancestors allows them to send you healing energies, and words of wisdom, and synchronicities, and what have you. Basically, the ancestor bridge is you saying: *Hey, ancestors. I'm all in. Let's level-up, and cocreate amazingness together.*

It's best to sit in front of your ancestor altar when you are building your ancestor bridge, because your ancestor altar is your focal point of ancestral mojo. But if you haven't created an altar to your ancestors yet, don't sweat it. Your ancestors can hear you wherever you are.

- Visualize a golden light emanating from your heart and extending out beyond your body, and beyond this realm, and into the spirit world.

- As you run that energy from your heart, and into the spirit world, say out loud: "Ancestors, I am opening up this bridge as a sacred portal between us. I welcome your wisdom, and your guidance, and your love, as well as any requests you have of me. I honor our connection, and I am so excited to share this journey with you."

Now that you've created your ancestor bridge, here's how you put it to use:

- Take a few deep breaths, and say: "Ancestors, send a sensation through my body, so that I can feel it."

- Pay attention to any sensations in your body, such as a heat, or chills, or pressure, or itchiness. When you feel it, say "I feel _____, ancestors. Increase my receptivity even more."

- Again, notice what you feel. Then say: "I feel _____, ancestors. Increase my receptivity even more."

- Repeat this process five times, total.

- Keep practicing this technique by asking your ancestors for signs. Ask them to bring a color into your mind that you can see, or to bring a word into your thoughts that you can hear or read.

Every time you hear, feel, or see something, tell your ancestors—out loud—what you are perceiving, and then ask them to increase your receptivity even more.

This spirit hack teaches you how to be present with your ancestors. The more you use this technique, the stronger your connection with your ancestors will be, and the more access you will have to them.

ANCESTRAL SUPERVISION

used to live in the upper unit of a fourplex in LA. My downstairs neighbor hated my drumming, hated my singing, hated my friends, and hated me. Though, let's be clear, people don't actually hate others for the reasons they think they do. People hate others because they can't control them to act in ways that would make them feel safe, based on what they already know and on how they've been programmed. It's a control thing. Anyway, this neighbor who thought he hated me hired a Moroccan *shawafa* to put a curse on me. Except, she couldn't. It got back to me that the Moroccan woman passed out cold during the ritual, and that when she came to, my ancestors wouldn't let her complete the spell. Her powers were useless in the face of all my ancestral protection.

Ancestral supervision isn't a given. It doesn't work like that. Unless we initiate a connection with our ancestors, and cultivate a connection with our ancestors, we're on our own. And that disconnect has a lot of people feeling like fish out of water wherever they are, because a part of them is always on alert for something bad happening. It's very disorienting when we are not operating with ancestral supervision. P.S. When I use the word "supervision," I don't mean the matrix's hierarchical manipulation of the word. I mean the OG Latin version; I mean what the word actually means, as in *super-vision,* as in many multidimensional eyes watching your back. I have that. I travel all over the world, and I always feel at ease, because I know my ancestors are always guiding me.

That Time My Ancestors Saved My and My Friends' Lives

When I was in Tel Aviv, my friends and I used to have lunch at the same little coffee shop on Allenby Street every afternoon. One day my ancestors sent me a bunch of signs indicating that we shouldn't go there.

First off, my friend knocked a glass off the counter on our way out of the house. It shattered all over the floor. That was my first inclination that there was a chink in our plan.

"Watch out!" said a workman as I passed a little too close to a ladder leaning up against a store wall.

As we rounded the corner that took us to Allenby Street, I noticed a couple arguing loudly on the sidewalk. A minute later, I reached for the door of the café, and I heard a voice in my head say, very clearly: "You should find a different place to eat, *now*."

I told my friends that we needed to go to another restaurant. It took some convincing, but they finally acquiesced. As we were ordering our food, we heard an explosion. A suicide bomber had blown up our little café on Allenby Street. That was a pivotal moment for me. That was when I really got how important it is for me to listen—I mean, like *really* got it, you know?

GET FULL OF YOURSELF

Codependence creates a lot of suffering in our relationships. People put all this pressure on their family members, and all this pressure on other people in their lives to fulfill the emotional needs they haven't learned how to give themselves.

A woman came to one of my workshops and asked me for advice on getting over her homesickness, as though homesickness is a thing, which it isn't. I explained to the woman that her issue had nothing to do with homesickness. Her issue was her choice to identify her feelings as "homesickness," which was based on the false belief that her family was the source of her balance, and her sustenance, and her nurturing, and her being grounded, and that the only way for her to experience these energies was to be at home with them. Her issue wasn't geography. Her issue was that she wasn't full of herself, meaning that she wasn't taking responsibility for giving these energies to herself. She was projecting that responsibility onto her family, thereby putting the burden of fulfillment onto their shoulders.

When we don't fill ourselves up with the sustenance we crave, we become vacuous energetic shells perpetually looking for someone else to fill us up. It's a precarious setup, because—like I always tell my clients—if you are not full of yourself, then someone else is going to come along and fill you up with a bunch of their own bullshit. And when you're full of that, that's where the discord comes in.

DISCORD

Because human beings are driven by our need to be liked, and by our need to belong, a lot of our relationship dynamics are marked by discord. Like, a lot. We generate discord when we allow ourselves to connect with energies that are not in alignment with our highest truth, or our highest happiness, or our highest well-being, or our highest harmony. Basically, when we compromise what is best for us, and what is resonant with us, to just go with the flow, or to be part of the in crowd, or to people-please, or to belong, we are generating discord.

Let me give you an example. Let's say you're at a dinner party with friends, and the conversation is predominantly negative—lots of judging, and gossiping, and complaining, and that sort of thing. You feel yourself contracting and bristling in the face of all the negativity being exchanged, but you do nothing to redirect the conversation toward a more positive trajectory. That conversation is generating discord, and when you will leave that conversation you will be in a state of discord. It doesn't matter whether you chimed in with your own complaints, or your own judgments, or not. You still immersed yourself in those vibrations, and you enabled those vibrations, and because those vibrations are not resonant with your highest truth, harmony, or well-being, or your greater knowingness, now you are in discord.

This type of discord is an expression of the larger issue of denial, which we are dealing with on the planet as a collective. We can no longer pretend that we don't know what we know; which means we can no longer pretend that we don't know that our actions have consequences. As quantum creators, we must take responsibility for the input we are allowing into our vessels, and our energetic fields, and into the world at large, just as we must take responsibility for shifting and lifting that input, and for evolving our interactions and our social constructs, as well as for evolving ourselves and the world.

It would be one thing if we lived in a singular-dimensional construct/vacuum, where discord was simply a feeling state or frequency with no implications or offshoots to deal with. But that's not how quantum reality works. Discord opens the door to more discord, and to more darkness, because discord is a multidimensional magnet for underworld parasites.

UNDERWORLD PARASITES

Underworld parasites are basically spirit bugs whose purpose is to keep the darkness dark. They gain access to our systems through discord, where they feed off our negativity to empower the darkness, and to attract more discord into our lives, so they can empower the darkness some more, and attract even more discord into our lives. Wash, rinse, repeat. Once they've embedded themselves in our beings, the underworld parasites seize control of our minds, where they hijack the algorithms of our thoughts, and manipulate us into making misaligned choices to keep us in a perpetual state of imbalance.

Underworld parasites wreak havoc on our lives by blocking us from opportunities we are aligned with, and by linking us with dysfunctional people, energies, and situations that are a vibrational match for the discord that attracted the spirit bugs in the first place. Underworld parasites attract other people to us who are also in discord, so that—together—we will create exponentially more discord, to keep the underworld alive and kicking.

The longer we stay in discord, the more access we give the underworld parasites to our being, which means the more damage they do and the harder the whole mess is to correct.

It's just all the more reason to stay aligned, and to stay in accord. That means steering clear of the kinds of disruptions that create discord, like complaining, criticizing, gossiping, shit-talking, showing off, bragging, degrading, disparaging, etc. If our words are not lifting and shifting, then we need to look at the junkery inside us that is inspiring us to speak to hurt, and to speak to divide; and we need to examine the insecurity that it's attached to. But what we definitely do not want to do is to spread those discordant vibrations throughout the quantum field by engaging in low-vibe exchanges just to pass the time.

Spirit Hack: Shamanic Harmonic Ninja Sorcery

Shamanic harmonic ninja sorcery is a great way to take responsibility for your environment, and to shift low-frequency conversations into vibrational alignment, and to protect your field from discord and underworld parasites. Because, *ew*.

There are no hard-and-fast rules to utilizing shamanic harmonic ninja sorcery to combat discord, but here's the basic gist: when you find yourself in a conversation marked by complaining or negativity, you want to redirect the conversation onto a more resonant trajectory as quickly as you can.

First, you intercept the dissonant vibrations by acknowledging what the person is saying. So, you would say something like: "I hear everything that you're saying," because you don't want to dismiss the person or their perspective entirely, you just want to help guide them toward a more harmonious expression.

Then, you ninja the conversation onto a more positive path by inviting whoever was doing the complaining to see the situation from a different angle.

So, you would ask things like:

- "What is working for you about the situation?"

- "What is the situation teaching you about yourself?"

- "How will you handle the situation differently next time?"

Or, if you find yourself with people who are gossiping, or putting other people down, you can steer the conversation onto a more aligned trajectory by offering a positive reframe on the person or the situation. Or, you could talk about a time in your own life when you were navigating something similar to whatever your friends are complaining about, and share about what it taught you, or share about what in your life was informing it, so as to help the people you're with expand their understanding of the situation.

When we are using shamanic harmonic ninja sorcery, we are playfully guiding others to expand their perspective, and to tap into a more positive, coherent frequency. The purpose is not to shame, or to make anyone else wrong. The purpose is to raise the collective vibration, and to create a frequency of harmony and a field of accord in which everyone is safe to connect, and share, and enjoy, without attracting extradimensional pathogens into their fields.

SIGNATURES ARE A THING

So many people want to find a partner to share their life with, but they get really hung up on all these details, like what color their eyes are, or how tall they are, or whether they meditate, or eat gluten, or use fluoridated toothpaste, or call their mother, or own their own home, or whatever. That's all fine, you could meet someone who fits every requirement on your vision board—you guys do CrossFit together, it's great that you're both vegan, and you both have rescue dogs, and you both love the Beatles—but unless your signatures are aligned, that relationship is going to be discordant.

When people's signatures are aligned, it's easy for them to be together. They move at the same pace, and in the same flow. They feel uplifted in each other's company, and their relating is always smooth. These relationships help keep us in harmony, and these relationships help keep us in accord.

Then there are those people who drain us, and stress us out, and rub us the wrong way, and leave us feeling drained, or frazzled, or off—not because of anything they say or do, but because of the frequencies they generate. This is what happens when our signatures are misaligned.

A lot of relationship friction is a result of misaligned signatures. It's not that anyone is doing anything wrong, or that anyone is behaving in such a way that needs correcting. The discord is happening on much subtler and more fundamental energetic levels, which means that simple behavioral adjustments aren't going to shift them. We're not meant to be in relationship with everyone.

ALONE GETS A BAD RAP

A lot of people would rather be in discordant relationships with people who drain them and treat them badly than be alone. People are terrified of being alone because people don't want to face their shit. They would much rather keep themselves preoccupied with relationship drama, and relationship distraction, than be with themselves. Because if people were willing to be with themselves, they would start to see where they were getting in their own way, and where they're dropping the ball, and where they are not being honest; and then they would have to take responsibility for these things; and then they would have to make different choices and adjust their lifestyle. And that's inconvenient, and that's uncomfortable; so people avoid it. This is why people choose to stay in discordant relationships, and muck up their lives with parasitic energies and all the rest of it. These people think, *Well sure, my partner ignores me, and treats me like a child. And yes, our relationship is painful, and tumultuous, and disempowering, but at least I'm not alone.*

Being alone is stepping into the unknown. When we avoid taking that journey inside ourselves, we become fragmented, and we become distorted. When we can't be alone with ourselves, it's like being in a big room where someone's shoved all the things they don't want to deal with under the rug. So, if you want to get something from the other side of the room, you can't just walk in a straight line across the shortest path to get to it. You have step over all these lumpy things that are poking out from under the rug. You have to maneuver around these things, which catch on the hem of your pants, and trip you, all because you haven't put just a bunch of stuff under your rug; you've also created actual obstacles for yourself, inside yourself.

When we connect with others to avoid being alone, we are not able to connect authentically, from a place of wholeness. We are just looking for some walking, talking Spackle to fill the holes in our consciousness, and to fill that gaping void where we're holding on to pain and belief structures that we could actually heal and move on from, if we would just choose to be present with ourselves, and to examine the parts that hurt, and that scare us, and then fill them up with our own love and acceptance of our own damn selves.

Your autonomy is a necessary function of your development as a human being. One of the biggest reasons why relationships fail is because as soon as people get into a relationship, they ditch their autonomy, but that's when they actually need to be doubling down on it. To have a relationship that works—meaning that it's healthy, and it's communicative, and it endures, while serving the highest well-being and interests of both partners—we must be independent, and we must be autonomous. It's not your partner's responsibility to convince you that you're beautiful, or to rub your shoulders after work, or to make you happy. No one can make another person happy. Happiness doesn't come from other people. Happiness comes from ourselves. This is why it's so important to be what I call *relationship independent,* where you are the one filling your own vessel, and you are the one taking responsibility for your own happiness. When we rely on others to fulfill our needs for us, we create expectations. It's all well and good if you want to distort the shit out of your relationship, and spend all your time fighting, and arguing, and disappointing each other, and being miserable. But if you want to stay on the lit train and live a happy, fulfilled, poprocks, amazing life, you better leave those expectations at the door, babe.

SUSTAIN THYSELF

We must learn to be self-sustaining—not just for our own healing and our own well-being, but also out of respect for our loved ones, and the relationships we share with them. When we walk around un-whole, looking for others to fulfill our emotional needs, and to fill our voids, and the cracks in our consciousness, our relationships become discordant, because they are not free.

We betray our authenticity when we sign on to discordant relationship dynamics, and when we sign on to codependent relationship dynamics. When we are not truly in alignment with the vibrational frequency of that relationship, we must adjust ourselves to make it seem like the relationship fits. We contort ourselves into emotional, psychological, and spiritual knots to make the relationship "work." When we change or we compromise who we are to trick the person we are with into loving us, we are eating what I call *compromised pie.* And, let me tell you, compromised pie tastes like shit.

Back When I Ate Compromised Pie

Because I was abused as a child, and because I was bullied as a child, I attracted a very abusive, very tumultuous relationship as an adult. Even though it was extremely painful, and it was extremely volatile, I stayed in that relationship for several years. The reason I stayed in that relationship for so long was because I was so focused on giving to my partner, and on helping my partner, and on pleasing my partner, that I completely lost sight of myself, and I couldn't see how much I was compromising my truth to stay in this abusive dynamic.

We used to fight, like, all the time. And I would get so furious with him for taking advantage of me, and for not appreciating all the things I did for him, and all the things I sacrificed for him. I would scream at him for constantly taking, taking, taking from me, but I wasn't acknowledging that I was the one who was doing all the giving, giving, giving. The truth is that I had no right to be yelling at him, or complaining about him, because I was just as responsible for our toxic dynamic as he was. The only person I could rightly complain about was me, because I was the one who compromised myself to get love, and I was the one who compromised my truth to stay in that relationship, and I was the one who allowed myself to be treated that way.

That relationship was so valuable because it taught me that it's not anyone else's responsibility to acknowledge me, or to praise me for being kind, or generous, or powerful, or what have you. It taught me that it's my responsibility to fill my needs, and that I can choose to do, or say, or give whatever I want, but that I have no right to get upset if someone doesn't respond to those gestures the way I want them to. That expectation shit will kick you in the ass every time. Mostly, that relationship showed me how inauthentic I was being, and it taught me to stop eating compromised pie. It taught me that I don't need to shape-shift myself into anything different than what I already am to be someone who someone else would want to love, and that all I need to do to be someone who someone else would want to love is to just be comfortable being me.

SEXUAL BLOCKS ARE A THING

You would be shocked to know how many people I work with as a shaman who have blockages in their sexual energy. It's basically an epidemic, and it's a huge problem, because blockages in our sexual energy create blockages in our lives.

Sexual energy is expression energy. That's all that sex is. Sex is expression through communion, and connection, and communication with another human being through the body. Sex is an opportunity for humans to experience pleasure. Pleasure is an extremely powerful energy. Pleasure awakens very healthy, very nourishing energies and feelings inside us. Pleasure allows us to feel safe and secure. Pleasure allows us to feel comfortable with who we are, which allows us to communicate more freely, and more efficiently, and more effectively. When we are comfortable in our sexuality, and in our sensuality, and in our intimacy, we are more easily able to connect with others. We are able to open up new gateways of perception, because we are not afraid. Sex connects us to our inner sanctity, and our inner well-being, as well as to our youth and our vitality. Sex is poprocks.

When we block our ability to communicate pleasure, and ecstasy, and bliss through our body, we shut down our sensitivity, and we shut down our sensuality, and we shut down our sensorium. We cut off our ability to sense and to feel, and we become numb to the world, and to other people. When we shut down our sexual energy, we block ourselves from attracting the kinds of experiences that would bring joy, and pleasure, and ecstasy into our lives. We also block our receptivity channels, which translates into financial issues and scarcity consciousness. Sexual blocks are a big deal, because they create a lot of havoc in a lot of areas of our lives.

HOW THE MATRIX SULLIED SEX

The matrix uses religion to program humans to believe that sex is sinful, and that sex is dirty. The program triggers guilt and shame, which has us feeling like we should be punished anytime we have sex. And so we self-flagellate mentally, and emotionally, and spiritually, as well as physically, which is how we manifest disease.

When I was a kid, my stepmother caught me masturbating in my room. She totally freaked out. She grabbed a pair of scissors, dragged me out into the hallway, made me pull out what she called my "ding-a-ling," wedged it between the blades, and hissed: "If I ever catch you doing that again, I'm going to cut it off."

To this day, I remember feeling the coldness of those sharp blades against my skin, and the pressure of that metal as she tightened the scissors to make her point. I remember feeling terrified that my stepmother was going to cut off my penis. But for the life of me I couldn't figure out what I did wrong. I mean, I knew my stepmom was Catholic, and that she thought sex was dirty, and bad, and wrong, but it didn't make sense, considering that I knew she and my dad kept an extensive collection of Swedish erotica tapes hidden in their armoire. It didn't add up. If sex was so bad, and if sex was so wrong, then why were she and my dad watching these videos of people doing it in all these weird ways?

This is the contradiction that repression creates. It's very confusing, especially for kids whose parents are telling them not to be sexual, and that sex is a sin, but then they're all doing all sorts of weird, twisted shit, and hiding it, and lying about it. The matrix uses repression to keep humans blocked sexually. The repression field is what triggers humans to operate in extremes. That's why we have all these people pendulating into these really out-there, perverted forms of sexual expression. Because they have so many blocks from so much disruptive programming, they cannot allow themselves to simply enjoy the beautiful feelings, and the connection with another soul on a physical and spiritual level. It's really sad, because our nature as human beings is to express, and to communicate. That's what every being in the world does—every animal, every insect, every flower, every tree—they all express themselves fully and completely, without rules and limitations, for that is the natural way.

CONQUEST CULTURE

S exual repression has given way to conquest culture, wherein men base their value, their self-worth, their masculinity, and their reputations on how many chicks they've banged. This includes body-hopping. Body-hopping is when a guy leaps from one minirelationship to the next, with each one lasting about as long as the dopamine high. The second those hormones wear off, and the excitement fades, and the man is faced with an actual person with fears, and flaws, and human emotions, and blackheads, it's *Sayonara, baby!* and off they go to swipe their way to their next conquest.

Then there's the boys' club that men never seem to outgrow, where you have guys bragging about fucking the most women, and about fucking the hottest women, and about all the depraved ways they violated all these women. It's all being driven by the same insecurity that drives every man, which is: *Is my dick big enough? Is my Benz fly enough? Do women want to fuck me?*

And what these men need to realize is that no number of women, and no perfect-ten supermodel, is ever going to be able to silence the noise of all that self-hatred, and all that self-doubt, if they don't man up and develop the courage to not distract themselves with the chase, and with the swiping, and with the ego boosts, and with the dopamine rushes, and to instead go inside and fill themselves up with themselves.

CONNECT WITH YOUR FEMININE, DUDE

Given the extent to which men are programmed to suppress their feminine and are deprived of feminine energetics, it's no wonder men aren't relating to women from a healthy place. It certainly doesn't help that men are deprived of affection in this culture, and that men are dissuaded from expressing emotion in this culture. Men are not given the same freedoms as women are to emote and to be forthright with their feelings.

"If you want to be emotional," my father used to say to me, "I'll give you something to be emotional about."

That was about as much emotional intelligence training as I got in my house growing up.

The system programs us to believe that emotions are a sign of weakness, especially in men, who are not only discouraged from emoting, but who are also discouraged from expressing affection. Men who exchange affection with other men are considered effeminate, and are accused of being faggots, and fairies, and flamers, and homos, and gay. The affection deprivation starts in the family, where when a boy reaches a certain age, his father stops being affectionate with him, if he ever was in the first place. This means that most boys grow up receiving affection only from their mothers. As adults, men get affection only when they are in a relationship, and then, only when they have sex, and when they have kids—for the first few years, anyway. This has men operating from elevated levels of testosterone because they aren't receiving any kind of touch or connection that would help balance them out. This has men seeking to fill their emotional needs through competition, and being right, and picking fights, and by proving how smart they are, and doing things to make their women clap for them.

It's just another one of the many blocks and distortions that keep men and women perpetually seeking outside of themselves for validation, which—as we've already established—is a zero-sum game that's getting us nowhere. The bottom line is that men and women are not communicating correctly with each other, and if we are going to survive the Blackout, this disconnect must be healed.

YOU'RE NOT A DUDE, BABE

But men are not the only ones who are disconnected from their feminine energy. Plenty of women are unconsciously posturing as men, and trying to pass themselves off as one of the guys. But women are not, in fact, any of the guys. Women are women; and men and women are very different. They are different biologically, they are different chemically, they are different hormonally, they are different psychologically, they are different neurologically, and they are different spiritually. And it's really important for humans to acknowledge these differences, and to start getting real about it.

One of the great downsides of the feminist movement was that it convinced women that the best way for them to survive in this world is to act like men. So now we have all these smart, capable women who are operating the way they think men operate, because they want to be liked, and they want to be seen, and they want to be heard, and they want to be valued, and they are programmed to believe that the only way they can experience any of these things is to take on a masculine identity, which is false. Women's greatest power, and women's greatest impact, and women's greatest influence, lie in their femininity. Women lose themselves when they buy into this dissociative masculine role-playing, which only creates blocks for them while shutting down their powers and abilities, and throwing the collective gender balance into chaos.

SEXUAL SUCCUBUS IS A THING

One last word on engaging sexually, because it's important.

When we have a lot of casual sex, and we have a lot of disconnected sex, we attract underworld entities called sexual succubi. The sexual succubus is a spirit that attaches to a person's energetic field with these suction-like appendages, and that uses them as a feeding vessel by way of all the darkness and energetic distortions they take into their being through mis-aligned sexual encounters. These succubi attach to the sexual glands while infecting the mind of the host with guilt and shame, and attracting darkness in our lower chakras, where it accumulates, thereby generating more guilt and more shame with every sexual act. These emotions, which are tools of the darkness, signal the subconscious mind to manifest disease and illness, because we feel like we should be punished.

The sexual succubus is the origin point for all sexually transmitted disease. The only reason sexual pathogens even exist on this planet is because religion teaches us that God punishes sinners, which programs people to believe that (a) God punishes; and that (b) it's actually possible for us to do something that would make us deserving of punishment—as though God is anything but perpetual, constant, ever-flowing, never-ceasing, infinite unconditional love and acceptance for each and every one of us for every single second of every single day for all eternity. Needless to say, these suppositions are false, and it is high time that we freed ourselves from their detriment once and for all.

Spirit Hack: Second Chakra Scrub

Sexual succubi are super common, what with the ubiquity of dating apps and hook-up culture, and humans' generalized cluelessness about the energetic implications of their unconscious sexual interactions. Because these underworld creatures are the source of so much discord, and so much destructive behavior, and because they are the energetic impetus for physical disease, it is very important to clear your biological space suit of any sexual succubi, or underworld spirits, on the regular.

For this spirit hack, you're going to need a smooth magnetic stone—like hematite, or pyrite, or lodestone. Make sure it's smooth, and preferably, polished. Also, some massage oil.

- Situate yourself so that you are lying down comfortably on your back, and apply a small amount of massage oil onto your pelvic/ lower stomach area.

- After you've covered the area with the massage oil, take your magnetic stone and rub it over your lower belly in gentle, even, counterclockwise circles until you feel notably lighter, and calmer, and at peace.

This process magnetically draws out the parasites, and the pathogens, and the energetic invaders, as well as the imprints they leave in the body, and in the energetic field. It can also bring tough emotions to the surface, so be very gentle with yourself as you engage this process.

COPULATE CONSCIOUSLY

If we are to come into alignment with our sexual energy, and allow it to flow, unhampered by programs, pathogens, and toxicity, we must be conscious in our sexual engaging, and we must be heart-centered in our sexual engaging. It doesn't matter if it's a fling, or a one-night stand, or a hook-up, our every sexual engaging must be devotional. Everything should be done with devotion—every kiss, every caress, every merging, all of it.

When you kiss your lover, you should kiss with devotion, as though you were kissing yourself. How do you want to be kissed by your beloved? That is how you kiss. How do you want to be touched by your beloved? That is how you touch. You honor your every lover as your beloved, just as you honor yourself as your beloved, and just as you honor Spirit as your beloved. When we love like this, we create a vibrational field so vast, and so powerful, that no sexual succubus can penetrate it. Plus, we get to experience that poprocks, giant sexual energy that makes this Earth realm so fun.

9

CONNECT SOME MORE

Connecting is not just about sharing time, space, energy, attention, and presence with our friends, and our families, and our fellow human beings. Connecting is also about sharing time, space, energy, attention, and presence with nature, and with the other life forms we share this planet with, as well as with our biological space suit. That's right. Connecting is also about dropping in with your bod. But, first things first . . .

HUMANS AREN'T THE ONLY EARTHLINGS

The majority of human beings on the planet are extremely disconnected from nature. *Extremely.* Most people know absolutely nothing about the natural species existing in their own backyards. They don't know the names of their plants, or the names of their neighborhood's plants, or the names of the trees they're driving past every single day, or the names of the insects that are living in their very own gardens. Nor do they have a clue as to what kinds of animal species share the ecosystem with them. That's some bullshit, right there. How are you going to live in the same place for an extended period of time, and share your environment with all these different types of living intelligences, and not even bother to educate yourself about any of it, let alone put in the effort to connect with it, and to commune with it?

Humans are narcissistic. We act as though we are the only Earthlings—as though we are not actually sharing the planet with eight million other living, breathing species of life. This collective self-absorption keeps humans indifferent to the well-being of their fellow Earthlings, and oblivious to the ways their actions are affecting their fellow Earthlings, as well as to how they are affecting Gaia herself.

Remember, Earth is not just a spinning rock hurtling through space. Earth is a beautiful spirit named Gaia. Gaia is conscious, and Gaia is intelligent. People are not aware of the consciousness of Earth, and people are not aware of the consciousness of nature, because we are not taught such things in our educational institutions. This is unfortunate, because humans are not only missing out on a lot of the insight, and the power, and the connection that they could be harnessing by engaging this consciousness, but they are also harming the very consciousness they are ignoring.

If humans were connected to the consciousness of the planet, there would be no more mining. There would be no more clear-cutting of forests, or of sacred jungles. Nor would the ocean be riddled with single-use plastics, which wouldn't exist anymore, either. Humans would not be able to inflict such harm upon their home planet if they understood that Earth is an intelligent being who feels the effects of the rape and the plunder we continue to perpetrate upon her by way of our greed and our reckless consumption. The truth is that every time we disrespect the planet, we are disrespecting Gaia herself. Given that Gaia exists to give, and give, and give, and give, and give so that we, and every being on this planet, can survive and thrive upon her surface, it's just good manners not to shit all over her.

That Time I Learned to Trust Nature

When I was younger, my guides encouraged me to study with a shaman friend of mine to help build my connection to spirit. One day he and a group of elders took me high up into the mountains near Lake Tahoe. They blindfolded me and led me deep, deep, deep into the forest. I walked for a very long time, with an elder on each side, guiding me by the elbow, telling me when to step over a root, or around a rock, or to duck under a branch. At a certain point, we stopped walking. The men set a timer, and told me to remove the blindfold when the alarm sounded, and that I had until sundown to make my way back to wherever they were.

"Use your resources," the elders instructed as they left the forest, and their voices got farther and farther away; and I stood blindfolded, wondering where the hell they'd taken me. "Trust in spirit. Trust in nature."

I was in the middle of the Sierra Nevadas, surrounded by nothing but trees, and rocks, and shrubs, and dirt, and sky. I had no idea where I was, no idea which direction I'd come from, and no idea how to get myself out of there.

The first thing I did was look for signs from spirit—like a stick, or a stone, or a marking etched into the bark of a tree—basically any kind of symbol I could connect with and use as a bread crumb to get myself out of there. But there were no signs, and there were no symbols, and there were no bread crumbs, and there wasn't actually anything there at all to help me get out of that forest. Or, so I thought.

I paused, and I remembered the elders' instructions to use my resources, and to trust in spirit, and to trust in nature. I prayed to the nature spirits and asked them to help me find my way to my friends. A couple minutes later, a beautiful bird with bright blue wings and a yellow beak flew onto a branch in a nearby tree, and started chirping loudly.

"Are you here for me, bird?" I asked, at which point, the bird flew to the branch directly above my head, and chirped again.

That's when I realized that the bird was actually a spirit who had come to help me find my way back to the elders. I followed the bird as it flew to a nearby tree, and I continued to follow it as it flew from tree, to tree, to tree, to tree. There were moments when doubt overcame me, and I would stop, and wonder if I was going in the wrong direction. And then the bird would chirp, and chirp, and chirp until I started walking in the direction it was flying again. And then, just before the sun dropped down behind the mountains, that bird led me straight to the elders—like, directly to them.

That experience really helped deepen my connection to the spirit world, and to the elements. It allowed me to detach from the idea of having to depend on other humans, because it showed me that I can trust in nature, and that I can trust in spirit. I now trust spirit and nature way more than I trust humans. Not that I have anything against humans; it's just that we're so complicated. Nature doesn't say one thing when it means another thing, because of insecurities and personality defects. Nature just offers facts and information. It's very simple that way. People, not so much.

NATURE KNOWS SOME SHIT

Because shamans are aware of the life in everything, and of the intelligence in everything, we engage that life and that intelligence whenever we get a chance. Nature is such a powerful teacher, and such a powerful ally. So when the wind blows across my skin, I receive the gust like a tap on the back from a friend.

"Hey, wind," I'll say. "What's going on? Got anything to share with me?"

I always ask the wind if it has any information to share with me, because the wind carries all our thoughts, which means the wind knows what everyone is thinking, and dreaming, and worrying about. But most people feel the wind blowing across their face, and they're just annoyed with it for messing up their hairdo.

Nature has so much wisdom and knowledge to share with us, if we would just get present and be still with it. Like, it's really not that complicated. You don't even need spirit hacks or shamanic techniques; you just need to be in nature, and to not talk, and not be on your phone, and not multitask, and not check out, and just be fully and completely present with nature. But getting people to be fully and completely present is a whole other thing, so it's good to have the spirit hacks.

I once took a trip with some friends to visit this little beach in Turkey. While my friends were talking about how lovely it must have been to live there back when it was a thriving village, I picked up a stone and allowed myself to be fully present with it. That stone showed me the Ottoman soldiers sailing into the harbor in full body armor, and it showed me the blood pouring into the sea. My friends couldn't believe that anything so violent could have occurred in such a peaceful setting. So we asked the tour guide, and she said that I was spot-on, and that there was indeed a very bloody battle that took place on that beach. So, that stone knew some shit.

Trees, as well. Big-time. Trees are pretty much overflowing with wisdom. I once had a redwood tree show me the memories it had stored in its rings, and I saw all the people who had passed by it throughout the decades. Trees remember everything. Then the tree asked me to bury some quartz crystals in the soil near its roots to help amplify its power, and its strength. Of course, I came back the very next day with a bunch of crystals for the tree. Trees are badass. They can weave their energy in with our own human energy fields, and direct powerful healing frequencies into our bodies. I've always had great respect for trees. If humans would just take the time to listen to the trees, and to commune with the trees, we could adapt and grow so much more quickly as a species. There are so many things the trees have to share with us, but humans can't access the trees' vast storehouse of knowledge until we learn to log in to them.

Spirit Hack: Log in to Nature

Most people have no idea how much wisdom, knowledge, power, and healing nature has to share with them, because most people spend more time logging on to their smartphones and their social media feeds than they do logging in to nature.

Logging in to nature activates our connection with the nature spirits, and opens up our channel of communication with the elemental kingdom. Ideally, you want to do this spirit hack while you're in nature, to get deeper access. Because, when you're in front of a tree, and you log in to nature, you can actually pull tree energy into your body. Same if you are invoking earth energy while you're lying on the grass, or mineral energy when you're lying on the dirt. But you can do this spirit hack anywhere and still tap into the energy frequency of whichever aspect of nature you're choosing to connect with; it's just way more powerful when you're in nature.

- Hold your finger in the air in front of the tree, or the flower, or the ocean if you're out in nature. If you're in your apartment, or in line at the DMV, that's fine; just put your finger in front of your face.

- Draw a square in the air, exhaling sharply with each stroke.

- Next, draw a triangle in the center of the square, again exhaling sharply with each stroke.

In shamanism, we use the square to establish a structure for our spirit hacks. The triangle represents the energetic trifecta of love, wisdom, and power and functions as a high vibrational antenna of intelligence for knowledge and information to travel through.

- Say: "Activate. Log in to nature, so I can feel it in my body."

- When you feel the energy shift, you know you're logged in. If you don't feel anything, say: "Increase nature in my body, so I can feel it."

Now that you're logged in to nature, you can engage nature however you want. You can ask questions, or request a healing, or what have you. If you're in an urban environment, you'll want to add another step to this spirit hack and invoke, or call upon, the elemental spirits to collaborate with you.

Invoking the Elementals

- Say: "Restore elementals."

In doing so, you invite the spirits of the elements to tap into the frequencies of the elements in your body—the earth that is your bones, the air that is your breath, the water that is your blood, and the fire that is your muscles.

- Once the elementals have been invoked, you can direct these powerful healing helpers however you want.

You can say: "Elementals, restore and repair my body."

Or: "Elementals, align my body structurally."

Or, even: "Elementals, heal whatever part of my body needs it the most, so I can feel it."

It's a good idea to add ". . . so I can feel it" to all kinesthetic spirit commands, especially when you are first starting your shamanic training.

The elementals are great at restoring and repairing, so you can ask them to help heal your sprained ankle, or to fire up your digestive system, or to boost the collagen in your face and neck. But even just invoking the elementals, and inviting them into your field without giving them a bunch of tasks to do, will calm your nervous system and help level out your moods, and synchronize your heart rate with the vibrational frequency of the planet, which allows your body to heal and rebalance itself.

GET GROUNDED

A lot of people spend the majority of their lives in their heads. They are consumed with thoughts, and ideas, and concepts, and noise; and they are completely disconnected from their bodies, and their environment, and Earth beneath their feet. People are ungrounded.

Being ungrounded makes us more susceptible to the influence of external sounds, movement, activity, and frequencies, which can create a cacophony of disruptive input that overwhelms the body and the being. This surge of incoming data distorts the brain's functioning so that it becomes fragmented, and has to juggle multiple distractions at once, in addition to whatever it's actually trying to deal with—like making your leg move, or regulating your heartbeat, or whatever.

It's very easy to get ungrounded when we are so disconnected from nature. Grounding is really as simple as putting our feet in the dirt, or jumping in a lake, or lying on the grass. When we connect with nature, we ground. But not everyone has access to grass, or dirt, or lakes 24-7, which means we must make grounding a practice.

Spirit Hack: Get Grounded

Grounding is a fundamental spirit hack you want to get in the habit of doing at least every day. You definitely always want to ground before leaving the house in the morning. It's also good to ground before you go into a crowded public place, or anywhere you know where there is going to be a lot of different kinds of input or stimuli. Or if you're going to engage a challenging personality, or you know you have to have a tough conversation, grounding will support you in holding your center, so you're not giving your power away to emotional triggers.

- Stand up straight and visualize a stack of electric aqua-blue circles—like rings—around your body. The more circles you envision around you, the more grounded you will feel.

- Now, you want to turn the circles on. Say: "I activate circle one. Circle one, ground me into Earth."

- Repeat the process for circle two, and circle three, and for all your circles.

- After you've activated all the circles around your body, envision the same electric aqua-blue circles as rings stacked above your head.

- Now, turn on the circles. Say: "I activate circle one. Circle one, lift me out of the maya."

- Repeat the process for all the circles you have stacked above your head.

- Now that your circles are activated, you want to link them up. Say: "Create an energy surge connecting me from heaven to Earth, so that I can feel it in my body."

It is just as important to ground into the heavens as it is to ground into Earth. By connecting heaven and Earth through your body, you create a clear, deliberate channel, stretching between these two polarities. The act of grounding through both of these gateways generates feelings of security, eliminates distraction, and sets a high, strong focal point for your mind.

The more grounded we are, the easier it is for the body to regulate itself, because it's not distracted trying to catalog a bunch of extraneous input. When the body is grounded, it generates an energy frequency that optimizes communication among our cells, our organs, and our brain, which allows the system to function much more efficiently.

When we are not grounded, we're scattered. Our energy whizzes all over the place. It's not organized, and it's not contained, and it creates chaos and energetic disturbances in the environment. To this end, the matrix loves an ungrounded populace, because an ungrounded populace generates a whole bunch of discord for the darkness.

URBAN DISCORD BY DESIGN

The system designs our cities to generate discord by laying out more buildings and more infrastructure than nature. Our urban enclaves are extremely imbalanced. The planet is animated by elemental spirits—by fire spirits, and water spirits, and earth spirits, and air spirits. There are no concrete spirits, and there are no fluorescent light spirits, and there are no EMF spirits, and there are no BPA spirits. This misalignment in our environment—where the man-made particles, and pollutants, and structures are not being harmonized by enough trees, and parks, and plants, and butterflies—is taking an extreme toll on people's health. This is why so many people are dealing with adrenal fatigue, and thyroid issues, and digestive problems: the biological space suit isn't recognizing its environment, and the biological space suit is so starved for nature, it is functioning in a near constant state of low-grade panic, which manifests as an increasing number of health problems.

Spirit Hack: Shamanizing Urban Energy Disturbances

My shamanic work takes me all over the world—to lush, quiet villages nestled in beautiful natural settings, and to big, bustling metropolitan cities that are awash in lines, and boxes, and concrete, and noise, and toxicity, and pollution, and discord. I might be a powerful shaman, with a massive spirit force in my corner, but I'd be lying if I said that cities don't take their toll on me.

This is a technique African shamans use to clear negative energy. I find this spirit hack really, really helpful when I'm in an urban environment and I'm feeling bombarded by a lot of stimulation, a lot of sensory input, and a lot of toxicity. This spirit hack breaks up energy disturbances and prevents them from accumulating in the body.

- To clear any negative energies in your environment, or your bio-logical space suit, clap your hands in counterclockwise circles about six inches in front of your chest. Five to ten circles should do the trick.

- If the energy disturbances are more acute, and are lodged in your body, clap your hands over the area where you feel the distur-bance, like the head, the heart, the throat, or the stomach.

You can use this spirit hack anywhere, any time you feel yourself af-fected by negative energy, or any time you feel energy disturbances in your body—like after you have an intense conversation and you feel a lot of heat or tingling in your chest and throat. This is the hack you want to use to clear that.

I taught this spirit hack to a friend of mine who works in a correctional facility. She used to come home feeling like she'd been flattened by a Mack truck, she was so drained. She loves this spirit hack and uses it all day to clear energetic disturbances, which are plenty, given her work-ing environment. Now she comes home feeling strong, energized, and up-lifted. She loves this spirit hack so much, she taught it to her coworkers, and now they all use it to keep their energy clean and clear.

SYNTHESIS

Most people don't even realize how disconnected they are from nature because most people's synthesis is out of whack. I see it all the time— the bobbleheads stumbling around their environment in these spazzy, discordant, fragmented states, clueless as to the quantity of input they're not registering, because their sensory mechanisms are not communicating properly with one another.

Energy communicates through synthesis. When our synthesis is strong, we feel energy. You know when you get scared, and you feel chills running up the back of your neck? That's synthesis. Those chills are an expression of your intuition, which is your spiritual body communicating a potential threat to your emotional body, which communicates fear to the physical body, which manifests through goose bumps, which alert you—the connected whole—to the situation at hand. Those chills are a function of strong synthesis.

Most people's synthesis is weak. When synthesis hasn't been developed or cultivated, or when the synthesis has been deliberately taken off-line by the darkness, the spiritual body can't communicate with the mental body, which can't communicate with the emotional body, which can't communicate with the physical body. The physical body therefore becomes this dense, numb shell, shuffling an empty, unfeeling robot around a planet they're barely engaging, or even really aware of.

NEGATIVE ENERGIES TRICOLORÉ

There are three types of negative energy frequencies I clear from people's fields. There is the black sludge, which is the darkness we take in when we accept words, or thoughts, or images, or ideas into our being that are contrary to truth, and to love. There is the red energy frequency, which glows like neon light. The red energy is all the anger people hold on to, and stuff down into their musculature, which causes inflammation in the body. And then there's the green gas. The green gas is the energy the darkness uses to shut down people's synthesis and sever their connection to the spirit realm. This green gas is what allows humans to give up their sovereignty, and to be turned into zombies taking commands from the darkness, and playing out the system's propaganda. They don't realize that their piousness, and their righteousness, and their refusal to consider other points of view are all side effects from this gooey, green underworld toxin that's distorting their system, and shutting down their synthesis.

Spirit Hack: Synthesize!

In order to turn on your synthesis, you have to clean out all that green gas, and all the effluvia, and the other negative energy frequencies that people like to hold on to. This spirit hack cleans that shit out.

- With your feet planted firmly on the ground, take a strong stance. You want to do this spirit hack standing up, so that you can practice being very present with your energy.

- Say: "Force fields up."

This command activates your conscious energetic field and directs it to project itself around you.

- Then, say: "Force field, utilize yellow electricity to create a powerful source of unconditional love to go into my brain, and to go into my body, and to connect with any energies that I am holding on to that are creating any blockages in my synthesis, and release those blockages out of my mouth and throat, through deep yawn, or deep cough."

- After you say these words, attune your attention to your breath. When you feel sensation starting to emerge in your throat—like, you feel heat, or tickling, or irritation, or throbbing—speak your sensations aloud. So, you would say: "I feel tickling in my throat," if, in fact, that was the sensation you were feeling.

At this point, you will probably cough a lot, or you will probably yawn a lot, and you might even burp (a little, or a lot) as your body expels the energies from your system. This is a good thing.

- Then ask Spirit to increase the sensations by saying, "Increase yellow electricity."

The yellow electricity functions to purify your energetic body through the synthesis of light frequencies and emittent tones, which combine to decongest dense, negative, low-vibrational frequencies.

Continue to increase the yellow electricity, and continue to speak your sensations aloud, and continue to release the energies out of your mouth and throat. The more you allow yourself to release, the stronger your body will grow, and the stronger your synthesis will grow, and the stronger your spiritual powers will grow.

Synthesis is a big deal. The human vessel is a complex, multidimensional system comprised of a mental body, a physical body, an emotional body, and a spirit body. For a being to thrive, all four pillars must be healthy, and all four pillars must be free from blockages, and all four pillars must be able to communicate clearly with one another at all times. But if those four bodies are not hooked up, and if those four spirits cannot connect with one another and share a conversation, that's when wires get crossed, and that's when communication breaks down, and that's when disease presents itself in the body.

DIS-EASE

Disease simply means *lack of ease* in the body. Dis-*ease*. It means imbalance has arisen and that there is a disruption in the system's usual functioning. Disease can manifest as illness, injury, discomfort, disorder, disturbance, what have you. Shamans treat disease very differently from the way Western doctors do. Doctors pathologize these manifestations and curse their patients by giving these manifestations names, and then declaring war on these manifestations.

Western doctors are trained in the allopathic medical model, wherein they catalog their patients' symptoms, lump them in a box, and then give the box a name that identifies the symptoms as a virus, or a disease, or an -*itis*, or an -*osis*, or whatever, which is then attacked, irradiated, or cut out. The thing is: the boxes aren't real. The boxes are made up by the system to homogenize people's symptoms so that they can be more easily standardized, and profited from.

The Western medical paradigm is archaic because it is still operating under the false belief that the physical body is its own autonomous entity that is neither influenced by, nor affected by, the emotional body, the mental body, or the spiritual body. The allopathic doctor is basically a dinosaur who treats the body like it's an island. This perspective is shortsighted, reductive, and incorrect. And because of it, instead of seeking to understand the symptoms as the body's primary means of communication, and then deciphering what those symptoms are indicating by considering them as parts of an integrated whole, Western doctors go about attacking the symptoms with aggressive languaging, like *beat* and *fight,* and with even more aggressive methods, which aim to kill, quell, silence, remove, or obliterate the symptoms. It's archaic, and it's reckless, and it's just another way our society's overemphasis on the masculine is messing shit up.

DOCTORS FIGHT. SHAMANS USE DIPLOMACY.

Shamans see physiological symptoms as indications of a deeper imbalance in the spiritual, emotional, and mental bodies. We see symptoms as invitations to take a journey into the unknown. We see symptoms as pieces of a puzzle, and as a call to go on discovery to find the original source of the imbalance. Only after we determine the root of the imbalance do shamans intercede to help restore harmony to the system as guided.

For example, let's say a woman comes to see me because she is having pain in her ovaries. I don't have to even see her to know that the problem isn't her ovaries. The pain in her ovaries, from a shaman's point of view, is her emotional body tugging at her sleeve, trying to get her attention. That is the purpose of physical symptoms—to alert us to an internal imbalance, which is always some kind of communication breakdown between the emotional body, the mental body, and the spiritual body. Pain means we are not in synthesis. Therefore, the way to correct my client's dysfunction is not

257

to attack the ovaries, or to fight against the discomfort that is manifesting through the ovaries, or to numb the discomfort that is manifesting through the ovaries. The way to correct the dysfunction is to decipher what inspired the malfunction in the first place.

This is why it is so important that our synthesis is strong, because the only way to get that kind of information is from her spirit. The spirit is the aspect that is minding the whole system in all its multidimensional complexity. The spirit is the aspect that has the ability to sync up all the disparate parts, and to facilitate clear communication among them. When our synthesis is on point, the spirit can speak freely with the mind, which can transmit the information to the emotions, which the emotions can transmit to the body, which is how healing takes place, and how my client's ovaries stop hurting.

IT'S ALL ABOUT THE ROOT

Allopathic doctors consider only a very narrow array of factors when it comes to the causes they attribute to disease. Like, they blame most cancer on genes. But just because genetic codes are passed down doesn't mean they have to be activated. We all carry lots of ancestral coding that never gets activated in our lifetimes. Genetic codes are activated by certain markers like emotional stress, emotional toxicity, environmental pollution, mental pollution, mental discord, etc. These markers are what cause the cells to morph and are what create the toxic internal environments in which these cells can multiply, turn into tumors, and grow, and grow, and grow, and grow. It doesn't matter what kind of hyper-extra-über-super-strength allopathic cancer killer you attack that tumor with, if you don't shift the internal environment; and the only way to shift the internal environment is to adjust the markers, and to address the root.

From a shamanic perspective, the root can be anything, including the words people tell themselves, the house they live in, or the people they hang out with. It could be their job, their partner, or their tendency to people-please and give their power away. Or it could be that they hate their life, and they hate themselves, but because they can't be honest about it, they create disease, because they don't want to be here anymore.

This is actually really common—that people get sick as a quick fix, and an easy way out of this reality construct. People would rather get sick than admit the truth, which is: *I don't really want to be alive.* The conscious mind can't process this level of truth, just as most human beings can't handle hearing this level of truth coming out of the mouth of a friend or a family member, so the conscious mind denies the truth while the subconscious mind turns it into an incurable disease.

When I go to hospitals and I work with people who have cancer, the first question I always ask is: "Why do you want this cancer?" That upsets some people. Kids, however, are not burdened by these kinds of hang-ups. When I work with children, and I ask them why they want their cancer, they tell me straight up: "Because I don't want to be here anymore."

PAIN

Western medicine is all about eradicating pain and discomfort by any means necessary. Western doctors don't understand pain. They don't understand the purpose of pain, and they don't understand how to deal with pain, so they just do that hyperaggressive masculine thing, where they attack the pain, or they obliterate the pain, or they numb the pain, much to their patients' detriment.

Pain is the body's way of communicating that there is an imbalance of energy in the body. The body has probably been trying to communicate the imbalance for a while in softer, subtler ways. But because most people's synthesis is weak, they are not able to perceive the body's signals, which means that the body has to communicate louder, and louder, and louder just to get their attention. That's when the body starts bringing pain into the mix, so that it can finally get you to stop ignoring it.

Western medicine denounces pain like it's a bad thing. When pain presents itself, doctors immediately try to numb the pain, or to eradicate the pain, or to cut out the pain, as quickly as possible. This is not the right approach to pain, because pain has valuable information to communicate. When we rush to get rid of pain, we miss the message the pain is trying to share with us. When most people have a headache, they take an aspirin, which gives them temporary relief by numbing the pain, so they can get on with their daily lives. In a million years, you couldn't pay me to take an aspirin when I have a headache, because I know that pain has something to tell me.

Spirit Hack: Sound Your Pain

Dialysis was excruciating. It wasn't just the actual dialysis treatment itself that was so painful; it was the angioplasty. Angioplasty is this procedure that involves cutting your arm open. People who are on dialysis have this procedure done every two weeks. I was on dialysis for eight years, so you can do the math to get an idea of how many times they cut into my arm. Because of all the angioplasty, I had multiple aneurysms and almost had my arm amputated.

While I was on dialysis, I used to experience this intense full-body cramping—like, the way someone might get a cramp in their leg, or their foot. But I would get them in my face, and in my neck, and in my fingers, and in my toes, and everywhere, all at once. The only way to get rid of cramps is to drink water, but I couldn't drink any water while I was having the treatment, so all I could do was scream it out, or let the pain take over my whole being until I passed out completely.

That's how I learned that all pain is trapped sound. Every pain you feel has its own corresponding sound. The way to relieve pain when it arises is to focus your full attention upon it and to let its own particular sound move through you. It is no use trying to control the sound, and it's no use concerning yourself with how the sound actually sounds. You just want to let that sound move freely, for as long as that sound wants to move.

NUMB THYSELF

The matrix doesn't want humans engaging our pain, or learning from our pain, or transmuting our pain, because that kind of empowerment doesn't drive the system. The system profits from our pain, which is why the system encourages us to dull our pain, and to ignore our pain, so that our pain will accumulate, and our pain will turn into suffering, and our pain will create long-term illness in our bodies, which will translate into profit for the pharmaceutical companies, and fuel for the darkness.

So the system created all these tools to help people run away from their pain—things like sugar, and cigarettes, and reality television, and caffeine, and opiates, and hook-up apps, and web porn, and alcohol. It doesn't matter which kind of medicine people are using to quell the pain; the pain is not being engaged, which means the pain is going to accumulate. A hundred percent.

ALCOHOL

Alcohol is unique because alcohol is a socially acceptable intoxicant. Alcohol is medicine that's allowed—medicine that comes along with the culturally sanctioned permission to check out.

Alcohol is an agent of the darkness. It allows people to disconnect from the matrix for just a moment. It's a breather—a way for people to let down their inhibitions, and to let down their guard, and to say things they wouldn't have the courage to say when they are sober. It's like this momentary relief from the pressure and the tension of the system that allows people to open themselves up in ways they feel like they can't when they are in the grips of the matrix. It also allows people to not have to take responsibility for their behavior, because they can just say they were drunk, and everyone gives them a pass.

But alcohol opens us up to random spirits, who joyride on our buzzes and our highs. That's why they call alcohol *spirits*, because it opens up our vessels to the beings who can't cross all the way over, which creates a whole, big bunch of discord.

I know a lot of shamans who work with plant medicines and who connect with the value of all kinds of intoxicating plants and beings—leaves, roots, fungi, herbs, amphibians, what have you. They use tobacco as a binder in ceremony. They mix specific roots with specific vines to tap into other dimensions of consciousness. They milk the sacred frog for its purifying poisons. They use all kinds of medicines found in nature. But they will not touch alcohol. Alcohol is the one intoxicant that so many shamans hold a hard line on not partaking in, because alcohol blocks our synthesis, and alcohol numbs us out, which is precisely why the system normalizes alcohol and glamorizes alcohol to the extent that it does.

BIG FAT PHARMA

Western doctors treat every illness, and every imbalance, and every disease exactly the same. They do a cursory overview of the physical body, diagnose a handful of physical symptoms, and then hand you a prescription for a bunch of pills that will temporarily mask your symptoms while stressing out your liver, and doing nothing to restore overall balance to the body.

Pharmaceuticals are created by the same shortsightedness that has doctors treating the body like it's an island. These scientists think they can take certain compounds out of a plant and synthesize them with chemicals in a petri dish in a laboratory, and not go creating bigger, long-term problems for the people who are taking these things. I mean, the arrogance is absurd.

Over half of the entire U.S. population is taking some kind of pharmaceutical drug to numb their pain. The pharmaceutical companies are the true drug dealers of the world. They really are. The only difference between a pharmaceutical rep and a dealer selling on the street is a fancy coat, and a spin job.

Doctors supplement their regular incomes with the kickbacks they get for the prescriptions they write. So when a doctor prescribes chemotherapy for a patient who's been indoctrinated into the cancer box, it might be because the doctor thinks chemotherapy will help (despite the dismal success rates), or it might be because it's going to get him a huge check from the company that manufactures the chemotherapy medicine, and the doctor stands to make a cool million a year off the patient, assuming he lasts that long. This is how the darkness has infected our health care system.

I work with a lot of doctors, and surgeons, and psychologists, and psychiatrists who are fed up. They have patients coming to see them because they are in pain, and because they are suffering; and these doctors want to understand why their treatments aren't helping, and why their patients aren't getting better. They want to know why their patient still has bipolar disorder, or why their patient is still having seizures. They are confused because they went to school for so many years, and they studied so many things, and still, their efforts are not working. They feel that they are not really accomplishing anything other than facilitating addictions to pills that don't actually heal their patients but that activate all sorts of other issues. These people come to me as a shaman because they feel like they don't have the tools they need to really help restore their patients' health. They are just alleviating symptoms in the short term, but they're not really facilitating long-term health or well-being, and they know it, and it makes them feel like shit.

Look, I don't mean to deride the entire Western medical world. The allopathic medical paradigm has its benefits and serves many valuable purposes. After I died, my kidneys were extremely compromised, and it wasn't like I could just shake a rattle and make some offerings to the kidney spirits, and tell the elementals to make it all better. Dialysis saved my life, along with dozens of operations, and procedures, and medications that Western medicine gifted this culture, including a kidney transplant. So I am very much a fan of Western medicine. I'm just disappointed in the Western medical world, because by refusing to consider the body as a whole, and by treating the body as a collection of separate, unrelated components, it is doing the people it's supposed to be helping a great disservice, and causing a lot of suffering in the process.

But let's be very clear: if your left arm starts tingling, and you start foaming at the mouth while the world gets fuzzy and hollow-sounding, get your ass to a doctor. Western medicine might not be perfect, but it definitely has its place.

DO NOT FUCK WITH THE NATURE CODES

As the Blackout continues to escalate, we are seeing people manifesting all kinds of allergies and all kinds of health issues that the species hasn't dealt with on this scale before—things like autism, ADD, Alzheimer's, candida, cancer, plus a whole bunch of mystery syndromes and illnesses that Western medicine doesn't even have names for. When I was a kid, food allergies were pretty rare. These days, half the people in any restaurant at any given time are allergic to half the things on the menu, like lactose, and gluten, and sugar, and soy, and nightshades, and what have you. All because, for some reason, our species feels the need to fuck with shit.

Genetic tinkering is straight-up arrogant, ignorant idiocy. There's really no way around it. When humans genetically modify food, and crops, and people, they are creating genetic markers that differ from nature's original design, and from nature's own coding system. Nature knows its own codes, because nature is intelligent technology—technology that humans really need to stop fucking with.

When we genetically modify anything, we change the atoms, we change the molecules, and we obliterate the synthesis. If I try to eat a genetically modified strawberry, the second that strawberry hits my tongue, my body is going to be confused.

What the fuck is this? the body asks. *This isn't the networking system that's supposed to go with my networking system.*

The berry's coding is off. The frequencies of the body's digestive enzymes are no longer a coherent match for the frequencies of the sugars in the fruit, which are no longer alchemically proportional with the fiber content. And so, because the body doesn't recognize this hodgepodged configuration of data and input, the networking systems don't boot up together. This creates all kinds of problems for the various processing systems, which aren't designed to handle these patterns of information, and this is how things get really out of whack.

Trans, Too

This applies to people who undergo gender reassignment surgery and are genetically modifying their bodies, as well. Like, of course it's fine if someone wants to medically transition to another gender, if that's what they're authentically called to do. It's great. But when people take pills to block their bodies' natural hormonal secretions, and then take more pills to stimulate completely different hormonal secretions, they are pulling in a whole bunch of very different energies that their system was not organically designed to be running.

People have to acknowledge this. And people have to learn how to work with these energies, and how to manage these energies, because people are forcing their bodies to function in ways their bodies were not actually designed to function. Being trans isn't about what kind of pronoun you choose to label yourself with, and get all huffy about; it's about learning to run very different polarity frequencies, and figuring out how to alchemize that energy in a way that works for you.

I REPEAT, DO NOT FUCK WITH THE NATURE CODES

It's really arrogant of humans to allege that they know better than God about how to design fruit, or rice, or chickens, or what have you. It's like saying *God got it wrong, and God didn't know what God was doing; but luckily we humans are here to fix God's mistakes with our almighty science.* It's also really shortsighted, because scientists have no idea what kind of long-term effects their tinkering is going to manifest. But I can promise you, those long-terms effects *will* manifest. When man takes it upon himself to change the nature codes when the nature codes have not themselves determined that it is necessary for them to change, then man is creating problems on the planet. They may take time to unfold, but trust me, they will unfold. You don't fuck with the nature codes.

From a shamanic perspective, the elemental kingdom is fine the way it is. If the elemental kingdom wanted to genetically modify itself, then the elemental kingdom would change its genetic structure of its own accord; but it doesn't, so it hasn't. Consumerism is driving genetic modification. Consumption is driving genetic modification. Genetic modification is about mass production, and mass consumption, and a hefty hunger for profit—that bigger tomato, that brighter tomato, that sweeter tomato, that rounder tomato—*boom!* That's more money for the agricultural corporations, which just so happen to be owned by the pharmaceutical corporations. Go figure.

A Side Note to Western Doctors Who Think Shamanism Is Woo-Woo Bullshit

I get really tired of Western doctors invalidating shamanism, and spirituality, and all these other things they haven't researched, haven't experienced, and don't understand. Aside from being reductive and wrong, it's extremely arrogant, considering that modern medicine wouldn't even exist if it weren't for the shamans, and the alchemists, and the mystics who preceded them.

So what I want to say is this: shut up, doctors. You know about your compartmentalized world of allopathic medicine, so why don't you just stick to that? Because you definitely don't know anything about spirituality, and you definitely don't know anything about the spirit world. So I don't want to hear your comments, or your opinions, or your ideas about the spirit world, until you do your own due diligence, and you embark upon your own discovery, and your own hypothesis, to come to an intelligent, informed conclusion. But if you don't do discovery, and you don't delve into these worlds to figure out what's what for yourself, then your conclusion that the spirit world is "woo-woo" and is "bullshit"—as well as all the other uninformed opinions falling out of your mouth—are simply closed-minded ignorance. And you need to acknowledge that, and shut your face hole, and stick to being a doctor. You stay in your world, and I'll stay in mine. If you want to leave your ignorance at the door, and come together to create a container, and explore a conversation, and an understanding so that we can share our knowledge to serve humanity, while respecting each other's realms of study and expertise, I'm game. If not, step off.

An uneducated person believes that the world is exactly as they perceive it, because they are ignorant. An educated person knows that there are many doorways, and that even if they haven't explored those doorways, and even if they can't perceive those doorways, those doorways still exist. An educated person doesn't shut down access to those doorways by condemning them as nonsense, and invalidating their existence just because they're not familiar with them.

PART III

THE GIANT AGE

10

RIDING THE LIT TRAIN

When I talk about the Blackout, some people get anxious, and apocalyptic, and spin out into this *It's too late, we ruined it* kind of doom-and-gloom thing. It's so funny when humans are like that—drama, drama, drama. You can choose to see it that way, sure, if you want to make yourself miserable and afraid, and if you want to create a doom-and-gloom reality that's already ruined. But given that the future is forged of the thoughts, dreams, visions, and desires every one of us is cultivating today, I really don't recommend it.

Here's the thing: it isn't ruined, and it isn't too late. That's just something people say to avoid taking responsibility for their lives and for the world, and to avoid making changes and being inconvenienced. The Blackout is an opportunity. It is an opportunity for us to level-up, and for us to experience a collective quantum leap by aligning the consciousness of the species with a higher intelligence. It is an opportunity to evolve the ways we engage and relate with one another, and with all life on this planet; and it is an opportunity to evolve our societal structures, and to create a new system that supports all beings in thriving, instead of just surviving. The Blackout is an opportunity for us to dream greater, and to use our powers as quantum creators to forge something new, and something giant—something that supports a poprocks planetary existence for all.

Actualizing the Giant Age: A Three-Step Shamanic Process

To actualize a Giant Age here on Earth, we must breathe into that concept as a reality.

1. BREATHE INTO THAT CONCEPT AS A REALITY.

The Giant Age is not an *if*, and the Giant Age is not a wish, and the Giant Age is not a hope. The Giant Age is a reality. Got it?

2. TAKE RESPONSIBILITY.

This means getting conscious, and getting real with ourselves about how we are operating as individuals, and how we are contributing to the world's challenges; and then making the necessary adjustments within ourselves in service to humanity and to the planet.

3. LEAD.

It is not enough for us to lift and shift only for ourselves. For us to turn this spaceship around, and welcome a Giant Age of peace, prosperity, health, and well-being for all, we must accept our roles as lit leaders of love, and help our brothers and sisters to lift and shift themselves.

FROM SURVIVING TO THRIVING

Thriving happens when we are held by a structure that supports us in living a balanced, healthy, juicy life, which includes time with friends, and time to ourselves and with our creativity, and time with our bodies and our sexuality, and time to learn new things—be it a language, or a musical instrument, or what have you. Thriving means our lifestyle affords us time and resources to devote to our purpose, and to create financial success, and to support the global community by serving causes that lighten humanity's load, as well as the planet's load. Thriving is day-to-day fulfillment, and balance, and well-being; and thriving is our birthright. And on this planet, in this moment, thriving is extremely rare.

As of now, and for most people, Earth is a prison planet, where we are born into slavery to drive a system that tells us we have to work to survive. This program has the vast majority of the populace trapped in survival mode, where their lives are driven by the hustle for basic needs, and the struggle to stay afloat. This lifestyle is what keeps humans vibrating at the frequencies of stress, tension, depression, and worry.

This is why people have bucket lists. Because their lives are filled with so many compromises, and so many have-tos, that they pinpoint a handful of meaningful experiences to squeeze in before they die so that their whole existence isn't a wash. As though sprinkling some sightseeing on top of a life spent in survival mode is going to make it poprocks.

The system is set up to keep us in survival mode because survival consciousness feeds the darkness. At its fundamental core, survival consciousness is scarcity consciousness. It is lack. When we are in survival mode, we are lacking in those areas that would otherwise constitute our thriving, because we are sacrificing them for the hustle.

ALIGNMENT VERSUS HUSTLE

A lot of motivational speakers and personal development gurus really want to sell you on the hustle. They're really amped, and they're really pumped, and they're really tan; and they all want you to know that if you want to be rich, and if you want to be successful, and if you want good-looking people to want to fuck you, then you gotta hustle, and you gotta hustle, and you gotta hustle some more. The thing is, you don't.

If we are hustling, that means we are not trusting that the universe has us. Hustling is a way that humans use to try to control reality to make ourselves feel safe, and to get what we think we need to survive. But because we are not actually smarter than God, and because we can't actually control shit, hustling doesn't actually lead us toward our highest, most amazing lives. It just narrows our options and burns out our adrenals.

When we are hustling, we are allowing fear to motivate us. We are using fear as an energy source to fuel our actions. Not only that, but when we are hustling, we are operating with an agenda, which means that our interactions with others are out of integrity. We are not connecting with people because we are authentically drawn to connect with them, and to authentically allow the natural alchemy of our energies to guide our interaction; we are "connecting" with them because we want something.

People hustle to make money, and they hustle for material things, and they hustle for power or social status. The point is, none of these things brings true fulfillment. They might bring temporary pleasure, or temporary satisfaction, but those feelings will inevitably be followed by long-term dissatisfaction, because the accomplishments were achieved through fear-based efforts, which means they were misaligned from the get-go. Only the progress we make when we are operating from alignment will lead us to sustainable fulfillment, and sustainable success.

The Giant Age is about alignment over hustle. Talk about a quantum leap in human functioning! When we are in alignment, we are operating in vibrational harmony with who we are, and what we are doing, and where we are going, which makes it easy for spirit to connect us with the people who are meant to help us move forward in our lives. When we are in alignment, our frequencies vibrate in such a way as to organically magnetize to us the people we are meant to meet, and the situations we are meant to meet them in.

When we're riding the lit train, we don't hustle. We simply align. We align, and we ground into ourselves, and our intention, and our purpose, and we trust that Spirit will connect us with the right people at the right time. The key to getting in alignment is staying in our heart centers, and vibrating from a place of joy, and a place of fun, and a place of ease, and a place of play in everything we do, without intensity, and without fear that it's going to be hard, and without allowing discord to disrupt our frequencies.

The Giant Age will be anchored by structures that support human beings' sustainable alignment. And so, instead of creating problems to create markets for social services to fix this, and to counteract that, in the Giant Age, the new system will support people in sustaining their alignment so that everyone can thrive.

THE END OF HIERARCHY

Our current structures will not survive the Blackout. That's not doom and gloom talking; that's fact. Because the current structures were built by the darkness upon the frequencies of separation and hierarchy, they will not be able to sustain themselves within the field of a collective consciousness devoted to unity and equality for all.

When I was in Iceland, I spoke to a group of CEOs at the Harpa. At one point during the talk, I handed everyone a plate, and I asked them to balance the plate on one finger. No one could do it. The plate kept falling to one side or the other. I explained to the group that this was a metaphor for the old paradigm business model that has the CEO making all the decisions, and doing everything, and driving the ship. I then explained that for a new-paradigm company to be healthy and successful, the foundation must be rooted in *we* consciousness, which means that every person on the payroll is holding on to that plate, and lifting it up high, in order to achieve that organization's mission, and to be successful.

Hierarchy is archaic. Hierarchy places a qualitative judgment on the roles people serve in groups, and in organizations, and in society. So if someone has a really creative solution to an ongoing issue occurring within a company, but he happens to be a janitor, no one is going to listen to him. Because when we are operating under hierarchy, we are operating under the false belief that some people's ideas, or opinions, or expertise, or presence on the planet is somehow more valuable than other people's. Hierarchy creates separation, and hierarchy creates a lot of distrust and resentment among human beings, and hierarchy doesn't even work. Hierarchy is why the Mayans died out, and why the Toltecs died out, and why the Egyptians died out. They were all powerful civilizations, but they destroyed themselves through hierarchy.

Any culture that positions a singular leader over the people, without empowering those people to serve the collective vision of the tribe, is bound to fail. If the chief is the only one determining the course of the collective, and if everyone else has to answer to that chief, then the tribe will collapse. For the tribe to succeed, the chief must empower every single member to embody their own personal power, so that they can contribute their own unique genius to the well-being of the tribe, and to the evolution of the tribe. This includes the fishermen, and the hunters, and the stone cutters, and the shamans. Everyone must be empowered to be who they are in order for the whole tribe to function, and to sustain itself; just as everyone must be valued as an integral part of that tribe for it to thrive.

THE BUTTERFLY EFFECT IS A THING

We are all passengers on this spaceship called Earth, which makes us one global tribe sharing this planetary experience together. Those who are operating under the false belief that human beings are separate, isolated entities, and that human beings are not all connected, are simply not understanding the full scope of the situation. Just as Western doctors see blood, bones, tissue, and organs as islands unto themselves, while shamans understand the body as a singular holistic organism comprised of intricately connected parts and systems working together in service to the whole being, shamans also understand Earth as a singular holistic organism, comprised of intricately connected parts and systems working together in service to the whole—meaning, every living being and intelligence on the planet. Everything that happens on Earth affects every single being here, without exception. And for us to actualize a Giant Age here on Earth, it is crucial for humans to recognize this.

Food insecurity in Yemen affects the people in Buenos Aires. Poverty in Somalia generates lack consciousness in Echo Park. That lack might express itself very differently, but the genesis is the same, as are the vibrational frequencies informing the circumstances through which the lack manifests. The people struggling in Asia and in Africa are our brothers and sisters. We are fundamentally connected to one another on various levels of our beings. This means that their struggle is our struggle, even though it is happening on a different level, on a different continent, and within a different cultural paradigm. So while someone is walking barefoot across a barren desert to find a root or a bug to feed their undernourished child, someone else is living in an urban environment, panicking about making their rent, or paying their car insurance bill. It's the same energetic frequency.

The thing is, the same goes for abundance, and vitality, and miracles. This means that as we lift ourselves into prosperity consciousness, and as we lift ourselves into abundance consciousness, the stronger and more steadily we are then able to hold those frequencies, and the farther out we are able to radiate those frequencies, and to transmit those frequencies to other parts of the world. So our financial freedom in Toronto translates to good fortune for someone in Bombay. You must always remember that you are not living just for you, but that you are participating in something much larger, and much more sacred, in service to the *we*.

FROM ME TO WE

Humans really need to stop perceiving everyone else as *other*—as though Muslims are other, and indigenous people are other, and Jewish people are other, and trans people are other. It is time for us to knock off the separation nonsense, already. Separation is one of the side effects of having a planet full of people who are disconnected from their sensorium, because they cannot feel their discord, and they cannot feel the planet's discord, and they cannot feel themselves, which means there's no way in hell they're going to be able to feel their connection to other beings. This disconnect and this separation have created a society full of people who care only about themselves, and who care only about what is happening in their own individual lives, and in their own individual geographies, and who are not understanding our fundamental connectedness, or our responsibility as planetary custodians. People need to get some perspective and realize that we are all part of a unified field of consciousness, and an interconnected web of synthesis, and that we, as Earthlings, are all responsible for this planet's upkeep and well-being, which means that it isn't all about *me, me, me*, but that it's actually about *we, we, we*. And if we continue to operate in this singular, separate, selfish, isolated way of thinking, then the forces that are sustaining the life and welfare of that *we* are going to come crashing down, and it's going to be game over for all of us. Straight up.

SEEING AS A *WE*

Humans are not operating as though we are a *we,* and humans are not treating one another as though we are a *we,* because humans are not actually perceiving one another as a *we.* Humans are still seeing each other as isolated individual components that are operating independently from one another, because the darkness has blinded human perception through the illusion of separation. We must train ourselves to begin to see one another as a *we* by perceiving each other through the eyes of unconditional love and acceptance. This means that instead of mentally identifying others by way of their differences, and by all the ways that they are not like us, and all the ways that we are not like them, we commit to perceiving and cataloging others by our similarities, and by all the ways that we are alike. The human experience is very vast, which means it's really not that hard.

But, it's not just about how we perceive other people—it's about how we treat other people. If human beings were to recognize that every person they see on the street is themselves in another body, they would have more love, and more respect, and more reverence for their fellow human. So even while we are still training ourselves to perceive as a *we,* it is important that we practice loving others as we would love ourselves, and that we practice loving others without reservation, and without withholding, and without stinginess, and without any less care or quality than the ways we love ourselves.

That Time I Knocked at My Door, Asking for Water

One time I was hanging out at my house with a couple friends—both were big-time ministers at a large spiritual center in LA. While I was in the bathroom, a homeless man came to the door, extremely dehydrated, asking for water. When I came out, my friends were in the kitchen, rummaging through the cupboards, looking for a plastic cup, or a plastic bottle, so they could give him some water.

"Don't be silly," I said. "Invite him in. I'll give him a glass."

Cut to my friends, freaking out, and trying to discourage me from inviting the man inside because he was dirty, and because he might hurt them.

"Don't be silly," I said again, heading for the door.

I invited the man inside, made him some lunch, washed his clothes, and gave him a bath. My friends didn't lift a finger to help. They hid in the back bedroom the whole time, and gave me shit for being inconsiderate of their feelings, and their comfort, and their safety.

"I cannot believe you have the nerve to call yourself spiritual people," I snapped, because I had had just about enough of their entitled whining, "and that you are only willing to share your spirituality with those who can pay for it, while withholding it from the ones who need it the most. You need to check yourselves, right now."

I mean, how are you going to call yourself a spiritual person, let alone a minister, when you won't even give a homeless person a glass of water? Is that some bullshit, or what?

OUR ENTITLED ASSES

Humans have gotten soft, and humans have gotten comfortable, and humans have gotten complacent, which has made humans afraid of change. The Buddha talked a lot about the nature of impermanence, and about the suffering that comes along with humans' tendency to cling. Entitlement is a protection mechanism that allows humans to operate under the assumption that everything is going to show up exactly as it always has, and exactly as we expect it to. Entitlement is fueled by the assumption that everything is going to stay the same. This assumption works for as long as it works. But then one day, life happens, and our corner grocery store stops carrying our favorite almond milk, and suddenly, we get frustrated, and we get bitchy, and we act out of character.

Entitlement is a cage forged of our desire to control, and micromanage, and stay comfortable. Entitlement is a limited dimension of our own creation that is reliant upon consistency, and uniformity, and same, same, same, which we must defend and protect to maintain. When entitlement takes over, we lose ourselves to the affront we are perceiving in the change we are resisting, which sends our sensibility, our compassion, our composure, and our sanity right out the door. We become the worst possible versions of ourselves simply because we are not getting what we want, or what we are used to. And yet the problem isn't the grocery manager for not stocking your favorite plant-based milk alternative; and the problem isn't God for not caring enough to prevent this from happening to you; and the problem isn't whatever planet is retrograding in your first house. The problem is you. The problem is that you haven't cultivated the flexibility and the pliability necessary to handle life when it shows up differently from the way you are expecting it to show up. The problem is that you are projecting your own responsibility for this assumption onto the grocery manager, and onto everyone else in your reality, because you don't want to own your inability to roll with the changes life is throwing your way.

The thing is, that entitlement shit isn't gonna fly as the Blackout continues to progress. I mean, let's be honest, that entitlement shit barely flies now. But with the shifts the planet is currently facing, we must be pliable, and we must be flexible, and we must be easy with the unforeseen twists and turns coming down the pipeline. This is why so many of the great Asian spiritual traditions talk about being fluid like water, and being flexible and able to bend like the reed. As the illusion of linear reality gives way to the quantum truth of the matter, more and more doors will begin to close, just as more and more and more begin to open. And so, as multidimensional beings, we must be formidable in many modes, and in many models, and we must let go of any inclinations we might have to cling to any one construct.

The reality is that anything can change at any time. Life can change drastically on a dime, at any given moment, at which point your entire life can be vastly, hugely, massively different. A country that has never experienced war can come under siege. Your favorite restaurant could shut down tomorrow. Your house could be demolished in a landslide. You could inherit a huge chunk of money out of the blue. Your life partner could die, or decide they want to be with someone else. You could trip, land wrong, and shatter the hand you use to earn your living. You could accidentally rear end the person who turns out to be your soul mate. Change happens. This does not mean we should live our lives in fear, waiting for the other shoe to drop, or for some big, bad, scary thing to happen. But we have to get real with the fact that life is constantly shifting, and we have to resource ourselves to be able to deal with that. I mean, if we want to ride the lit train into the Giant Age, that is.

EMBRACE CHANGE

Our collective resistance to change is the reason we are seeing so much widespread social conflict on the planet. It's what happens when you have a bunch of entitled people wasting so much precious energy fighting for irrelevant ideas and outdated concepts while defending dying structures and institutions that aren't serving us. This is why we have people fighting to keep gay people from getting married, and fighting to prevent women from breast-feeding in public, and fighting for the right to cut off their baby's foreskin. No one is even stopping to ask themselves what it is they are actually arguing for, or what it is they are defending, or why. We've all just gotten so used to whatever it is that we've gotten used to, that we don't want to have to go through the hassle of getting un-used to it. So we fight for the right *not* to change, and we fight for the right *not* to grow. But instead of being honest about our stubbornness, and our stuckness, we look for rationalizations and proof points that we can wield to make the people who believe differently than we do the villains, and to victimize ourselves in the face of their attempts at progress.

This is how our outdated ideologies, and ideas, and allegiances, and beliefs, and behaviors, and habits have become our blankies. They are like these ratty, threadbare, old security blankets that we cling to with made-up stories and righteous indignation as a way of trying to control our realities, even though these blankies are dysfunctional, and these blankies are stunting our evolution.

LET GO; GET LIT

When we are unwilling to embrace change, and we are unwilling to adapt to change, we block ourselves from evolving, and we block ourselves from having what we want, and we block ourselves from riding the lit train, and from living giant, poprocks lives. A lot of people have negative associations with change because it can be scary, and uncomfortable, which means that when change comes knocking at their door, they dig in their heels, and they tighten their grip, and they refuse to give up the comfort, and the familiarity, and the convenience of what they already know, and of what they are already used to. This resistance to change and this resistance to exploring unknown territory create a lot of conflict and a lot of discord for people, considering that impermanence is the fundamental nature of this reality construct, and that our evolutionary momentum is only accelerating.

Evolution is the purpose of life. We exist to evolve. Without the possibility of evolution, the mind would not devote itself to the task of keeping us alive. What would be the point without the possibility of a greater vision or model to develop into? Change is a necessary part of life, and a necessary part of the evolutionary process, as well as the only constant in this reality. Nothing is permanent. Everything shifts, and everything transforms, and everything dies, and everything is reborn. This means that if we want to live poprocks lives, and if we want to ride the lit train into the Giant Age, we'd better get good at letting go.

We cannot allow the new to come into our lives until we let go of the old. That's just basic spatial relations. Where would the new fit? The act of letting go of what we are accustomed to clears the space for something greater to come into form. In the same way that we celebrate the arrival of blessings and novelty, we must also celebrate the act of letting go, and we must ritualize the art of letting go as an integral part of the process of welcoming even more amazing things into our lives. This means changing our approach to donating, and recycling, and gifting, such that we are really revering the process of clearing space, and of untethering ourselves from yet another material fixture, as a necessary function of the sacred act of creation.

OVERPOPULATION IS A THING

Every other species on the planet procreates for one reason, and for one reason only: to ensure the survival of the species. It used to be the same with humans, but then we got really complicated, and really copious, and really disconnected from our sensorium; and then the spirit of narcissism hopped into the mix, and now humans procreate to solidify an identity for themselves, and to be on trend, and to have something to dress up in cute outfits, and post pictures of on social media. Also to ensure the survival of their own personal bloodline, and to create some sort of enduring genetic legacy that they think is going to translate into immortality. But what humans are definitely *not* doing is procreating with the intention of consciously nurturing the consciousness they are bringing to this planet as an edifying contribution that will add value to the greater global community.

The survival of the species isn't in question anymore. At least, our survival isn't in question because of any kind of population deficit. In fact, the species is facing quite a few threats to our collective survival. It's just that *not enough humans* is not one of them. It's quite the opposite, actually, as overpopulation is a very real and very big problem that humans must address if we are going to rebalance this planet before it's too late.

The rate at which human beings continue to multiply as compared to the actuality of available resources on the planet is a real issue. This is not a problem that will remain confined only to those who are impoverished, or only to those who are elsewhere. This is a problem that is already affecting all of us on various energetic levels, and this is a problem that is creating suffering on the planet now. Not only that, but this is a problem that opens the door to the dimensional potentiality where resource depletion inspires mass migrations. Large groups of people attempt to cross borders in order to feed their families, which leads to conflict with those wanting to protect their resources for their own, which leads to a big, bloody mess. The solution is not more children on the planet.

So many women come to see me because they want to have a baby. They've jumped through all these Western medical hoops, and they've spent all this money undergoing all these fertility treatments, and they still can't get pregnant. A lot of times, they can't get pregnant because one of the ways the Earth is attempting to self-correct is through humans' fertility mechanisms. But humans are entitled, and humans are used to getting what we want, and a lot of women really, really, really want to have a baby. So they try to force the issue through science, even though their bodies aren't actually on board, and even though the last thing this planet needs is another baby. The amount of resources that go into this entire branch of science that exists to figure out better and faster ways to override the body's natural inclination to *not* multiply could be used to facilitate so much helpful, positive change for so many other beings on this planet.

We do not have enough resources to continue operating the way we have been operating. We humans are going to have to adjust our behavior if we are going to survive the Blackout, and dream the Giant Age into form. This means chilling out on the breeding, which means letting go of the entitlement that has people thinking it's okay to have six kids when they can barely afford to feed them, or clothe them, or pay the bills, let alone carve out the time to exercise, or meditate, or do what it is their own spirit needs them to do to thrive. Those six kids are taking up valuable resources on an already imbalanced planet. Straight up. I mean, how do we think Earth is going to correct itself if we are not willing to take action to correct it, or—at the very least—to *not* take action to make it worse?

Adoption is the obvious solution to the fertility issues sweeping the populace. I mean, it's a no-brainer. We have millions of children without parents, living in orphanages, or on the streets; and we have millions of couples wanting children. Adopting children who already exist and who happen to be in the market for a family of their own creates a lighter carbon footprint and serves everyone's needs and desires, as long as people are willing to let go of their narcissistic identity hang-ups, and stop making it all about their DNA, and their bloodline, and their fractal fabulousness. The Blackout is real, people. It's time to serve the larger human construct and get over our damn selves.

THE FIFTH ELEMENT

Another way the Earth is course-correcting is through the *fifth element*. Gay people are known as the fifth element in the West African Dagara tradition. The Dagara shamans believe that gay people are gifts from Spirit, sent to restore balance and harmony to the planet, and to open new doorways of consciousness for the species. In addition to helping ease humanity's overpopulation issues, the fifth element are helping to model for all humans the ability to love beyond limitation, and to love beyond labels, and to love beyond indoctrination.

The conditions and limitations that human beings continue to place upon love are based upon antiquated ideas that have been bestowed upon us by religion (aka: the darkness). The reason people are still clinging to these outdated belief structures is because of our collective fear of change—because it's been a certain way for a really, really long time, and because it's easier to just stay on autopilot, and to just keep believing the same old way, even though we have no idea why we are even believing this way in the first place.

Most cultures and religions view homosexuality as an abomination because they are taking their culturally indoctrinated aversion to it out of context. Take Christianity, for example—a religion that holds a hard line against homosexuality, because it's prohibited in the Bible. The thing is, homosexuality is not prohibited in the Bible because the people who wrote the Bible were judging it, or claiming any moral high ground against it. Whoever wrote Leviticus wasn't dissuading Christians from guy-on-guy sex because they thought guy-on-guy sex was bad, or wrong, or sinful. They were just trying to protect the people from the plague that happened to be ravaging the village at the time that part was written. That's why the Bible also prohibits things like mixing wool and cotton, and lying with a menstruating woman. *Duh.* If a deadly epidemic that happens to be passed through bodily fluids is sweeping through town, then yeah, I'm going to take any steps I can to avoid exposing myself to it. That means not sticking my cock in some other guy's ass, and not getting my wife's period blood all over me—not because menstrual blood is unclean, but because it might be infected with a deadly bloodborne pathogen. I'm also not going to go rubbing up on people with rashes. When wool and cotton are woven together, and worn on the body, they can irritate the skin and create bumps that fill up with pus, and that transmit the disease, which effectively meant that—in those times—your cardigan could kill you. What it didn't mean is that your cardigan was a sin.

These passages have been misinterpreted throughout the centuries by people who didn't understand the context or the conditions in which they were written, and who then took it upon themselves to ascribe these ideas to Jesus, along with the intolerance that was erroneously attached to them. But Jesus never said these things, and Jesus wasn't intolerant, and Jesus certainly didn't have issues with gay people, or period blood, or merino-cotton blends.

ENTITLEMENT = ARROGANCE = APATHY = UGH

I t is humans' entitlement that has us thinking that we can have as many children as we feel like, and that our children are exceptions to the overpopulation situation, because they are ours, which makes them just a little more special than everyone else's resource-sucking kids. It is our entitlement that has us still driving SUVs, and still watering our lawns in the middle of the day, and still having lawns anymore at all, when we really need to be planting food and healing herbs. It is our entitlement that has us eating endangered ocean creatures, and buying clothes made in Southeast Asian sweatshops, and not bringing our own damn bags to the grocery store. And it is our entitlement that is keeping us from confronting our bullshit, and confronting ourselves.

Humans are arrogant, which makes us reticent to acknowledge when things are wrong, or when things are out of alignment, because it threatens our fragile little egos. This arrogance and entitlement have the vast majority of us refusing to look at the imbalances threatening our world. This denial is what allows people to consent to the machinations of the matrix, and to mass media indoctrination, and to aggravated stimulation, and to brain sting, and to all the rest of it. It's what has a lot of people shuffling around like distracted, brain-dead bobbleheads, feeding the system with their attention, and their currency, and their discord, and their life force, and not giving a shit about how their actions are affecting the world and feeding the darkness.

Most people in the West are dropping the ball by not actively participating in our culture. We have become so sedentary, and our wills are so weak, that we are not taking action to shift the injustices we clearly see. It's very much an *out of sight, out of mind* situation, which has made us a neglectful culture, and a lazy culture, and has us scrambling for bigger distractions, and better distractions, and louder distractions so that we don't have to feel the pain of the world's suffering, and so that we don't have to look at how our actions are contributing to the world's suffering. That's entitlement, and that's a problem.

Just Because You Can Do Scorpion Pose Doesn't Mean You're Not Entitled

When I'm in New York, I often stay with a yogi friend of mine who considers herself woke because she can do a handstand, and juices kale, and went to India once.

I flew into town to lead a workshop, and my friend said to me over dinner: "Do you really have to go back to Turkey? I worry about you living so far away, in such a dangerous part of the world. I worry for all those people."

"No, you don't," I said, because she was full of shit. "You don't worry about me. You're just annoyed that I'm not here, in your same time zone, and in your same borough, to give you healings, and to tell you that your alpaca blanket coat is fabulous. But, babe, let's be real, you do not give a shit about what's going on in Turkey."

"You're right." She shrugged. "I don't."

SAVE THYSELF

The darkness has been using religion as a way to program humans with the savior myth since they bound the first Bible. As soon as that story started picking up steam—the one that purports that Jesus died for our sins, and that he's going to come back from the dead so he can save us—humans pretty much stopped showing up for themselves. I mean, why bother, when a superhero, or a messiah, or a knight in shining armor can just as easily come rescue us, and we don't have to break a sweat, or pull a muscle, or anything?

It's the fallacy of being rescued, or of being saved by some external force, that has humans continuing to propagate such large-scale pollution on the planet; they just assume that things are going to be taken care of for them, and that someone else is going to deal with it, and make it all better. This is why our ocean is littered with single-use plastics, and why we continue to manufacture single-use plastics, because our species is in complete denial of the very real damage we are doing to our home planet; and our species is in complete denial about how this damage will affect every one of us in the long term. People are not taking responsibility for their lives, or for our planet, because people are under the delusional belief that everything is just going to fix itself, or that someone, or something, is going to sweep in and fix it for us.

This setup is preventing humans from allowing ourselves to recognize our power. We are too busy waiting to be rescued. This savior fantasy is limiting our species from evolving, because instead of taking responsibility for our Earth situation by taking responsibility for the individual energy that each of us, ourselves, is transmitting into the collective by way of our words, thoughts, and actions, we just sit back, smoke a bowl, and space out on a screen while waiting for some kind of superhero to come rescue us. We don't even give ourselves the chance to step up to the plate, and confront the situation, and be blown away by what we can overcome, and by what we can accomplish, and by what we can create.

That Time Superman Never Came

When I was twelve, I spent the entire summer locked inside my room as punishment for unwrapping my Christmas presents early, playing with the toys, and wrapping them back up again. My dad and my stepmom beat me until I bled, and then six months later, they took away all my toys and emptied out my entire room. The only thing they left was the bed. I got claustrophobic spending all day and all night in an empty box, so I would stick my head out the window, and call out for Superman.

"Superman!" I would yell into the wind. "Superman, if you can hear me, please come get me."

I called out for Superman every day. I waited, and waited, and waited, but Superman never came. After those three months were over, and I made it to the other side of that horrible experience, I realized that it wasn't actually Superman I was waiting for; it was me. Because I was still here, and I had gotten myself through it on my own.

That experience really shifted my perspective. After that, I still took the beatings, but instead of allowing that violence to turn into anger, or hate, or destruction, I turned it into love; because I knew that love was the one thing they could never take away from me.

THE HELPLESS THING REALLY ISN'T HELPING, THOUGH

Here's the thing: no one is coming to save us. There will be no superheroes, and there will be no messiahs, and there won't even be any aliens—not because aliens don't exist, but because other planetary kingdoms view humans as a hostile species, because we kill our own kind. It's not like extradimensional beings don't have plenty of mad wisdom, and knowledge, and technology to share with us, it's just that—given how easily and how often we kill one another—it's ridiculous to think that they could land their ships on our planet and we wouldn't freak out, and bomb the shit out of them.

It is our responsibility to save ourselves. It is our responsibility to allow ourselves to feel the pain of the world's suffering, and to acknowledge which of our actions and behaviors are contributing to the imbalances and the issues that are causing that suffering, and to adjust our actions and behaviors accordingly.

It is also our responsibility to educate ourselves as to how we are going to survive in the face of so many radical shifts in resources and living conditions, given the challenges we are facing as a species. Right now, survival means paying the bills, scheduling the carpool, buying organic greens at the farmers' market, and going to cardio barre twice a week. But as the Blackout unfolds, our concept of survival is going to change radically. We really need to be doing our due diligence so we can figure out how to navigate these impending shifts. But because people are so used to being taken care of, people are just assuming that someone else is going to deal with it, or that someone else is going to tell them how to deal with it, or that they'll be able to just download an app that's going to deal with it for them.

THE GOVERNMENT IS NOT YOUR FRIEND

Humans are not taking responsibility for their own well-being, safety, or ongoing survival because they are assuming that the government's got it handled, and that the government has their back, and that if something cataclysmic goes down, the government is going to take care of it for us.

People are under the impression that the government exists to protect us, and to tend to our needs, and to look out for our best interests, and to ensure our survival. This is false. The government was created by the darkness to serve the system, not the people. The government does not exist to safeguard your health, safety, stability, or well-being. The government exists to protect power, and to proliferate profit, and to control. Period.

Look at the food we eat. Instead of taking responsibility for our health, and taking responsibility for the ingredients we are putting in our bodies, and doing our due diligence by educating ourselves as to whether certain chemicals or ingredients are actually safe for us to be ingesting, we assume that if it wasn't safe, then the FDA wouldn't approve it, and it wouldn't be on the shelf at the grocery store. Except the FDA does not exist to protect the well-being of the populace. If it did, it wouldn't put its stamp of approval on things like sulfites, and aspartame, and red dye no. 3, and growth hormones, and sodium laureth sulfate, and genetically modified anything, which are all conclusively and unequivocally linked to a whole bunch of really fucked-up health problems. If you are asking me, the FDA exists to make money for the pharmaceutical corporations who profit off all the disease their additives, and their chemicals, and their pesticides cause. Straight up.

People really need to wake up to the reality of the situation, and to the true motives driving the system they're giving their power away to. Because while we sit around twiddling our thumbs, waiting for the government to save us, and to make it all better, we're dropping the ball by not stepping in and taking responsibility for the state of our world, and for the state of the Earth, and implementing some poprocks solutions.

CLEAN UP YOUR OWN DAMN MESS

It's people's entitlement that has them thinking that it's fine to pollute the planet, and that it's fine to throw trash out the window of their car while they're driving. I'm always amazed when I see this happen; and I always wonder what exactly people are thinking. That some trash fairy is going to just magically appear and sashay into the middle of the street, and sweep up their garbage for them, because they couldn't wait to park the car and walk all of two feet to put it in an actual trash can? I mean, what is the actual thought process going on there?

The answer is that there is no actual thought process going on there. It's a bobblehead thing. People are checking way out because they feel like it's all so overwhelming, and like it's all so out of control, and that shifting the planet back into alignment is some complicated ordeal that requires all this money, and all this technology, and all these geopolitical negotiations, when the simple act of putting our dirty Kleenex in the trash is exactly the kind of behavior that's going to shift this planet back into balance.

We do not have to take responsibility for solving all the world's problems, we just have to take responsibility for ourselves. *As within, so without* is a universal law. When we take responsibility for ourselves, and we make the adjustments we need to make, those adjustments trickle out into nature, and into economics, and into agriculture, and into all the rest of it. These seemingly small acts of personal responsibility and planetary custodianship are the adjustments that lift and shift the planet, and that bring the Giant Age into form.

THE RICOCHET EFFECT

The way we take responsibility for fixing our planet is by educating—by educating, and sharing from love. The reason people are feeling so overwhelmed, and the reason people aren't making the changes we need to be making in order to fix the planet, is that we don't think our individual efforts can actually make a difference. But if Martin Luther King Jr. had thought like that, or if Nelson Mandela had thought like that, or if Mother Teresa had thought like that, then our society would not have shifted the way their efforts have shifted it, and we would not have evolved as a culture in the ways that we have. The fact is that change starts with one person—with one person who has the passion and the courage to stand by their truth, and to educate people about that truth by sharing with love.

I've lost count of how many people I've taught to hug properly, and who have then taken it upon themselves to teach others how to hug properly. I have inspired many fractal lines of greater hugging. In fact, if there is any one contribution I can be sure I've made to the human species, it's definitely all the people I've taught to hug better and realer.

People in the West are not connecting correctly. The way people connect is very important, because when energies come together—even through something as fleeting as a handshake or a hug—those frequencies amplify one another exponentially. It's like a power surge. So when two people come together, each holding the frequency of love, that creates an expanded love frequency that resonates even stronger throughout the collective field of consciousness.

Most people greet one another for the very first time with a handshake. The handshake comes from the ancient Greeks, who used the gesture to indicate that they weren't carrying a weapon. It was a way of saying: *Hi, I am not going to murder you.* So the root of the handshake employed as a greeting is mistrust. It doesn't matter if we know the origin story or not; the gesture itself is still encoded with the energies of mistrust, which means the energy that we exchange, and the energy that we amplify every time we shake someone's hand in greeting, is mistrust. How can we expect to trust one another when, according to standard etiquette, this is the vibrational exchange taking place every time we meet one of our brothers or sisters? I mean, it's pretty fundamental, as far as the mechanisms of control that the system slips in to keep us from connecting with one another. That's why instead of shaking hands, I hug.

A lot of humans hug wrong. They pat the other person on the back instead of embracing them. It's the exact opposite gesture, because when we pat someone on the back, we're actually telling them that we're not available to connect. It's disingenuous. Not only that, but it breaks up the electromagnetic synthesis in the body, and so the feelings of peace and safety that would otherwise be generated from an act of true connection become fragmented and fearful.

A lot of men hug like this because we are indoctrinated to misinterpret affection as weakness. It's such a damaging program because it robs men in our culture of the chance to connect with their brotherhood. So men pound each other on the backs to prove that they are manly, and to prove that they are not gay, thereby depriving themselves and each other of the chance to connect through physical form and energetic synthesis that could otherwise be radiating positive vibrations between them, and then out into the field.

When I hug someone, and they pat me on the back, I tell them, "Don't pound me on the back. If you're going to hug me, embrace me—make the connection. When you pat me on the back, all you're doing is telling me that you don't want to connect."

That's how I teach people, who teach other people. I know, because they tell me. I taught my client's husband when he patted me on the back. And he said, "Oh, wow. This feels so much better. I had no idea. I was raised to hug that way, because that's how my father hugged. I'm never going to do that again. Thank you." And his wife told me that now he teaches all his friends not to pound, and that it's really endearing to see him educating other people. *Boom!* This is how change happens.

It seems like such a simple thing, because it is. Education is the simplest way to help people to change, and education is the simplest way to change our world. Especially when it's done through love's intelligence. I call it the ricochet effect. The ricochet effect is where we share our knowledge hacks with love, and we share it with joy, and we share it without making anyone else wrong, or telling them they're bad. We share in a way that allows others to feel good about what they are learning, so they will feel inspired to share it with others. And then that knowledge ricochets from person to person to person across the planet, and suddenly, our world shifts, and our world evolves.

DREAM THE WORLD GREATER

To manifest the Giant Age here on Earth, we must devote ourselves to a vision that supports the fulfillment of all beings, on all levels. If the whole world were to dream greater than the current dream, then our world would be better immediately. When our whole world learns to dream an inclusive, sustainable, peaceful, poprocks reality that supports all beings in thriving, then that is the reality that will materialize.

The darkness uses our attention to keep the current collective dream alive. The current dream cannot survive without our attention. So when we dream against the darkness—meaning, we dream a greater dream than the one the darkness is projecting onto our holographic reality—that is when our whole world will change.

If we want to see change on this planet—like, real change; like, transformation, and quantum leaps, and a Giant Age of peace, prosperity, and blazing poprocks litness kind of change—then we have to dream differently. We have to dream a different collective dream. That means perceiving the world through a greater lens, with the understanding that such a lens is a portal to that new reality. Therefore, it is our responsibility to frame our experience of reality through that lens—again, and again, and again—regardless of what sort of data reality is offering us. It is our devotion to our greater reality, and it is our commitment to consistently perceiving that greater reality, that allows it to manifest. So when life happens, and when life presents us with obstacles, or with challenges, we interpret those experiences, and we speak about those experiences with the understanding that they are happening in service to our greater dream, and we understand them as lessons and teachings that are guiding us toward that greater reality; and we do not doubt that—ever—not for one single second.

The truth is, reality is always showing us exactly what we need to grow and to manifest. All these people who are freaking out about the state of the world, and freaking out about who's in charge, and freaking out about what's going on in their realities, are not understanding that Spirit is giving us exactly what we need in order to grow and to manifest. This perspective emboldens us with the knowledge that everything we go through is happening for our benefit, and that everything is happening to serve the greater dream. So we don't judge our experiences as negative, and we don't let our experiences bring us down; we see them as opportunities for growth and for positive change. This is how we perceive our world greater, and this is how we learn to dream our world greater.

When I died, the spirits showed me the millions, and millions, and billions of realities that all exist right here, and right now. Each one of those realities is made manifest by how the spirit is dreaming. The dream decides which realities we manifest, and which realities we experience. So when we dream cleaner oceans, and we dream more efficient energy sources, and we dream deeper relationships, and we dream greater peace, and we dream optimal health, and we dream bigger love, those dreams become our reality.

YOU ARE THE DREAMER

We are all creators. Each one of us is constantly creating this reality construct that we are all housed in with our will, and our beliefs, and our attention. I cannot underscore enough the importance of understanding that we human beings are creating our world with our every thought, our every word, our every choice, and our every behavior. The way that we think, and the way we interact as a collective is quite literally making our world the way it is right now. So if you want the world to be different, your job is to dream it different, and to be, and to share, and to radiate every quality you want to see in the world in service to that different dream.

It is our world to fix, tribe. We cannot expect anyone else to do it for us. That means it is my responsibility to fix the world, just as it is your responsibility to fix the world. That means having the courage to feel the pain of the imbalances that are causing so much suffering in our world, and that are creating so much destruction in our world. It's not like Gandhi just woke up one day and decided out of the blue that he was going to help liberate his people from the British colonialists. He had to feel something to be inspired to take the action he took. Every leader has to feel the pain of life, because it is the agony of those imbalances that activates our devotion and that activates the leadership qualities lying dormant within us. We all exist in some segment of this societal construct, and each one of us has the power to make a difference in that piece of our collective puzzle. Talk is talk; it blows away like the wind. To take action, to stand for something we believe in—now, that's meaningful. That's giant.

It is time for us to take responsibility for our situation on planet Earth. No one did this to us. We did this to ourselves, and we did this to each other, which is why my greater dream includes a day when we let go of all the distractions and come together, and build a poprocks world of unified global citizens choosing to evolve our planet, as well as ourselves.

The Blackout is a blessing. The Blackout is an amazing opportunity for us, as a unified global collective, to choose to evolve through love, and to choose to evolve through consciousness, and to choose to evolve through our willingness to continue to adapt, and to continue to learn, and to continue to grow so as to become greater human beings, and to become a greater human species that lives in harmony with its resources.

We can choose to be those people, tribe. Shall we?

ACKNOWLEDGMENTS

I am so honored and grateful to my mother for giving life to me and for teaching me to be honorable and loving under all circumstances. To my great-grandmother Mamal for keeping our African heritage alive. To my sister Angelina for guiding me to stay in my course. To my niece Alex for making me a better person. To my niece Natalia for being brave enough to tell me the truth when I need to hear it. To my grandfather Leon for turning his back on shamanism and becoming a Seventh-day Adventist minister and for teaching me religion and showing me the beauty in it, as well as the hypocrisy. To my aunt Hazel, my uncle Ronny, and my aunt Ruth for reminding me to stay true to who I am, despite my family's opinions of me. To my aunt Shirley for introducing me to culture and giving me the strength to travel the world. To my friend Melanie Dawn, who believed in me, fought my father, and stayed by my side every day so that he wouldn't pull the plug while I was on life support. And to Stephen Clark for the hypnotherapy sessions that helped keep my mind from falling apart. To Abby Girvin, Sandra, and the rest of the Clark family for wrangling the friends and showing me such deep love. And to Mike Byrne, who supported me when I was sick and picked me up off the floor when I couldn't walk. To Ishanti and Bernie Diaz for seeing my truth and nurturing my shamanic path. Thank you to Gwyneth Paltrow for being my soul sister and guiding me through all of this. Thank you to Kelly Marks at Pure Public Relations for getting my message to the people of London. Thank you to Kelly Rutherford for always being there for me during difficult times. Thank you, Russ DeLeon, for supporting me in starting and writing the book, and for being a loyal friend. To my dad and stepmother, Geri, for an intense childhood that taught me to overcome any obstacle. And to all the bullies and the haters, thank you for giving me the ability to persevere. I would also like to give thanks to all my family members, friends, teachers, healers, and doctors who supported me on my journey, as well as to all the wise women who weren't afraid to put me in my place and teach me how to show up in my heart. To Marcus Hunt, who stayed by my side when I died. I'd like to thank Alexis Ware for helping me stay inspired to write this book and see it through. Sam and Aaron Ritter, thank you for your constant devotion in seeing me support the people globally. To Tanya Khani, my publicist, for believing in my message and for opening up doorways. To Hank Greenberg for your constant support in my health and your determination in seeing me fully committed to my path. To Michaelangelo L'Acqua, Anne Vincent, and Matt Kibble for helping me introduce shamanism to the mainstream. To Jimmy Chamberlin for being a badass bro and for keeping it real with me a thousand percent. I'd like to thank my literary agent, Coleen O'Shea, for just being amazing and walking me through the process every step of the way, as well as my publisher, my soul brother Joel Fotinos, and everyone at St. Martin's Press and Macmillan Publishers for believing in my vision of a greater world. And a special thanks to Dani Katz for honoring the promise we made all those years ago, and for helping me write a book that will put the power back in people's hands, and change the world. To all the people who have suffered, felt alone, confused, hurt, or lost when all they needed was love to come back, I dedicate this book to you. And to the tribe for keeping it lit and riding the lit train!

Thank you Andrew Dax for being Moses and parting the sea so I could deliver my message of love to the people in authenticity and grace, and thank you for believing in me and reminding me that I'm a honey badger. I would like to thank my UK publicist, Naomi White, for enabling me to spread my message and purpose for bringing forth change into the world as a shaman, because you see me, that was able to happen, and for that I appreciate you. Thank you Caroline Prothero for keeping me humble in remembering that it's not about me, it's about the people, always. Thank you Jasmine Hemsley for always letting me know that I can do it and guiding me on the process. Thank you Ruby Warrington for inspiring me to write a book and for connecting me with my book agent.